psycholinguistics and reading

psycholinguistics

Little, Brown and Company
Boston   Toronto

and reading

FROM PROCESS TO PRACTICE

CONSTANCE WEAVER

Western Michigan University

Library of Congress Cataloging in Publication Data

Weaver, Constance.
  Psycholinguistics and reading.

  Bibliography: p. 319
  Includes index.
  1. Reading. 2. Psycholinguistics. I. Title.
LB1050.W37   372.4′1   79-25685
ISBN 0–316–926868

And psycholinguistics can help to assert the right of children to learn to read with the aid of people rather than procedures.—Frank Smith

Library of Congress Catalog Card No. 79–25685

ISBN 0–316–926868

9 8 7 6 5 4 3 2

HAL
Published simultaneously in Canada
by Little, Brown & Company (Canada) Limited

Printed in the United States of America

contents

v

st of activities

list of illustratio

6   **How Is a Psycholinguistic View of Reading Relevant to Reading Instruction?**

7   **How Can We Assess Readers' Strengths and Determine Their Instructional Needs?**

8   **How Can We Help Readers Develop Good Reading Strategies?**

9   **How Can We Design a Psycholinguistically Based Reading Program?**

list of illustrations

ix

list of activities

preface

And reading itself, as a psycho-physiological
process, is almost as good as a miracle.—Edmund Burke Huey

As experienced teachers know all too well, there is no magic
formula for teaching reading. But some approaches are
more defensible than others, given what we know about the
reading process. The purpose of this book is to help teachers
better understand that process, in order to make sound instructional decisions.

The first part of the book is concerned with the reading
process and reading instruction: with the nature of proficient reading, and the implications for beginning reading
instruction in particular. The second part is concerned with
reading in the classroom: with how we can determine readers' instructional needs, how we can help them develop good
reading strategies, and how we can design (for any instructional level) a reading program that reflects an understanding of the reading process.

The book is intended primarily for preservice and inservice teachers who are concerned with reading and reading
instruction. More broadly, the book is appropriate for anyone interested in exploring the nature of the reading process. No special knowledge is required, because the technical
terms are defined in the text itself or in the summary of
English grammar presented in the appendix.

The basic thesis of this book is that reading is not a passive process by which we soak up words and information

from the page, but an active process by which we predict, sample, and confirm or correct our hypotheses about the written text. Suppose, for example, that you are reading the sentence **The cruel giant fell into the** . . . . What do you know about the word that follows **the**? First, you know it is likely to be a noun, a "thing" or substance (or a word that modifies an upcoming noun). Second, you know that this word probably denotes something that one can fall into. Without even seeing the word, you can narrow it down to a few likely possibilities: **water, well, lake, pond, river, hole,** and so forth. Thus you would need to look at only one or two of the letters in order to identify the word. And you could confirm (or correct) your tentative identification by seeing if the word makes sense with the following context. Such, in fact, is what proficient readers normally do.

In brief, then, this example illustrates the "psycholinguistic" nature of the reading process, the fact that reading involves an interaction between the *mind* of the reader and the *language* of the text.[1] It is this view which is explored in the pages that follow.

Over the course of several years, many people have helped to shape this book. First, I want to acknowledge and thank those who have contributed most to my understanding of the reading process: Kenneth and Yetta Goodman. Although they do not agree with everything said here, their influence clearly permeates the entire text. Without their research, a book like this could not have been written. And without Yetta's encouragement and inspiration, this particular text might never have come to fruition. I am especially grateful for her kindness and patience in commenting on two drafts of the manuscript. Naturally, however, I alone am responsible for the remaining errors and for the limitations of my knowledge and understanding.

Various colleagues have influenced my thinking and in some cases contributed directly to the text: Dorothy Bladt, Jim Burns, Michael Clark, June Cottrell, Ruth Heinig, Nancy Stone, Nancy Thomas, and especially Maryellen Hains and Theone Hughes. To all of these people I am deeply grateful.

---

[1] The term "psycholinguistics" comes from **psyche** (meaning 'mind') and **linguistics** (having to do with language).

Thanks go also to my students, to the many preservice and inservice teachers in my classes. Their questions, their reactions, and their experiences have contributed greatly to my own understanding. I would like to thank those among them who have provided some of the materials in the text: Martha Bond, Elizabeth French, Kayleen Hill, Cathy McCabe, Mary Sue Piper, Patricia Reeves, Mary Singleton, Kay Spade, Mary VanLangevelde, and Priscilla Weaver. Special thanks go to Candy Black and Victoria Pachulski for their extensive help with chapters 8 and 9, respectively. Without the contributions of these people and of my son John, the text would be barren indeed.

In addition, I would like to thank my typist, May Belle Harn, for her skill and dedication. I am also grateful to the many people at Winthrop Publishers who saw this book through publication: in particular, Paul O'Connell, chairman of Winthrop, who has given this project his continued support. Over the years, however, my greatest debt is to my friend and former teacher, Owen Thomas. He had faith in me long before I learned to have faith in myself.

C. W.

acknowledgements

Artley, A. Sterl. From *Phonics Revisited* by A. Sterl Artley, *Language Arts* (February 1977). Copyright © 1977 by the National Council of Teachers of English. Reprinted with permission.

Ball, Zachary. From *Bristle Face* by Zachary Ball. Copyright 1962 by Kelly R. Masters. Reprinted by permission of Holiday House.

Barr, Jene. Excerpt from *Little Circus Dog* by Jene Barr. Copyright 1949 by Albert Whitman & Company.

Bormuth, John R. From "Literacy in the Classroom" by John R. Bormuth in *Help for the Reading Teacher: New Directions in Research*, ed. William D. Page. Copyright © 1975 by the National Council of Teachers of English. Reprinted by permission.

Bradbury, Ray. From *Dandelion Wine*. Copyright © 1957 by Ray Bradbury. Reprinted by permission of Harold Matson Company, Inc. From *Golden Apples of the Sun*. Copyright © 1953 by Ray Bradbury. Reprinted by permission of Harold Matson Company, Inc. From *I Sing the Body Electric*. Copyright © 1969 by Ray Bradbury. Reprinted by permission of Harold Matson Company, Inc.

Brown, Claude. From *Manchild in the Promised Land* by Claude Brown. New York: Macmillan Publishing Co., Inc. Copyright © Claude Brown 1965.

Burling, Robbins. From *English in Black and White* by Robbins Burling. Copyright © 1973 by Holt, Rinehart and Winston, Inc. Reprinted by permission of Holt, Rinehart and Winston.

Carmer, Carl. From *Listen for a Lonesome Drum* by Carl Carmer. Copyright 1936 by Carl Carmer; renewal © 1964 by Carl Carmer. Reprinted by permission of Holt, Rinehart and Winston.

Carton, Aaron S. From *Orientation to Reading* by Aaron S. Carton. Reprinted by permission of Newbury House Publishers, Inc., Rowley, Mass.

Chomsky, Carol. From "After Decoding: What?" by Carol Chomsky, *Language Arts* (March 1976). Copyright © 1976 by the National Council of Teachers of English. Reprinted by permission.

Dahl, Roald. From "Poison" in *Someone Like You* by Roald Dahl. Reprinted by permission of Alfred A. Knopf, Inc.

Forester, Anne D. From "What Teachers Can Learn from 'Natural Readers'" by Anne D. Forester, *The Reading Teacher* (November 1977). Reprinted by permission.

George, Jean Craighead. Text excerpts from *Julie of the Wolves* by Jean Craighead George. Text copyright © 1972 by Jean Craighead George. By permission of Harper & Row, Publishers, Inc.

Goetz, Lee Garrett. From *A Camel in the Sea* by Lee Garrett Goetz.

Martin, Bill Jr. and Brogan, Peggy. From *Sounds of a Powwow* by Bill Martin, Jr. and Peggy Brogan. Copyright © 1974 by Holt, Rinehart & Winston, Publishers. Reprinted by permission.

May, Frank B. From *To Help Children Read: Mastery Performance Modules for Teachers in Training* by Frank B. May. Copyright © 1973 by Charles E. Merrill Publishing Company. Reprinted by permission.

McCracken, Robert A. From "Initiating Sustained Silent Reading" by Robert A. McCracken, in *Journal of Reading* (May 1971). Reprinted with permission of Robert A. McCracken and the International Reading Association.

McCullough, Constance M. From "Pioneers of Research in Reading" by Constance M. McCullough, in *Theoretical Models and Processes of Reading*, eds., Harry Singer and Robert Ruddell, 2nd ed., 1976. Reprinted by permission.

Nelson, Ruth. From "The First Literate Computers?" by Ruth Nelson. Reprinted from *Psychology Today Magazine*. Copyright © 1978 Ziff-Davis Publishing Company.

New York Times excerpt. © 1970 by The New York Times Company. Reprinted by permission.

O. Henry. From "Jimmy Hayes and Muriel" from *The Complete Works of O. Henry*. Copyright 1937 by Garden City Publishing Company, Inc. Used by permission of the publisher.

O'Brien, Robert C. From *Mrs. Frisby and the Rats of NIMH* by Robert C. O'Brien. Copyright © 1971 by Robert C. O'Brien. Courtesy of Atheneum Publishers.

Palermo, David. From *Psychology of Language* by David S. Palermo. Copyright © 1978 by Scott, Foresman and Company. Reprinted by permission.

Pearson, David P. and Johnson, Dale D. From *Teaching Reading Comprehension* by David P. Pearson and Dale D. Johnson. Copyright © 1978 by Holt, Rinehart and Winston. Reprinted by permission of Holt, Rinehart and Winston.

Rawls, Wilson. From *Where the Red Fern Grows* by Wilson Rawls. Reprinted by permission of Doubleday & Company.

Robinson, Francis P. From pp. 32–33, *Effective Study*, 4th edition, by Francis P. Robinson. Copyright 1941, 1946 by Harper & Row, Publishers, Inc. Copyright © 1961, 1970 by Francis P. Robinson. Reprinted by permission of the publisher.

Seton, Anya. From *Devil Water* by Anya Seton. Copyright © 1962 by Anya Seton Chase. Reprinted by permission of Houghton Mifflin Company.

Smith, E. Brooks; Goodman, Kenneth; Meredith, Robert. Adapted from *Language and Thinking in School*, second edition, by E. Brooks Smith, Kenneth S. Goodman, and Robert Meredith. Copyright © 1970 by Holt, Rinehart and Winston, Inc. Copyright © 1976 by Holt, Rinehart and Winston. Reprinted by permission of Holt, Rinehart, and Winston.

Smith, Frank. From *Comprehension and Learning: A Conceptual Framework for Teachers* by Frank Smith. Copyright © 1975 by Holt, Rinehart and Winston. Reprinted by permission of Holt, Rinehart and Winston. From *Psycholinguistics and Reading* by Frank Smith. Copy-

Acknowledgements   xviii

right © 1973 by Holt, Rinehart and Winston, Inc. Reprinted by permission of Holt, Rinehart and Winston. From *Understanding Reading: A Psycholinguistic Analysis of Reading and Learning to Read* by Frank Smith. Copyright © 1971 by Holt, Rinehart and Winston, Inc. Reprinted by permission of Holt, Rinehart and Winston.

Sperry, Armstrong. From *Call It Courage* by Armstrong Sperry. Reprinted by permission of Macmillan Publishing Company, Inc.

Van Ess, Dorothy. From *Fatima and Her Sisters* by Dorothy Van Ess. Copyright © 1961 by Harper & Row, Publishers, Inc. Reprinted by permission.

Weaver, Constance. From "Using Context: Before or After?" by Constance Weaver, in *Language Arts* (November/December 1977). Copyright © 1977 by the National Council of Teachers of English. Reprinted by permission.

Williamson, Joanne. From *The Glorious Conspiracy* by Joanne Williamson. Copyright © 1961 by Alfred A. Knopf, Inc. Reprinted by permission.

Wiseman, Bernard. Reprinted by permission of Dodd, Mead & Company, Inc. from *Morris Has a Cold* by Bernard Wiseman. Copyright © 1978 by Bernard Wiseman.

part one

the reading process and reading instruction

PART 1 of this book examines the nature of the reading process as well as some implications for beginning reading instruction. In chapter 1, you will be asked to consider your own views about reading. This exploratory introduction is followed in chapter 2 by a brief discussion of how reading instruction has commonly been viewed in recent years. Chapters 3 and 4 are concerned with word perception and identification. Chapter 5 then challenges the notion that reading is first and foremost a matter of identifying words. Finally, chapter 6 summarizes the nature of proficient reading and emphasizes implications for reading instruction. Part 2 discusses how to apply an understanding of the reading process in assessing readers' instructional needs, designing reading strategy lessons, and developing a comprehensive reading program appropriate for a wide range of instructional levels.

1

what are your beliefs about reading?

Our findings suggest that both teachers and learners hold particular and identifiable theoretical orientations about reading which in turn significantly effect expectancies, goals, behavior, and outcomes at all levels.—Jerome Harste

Questions for Study and Discussion

1   What kinds of errors (miscues) are typical of a *good* reader? What kinds are typical of a *poor* reader?
2   If a teacher believes that reading means translating written words into spoken words, how is he or she likely to go about teaching children to read?
3   If a teacher believes that reading means reconstructing the meaning that underlies written words, how is he or she likely to go about teaching children to read?
4   What is your own view of reading? How would you go about teaching children to read?

THE IMPORTANCE OF A DEFINITION

What *is* reading, anyway? Here are some answers from children (Harste 1978, p. 92):[1]

[1] To avoid numerous footnotes, references will usually be cited in the text itself by author, year or short title (when desirable or necessary), and page number(s). The full reference can be found in the bibliography titled "References." The bibliographic entries for each author have been listed chronologically.

In describing experiments and citing research, I have kept in mind the newcomer to psycholinguistics rather than the experienced investigator or scholar. Thus I have usually described experiments in the briefest of terms, and have often cited readily accessible and readable secondary sources rather than primary research reports. Furthermore, I have made no attempt to be exhaustive in my discussion of research. Rather, I have cited only a few studies that are of particular importance and/or that contain examples which can be profitably discussed.

"It's filling out workbooks."
"Pronouncing the letters."
"It's when you put sounds together."
"Reading is learning hard words."
"Reading is like think . . . you know, it's understanding the story."
"It's when you find out things."

There is considerable variation in these definitions. One emphasizes a medium of instruction, the workbook; others emphasize words or parts of words; and still others emphasize meaning. Of course, children do not often stop to define reading. Nevertheless, their approach to the task of reading is guided by what they think reading is.

Where do children get such definitions of reading? Often they simply infer them from what is emphasized during reading instruction. If the teacher spends a lot of time teaching correspondences between letters and sounds, at least some children will conclude that reading means pronouncing letters or sounding out words. If the teacher spends a lot of time teaching children to recognize words as wholes, at least some children will conclude that reading means identifying words or knowing a lot of words. Whatever the instructional approach, it is likely to affect at least some children's implicit definitions of reading and hence their strategies for dealing with the written text. And ironically, those children who are least successful at reading may be the very ones who try hardest to do just what the teacher emphasizes.

The instructional approach is crucial, then, if we want to help children develop productive reading strategies. But again, the instructional approach reflects a definition of reading, whether that definition be consciously formulated or only implicit. Figure 1.1 depicts the lines of influence.

Children's success at reading reflects their reading strategies; their reading strategies typically reflect their implicit definitions of reading; children's definitions of reading often reflect the instructional approach; and the instructional approach reflects a definition of reading, whether implicit or explicit. In fact, the instructional approach may reflect a

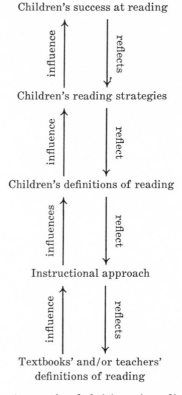

Children's success at reading

influence   *reflects*

Children's reading strategies

influence   *reflect*

Children's definitions of reading

influences   *reflect*

Instructional approach

influence   *reflects*

Textbooks' and/or teachers'
definitions of reading

Figure 1.1 *Importance of a definition of reading*

definition quite different from that consciously espoused by the teacher or the textbook.

The vital question, then, is *what* approach, and *whose* definition? If the teacher has only a vague notion of how people read and learn to read, he or she may in effect adopt the definition implicit in a given reading program, perhaps a basal reading series. In that case, the guiding definition may reflect more the publisher's knowledge of what will sell than scholars' and educators' knowledge of how people read and learn to read.

Fortunately, teachers can have far more influence on the instructional approach than they often realize. Armed with a viable definition of reading and an understanding of some of the instructional implications of this definition, teachers can use almost *any* reading materials to help children develop productive reading strategies. The teacher is the key. One of the primary purposes of this book, then, is to help teachers become knowledgeable enough to foster good reading strategies in children, perhaps despite the approach of the reading materials provided by the schools.

CHARACTERIZING READING AND READING INSTRUCTION

As people become increasingly knowledgeable about the reading process, they typically modify their definitions of reading. But first it is important to determine where one stands. The remainder of this chapter consists mainly of three activities intended to help you determine your own views of reading and reading instruction.

Activity 1. First, please read the following paragraph from David Palermo's excellent *Psychology of Language* (1978, p. 38):

At least four theoretical variants of the interpretive semantic theory have appeared in the literature since Chomsky first grappled with the problem of semantics. In the late 1960s, alternatives were offered by Lakoff (1968), McCawley (1968), and Ross (1967). Their arguments centered around the idea that it is not possible to separate the semantic and syntactic components of the grammar. According to these linguists, there is no single base phrase marker but, rather, sentence generation begins with the semantic component and subsequent interaction between lexical insertion and transformational rules leads eventually to the surface structure and the application of the phonological component. Thus, the focus of linguistic inquiry should give at least equal billing to the semantic component rather than merely relegating semantics to a role of interpreting the syntactic component. The generative semanticists, as these linguists have come to be called, have argued that the underlying structures in standard theory are too concrete. Once the presuppositions and implications of sentences are analyzed in more detail, it becomes necessary to postulate more abstract underlying structures which make the deep structures of sentences deeper and more complex. Ross (1974), for example, shows how a simple causative sentence such as "Dr. Grusel is sharpening the spurs" involves more than seven underlying sentence forms or propositions encompassed within its meaning including, for example, the presuppositions that Dr. Grusel and the spurs exist.

Were you able to read the paragraph, as requested? It should be interesting to discuss your response with others who have tried to read this same paragraph.

Activity 2. Probably the most effective way of determining how a person goes about the task of reading is to examine his or her reading miscues. A miscue is any departure from what the text signals. For example, if a reader substitutes one word for another, adds or omits a word, or reorganizes a sequence of words, he or she has made a miscue.

Compare David's miscues with Tony's, in the following two transcripts of a selection they each read aloud. In each case, do the miscues suggest that the child is using implicit knowledge of *sentence structure* (syntactic cues, like word order and function words[2]) in order to predict a word that is grammatically acceptable in context? Do the miscues suggest that the child is using *meaning* (semantic cues) to predict a word that is meaningful in context? Do the miscues suggest that the child is using *letter-sound correspondences* (grapho/phonic cues) to sound out words? Which child would you say uses a better combination of reading strategies? Again, discuss this activity with others, if possible.

In the transcripts an omission is indicated with a circle around

---

[2] Function words are the "little words" which glue the content words together. The main types of function words are as follows: noun determiners (like the, and like this in this boy); verb auxiliaries (like will in will win); prepositions (like by in by the lake); and conjunctions (like because and and). For a more thorough discussion of these and the other "parts of speech" (grammatical categories) see the appendix.

the word(s) omitted; an addition is indicated above the line with a caret pointing to the added word(s); and a substitution is indicated with the substituted word(s) simply written above the text. Underlining indicates that the reader repeated the word or phrase. The symbol © shows that a miscue was corrected; a © attached to an underline simply means that the reader backtracked and corrected the miscue. Where the reader made more than one attempt at a word or group of words, the attempts are numbered above the text. Where intonation suggested that the reader was uttering what he or she considered just part of a word, a hyphen is used (as in "Mo-" for **Mohamed**).

The reading selection is adapted from Lee Garrett Goetz, *A Camel in the Sea* (New York: McGraw-Hill, 1966), pp. 11–14. This particular adaptation is from *Fiesta*, one of the Houghton Mifflin readers (1971). The line divisions differ in the two transcripts because the story was typed differently for each child.

a. *David's Miscues*

1 Mohamed (mo-hah'med) loved to go swim-

2 ming in the sea. How lucky he was to live in a

    Sami   © willage on the right hand or
3 Somali (so-mah'lee) village right on the Indian

4 Ocean! The sandy shore rang with the happy

    ©
5 shouts and cries of the village boys and girls.

6 They liked to race one another into the surf,

7 splashing and spraying the water into a white

8 dancing foam before they dove into the waves.

        younger
9 Mohamed and his young sister, Āsha (ie'shuh),

10 spent all the time they could in the cool, clean

    swimming,   in the water
11 sea, swimming and playing water games. They

                                            s
12 were good swimmers because their mother had taught them.

13   Every day except Friday, Mohamed went to

14   school with the other village boys. The class

15   was outdoors, and the children sat on little

16   benches in front of the teacher in the shade of

            © twee   may
17   a tall palm tree. They did not have books, so

18   the boys repeated everything the teacher said,

            again
19   over and over, until they knew their lessons by
                  ^

20   heart. The girls of the village did not go to school,

21   for the people thought that school was not as

22   important for girls as it was for boys.

b. *Tony's Miscues*

      Mo-
1   Mohamed (mo-hah'med) loved to go swimming in the sea.
                              2 Sammon
                              1 Sam-
2   How lucky he was to live in a Somali (so-mah'lee) village

3   right on the Indian Ocean! The sandy shore rang with the happy
      soots
4   shouts and cries of the village boys and girls. They liked
                                          high
5   to race one another into the surf, splashing and spraying
                                              ^
            drase
6   the water into a white dancing foam before they dove into the
            Mola   yung   Asla
7   waves. Mohamed and his young sister, Asha (ie'shuh),

8   spent all the time they could in the cool, clean sea,

9   swimming and playing water games. They were good swimmers

10   because their mother had taught them.

expert _Molda_

11   Every day except Friday, Mohamed went to school with the

nother viner

12   other village boys. The class was outdoors, and the children

beaches _frose_   _shape_

13   sat on little benches in front of the teacher in the shade

14   of a tall palm tree. They did not have books, so the boys

ramped

15   repeated everything the teacher said, over and over, until

other classrooms hurt   _vengil_

16   they knew their lessons by heart. The girls of the village

17   did not go to school, for the people thought that school was

imprentice   _to_

18   not as important for girls as it was for boys.

Activity 3. Having tried to read a paragraph for which you may
not have had much background, and having compared the miscues
of two children, you should be able to select or formulate a definition
of reading that accords with your beliefs at the present time. Below
are some definitions and characterizations of reading and the reading process, arranged more or less from simple to complex. Which
one or ones come closest to expressing your own opinion? If none
of these is satisfactory, formulate your own. Then, as you finish
each of the chapters in part 1, return to your chosen definition and,
if necessary, modify it in accordance with your increased understanding of the reading process.

> a. Reading means getting meaning from certain combina-
> tions of letters. Teach the child what each letter stands
> for and he can read. (Flesch, p. 10)
>
> Johnny must learn, once and for all, that words are
> written by putting down letters from left to right, and
> that they are read in the same direction. (Flesch, p. 31)
>
> b. Reading is a precise process. It involves exact, detailed,
> sequential perception and identification of letters, words,
> spelling patterns and larger language units. (view de-
> nounced in K. S. Goodman 1967, p. 126)

c. The linguist's concept of reading is not the concept commonly held by the classroom teacher and the reading specialist—that reading is getting meaning from the print on a page. The linguist conceives the reading act as that of turning the stimulus of the graphic shapes on a surface back into speech. The shapes represent speech; meaning is not found in the marks but in the speech which the marks represent. (Strickland, p. 10)

In order to comprehend what he reads, the reader turns the visual stimulus of written language back into speech —overtly if he is inexperienced and immature, subliminally if he is a rapid, experienced reader. (Strickland, pp. 13–14)

d. Printing is a visual means of representing the sounds which are language. Meaning is in these sounds. We want to equip the child to turn the written word into a spoken word (whether he actually utters it or not) so he will hear what it says, that is, get its meaning. . . . we have never found anybody who did not think that the purpose of reading was to get the meaning. The only possible defense of skipping sound and going directly from print to meaning would be that printed words are directly meaningful—that the printed word *green* means the color, but this is not so. It is the spoken word *green* that designates the color, while the printed word designates the sound of the spoken word. Various linguistics specialists have recently been stressing this fact. (McCracken and Walcutt, p. xiv)

e. Corresponding to the auditory analysis of sentences the skill of reading can be viewed as the ability to extract from a *visual* signal the underlying structure of sentences. (Bever and Bower, p. 20)

f. Reading is a psycholinguistic guessing game. It involves an interaction between thought and language. Efficient reading does not result from precise perception and identification of all elements, but from skill in selecting the fewest, most productive cues necessary to produce guesses which are right the first time. The ability to anticipate that which has not been seen, of course, is vital in reading, just as the ability to anticipate what has not yet been heard is vital in listening. (K. S. Goodman 1967, p. 127)

g. Reading is the active process of reconstructing meaning from language represented by graphic symbols (letters), just as listening is the active process of reconstructing meaning from the sound symbols (phonemes) of oral language. (Smith, Goodman, and Meredith 1970, p. 247)

h. When the light rays from the printed page hit the retinal cells of the eyes, signals are sent along the optic nerve to the visual centers of the brain. This is not yet reading. The mind must function in the process, the signals must be interpreted, and the reader must give significance to what he reads. He must bring *meaning* to the graphic symbol. (Dechant, p. 12)

ACTIVITIES AND PROJECTS FOR FURTHER EXPLORATION

1. If possible, observe several teachers during reading instruction. What kinds of direct instruction do they give? How do they respond to children's miscues? Try to decide what each teacher's implicit definition of reading must be. Later, ask each teacher how he or she would define reading and how reading should be taught. Compare these interview results with what you observed and what you inferred from the observation. In each case, does the teacher's definition of reading seem consistent with his or her teaching practices?

2. If in the preceding activity you discovered teachers with widely differing instructional approaches and/or definitions of reading, it might be particularly interesting to try a further project with some students from the most markedly different teachers. With the teacher's permission, interview some of the poorest and some of the best readers from each class. If possible, tape record the

interviews for later study. Ask such questions as these adapted from Harste (1978, p. 90) :

What is reading?
What makes a person a good reader?
Do you know what your teacher thinks a good reader does?
Do you know anyone in your class who is a good reader?
What does that person do that makes him or her a good reader?

Compare the children's responses with their teacher's instructional approach and definition of reading. What correlations, if any, do you find? Do you find any evidence to support the earlier statement that those children who are least successful at reading may be the very ones who try hardest to do just what the teacher emphasizes?

3. To explore further your own views of reading and reading instruction, you might try the following questionnaire. Indeed, you might have friends and teachers try it. For each question, circle the number that most nearly represents your response. The designations are as follows: 1 strongly agree, 2 agree, 3 no opinon, 4 disagree, 5 strongly disagree.

    a. Teachers do not need to understand the reading process in order to teach reading.   1 2 3 4 5

    b. Learning to read means learning to associate written words with spoken words.   1 2 3 4 5

    c. In beginning reading, it's more important for a child to pronounce words correctly than for the child to get the meaning of what is read.   1 2 3 4 5

    d. Since learners need immediate feedback, a child should be corrected whenever he or she makes an error in reading aloud.   1 2 3 4 5

    e. A child should learn to read sentences one word at a time, without looking ahead or backward.   1 2 3 4 5

    f. Language is defined as a set of arbitrary vocal symbols used for communication.   1 2 3 4 5

    g. Children need to speak standard English before they can learn to read.   1 2 3 4 5

    h. In helping children learn to read, one should focus first on spelling-to-sound

correspondences, then on words, last on
phrases and clauses.   1 2 3 4 5

i. Children should be encouraged to sound
out unfamiliar words instead of guessing
at their meaning.   1 2 3 4 5

j. Learning to read is essentially a matter
of mastering various reading skills.   1 2 3 4 5

k. Children must read aloud with correct
pronunciation in order to understand what
they read.   1 2 3 4 5

l. Children will not be able to attack new
words unless they have been taught
phonics rules.   1 2 3 4 5

m. The English spelling system is based on
regular correspondences between letters
and sounds.   1 2 3 4 5

READINGS FOR FURTHER EXPLORATION

Harste, Jerome C. "Understanding the Hypothesis, It's the Teacher That
Makes the Difference: Part I." *Reading Horizons* 18 (Fall 1977):
32–43. Indicates that the teacher's definition of reading and approach to reading may be crucial in reading instruction.

Downing, John. "How Children Think about Reading." *The Reading
Teacher* 23 (December 1969): 217–230. Discusses five-year-olds'
understanding of reading and of key terms used in reading instruction.

Burke, Carolyn. "Oral Reading Analysis: A View of the Reading Process."
In *Help for the Reading Teacher: New Directions in Research,*
edited by William D. Page. Urbana, Ill.: National Council of
Teachers of English, 1975, pp. 23–33. By discussing various kinds
of miscues, Burke sheds light on the reading process.

Goodman, Yetta. "I Never Read Such a Long Story Before." *English
Journal* 63 (November 1974): 65–71. In examining the miscues
of one particular student, Goodman makes several important
points about the reading process and reading instruction. This
article is highly recommended by most of my students.

Barr, Rebecca. "Processes Underlying the Learning of Printed Words."
Elementary School Journal 75 (January 1975): 258–268. Summarizes research concerning the relation between instructional
methods and kinds of reading miscues.

2

how has reading instruction commonly been viewed?

Certainly, no thoughtful reader can leave this book without wondering how a child can learn to read as a skillful reader reads, when instruction focuses on letter-sound correspondences, word form, word meaning, and questions on the meaning of what was read.[1]—Constance McCullough

Questions for Study and Discussion

1   Why is it overly simple to say that we combine the meanings of the individual words in a sentence in order to arrive at the meaning of the whole?

2   What major grammatical signals help to clarify the meanings of words and the relations among words in a sentence?

3   How might we define sentence surface structure and deep structure?

4   What do psycholinguists mean when they say that we bring meaning *to* sentences instead of getting meaning *from* sentences? More technically, what does it mean to say that we impose deep structure on surface structure?

5   What do phonics, sight word, linguistic, and eclectic approaches to teaching reading all have in common?

6   How are word-centered reading approaches different from meaning-centered approaches, as explained here?

LEARNING TO READ

Everyone seems to agree that the ultimate purpose of reading is to arrive at meaning. However, we can identify at

[1] By "this book," McCullough meant the second edition of *Theoretical Models and Processes of Reading*, edited by Harry Singer and Robert B. Ruddell (Newark, Del.: International Reading Association, 1976). The comment is equally applicable to the present text, however.

least three basic views of learning to read, each of which places a different emphasis on the role of meaning:

View 1 Learning to read means learning to pronounce words.

View 2 Learning to read means learning to identify words and get their meaning.

View 3 Learning to read means learning to bring meaning *to* a text in order to get meaning *from* it.

The first view assumes that once words are pronounced, meaning will take care of itself. The second assumes that once the meaning of individual words is determined, the meaning of the whole sentence (paragraph, text) will take care of itself. The third assumes that meaning results not necessarily from the precise identification of every word in a sentence, but from the constant interplay between the mind of the reader and the language of the text. The latter is a psycholinguistic view.

Many people would find the first definition unsatisfactory, incomplete: it is not enough to pronounce the words. If we cannot also get the meaning, we tend to feel that we are not really reading. This, indeed, may have been your response to the paragraph on generative semantics (activity 1 in chapter 1). You may have been able to pronounce most of the words, yet felt that such word identification did not really constitute reading. If so, your view may be close to view 2, that learning to read means learning to identify words and get their meaning.

As noted, this view assumes that once the meaning of individual words is determined, the meaning of the whole sentence will take care of itself. Since such an assumption seems to underlie most of the reading approaches currently used in the United States, it is important to examine this assumption in some depth.

THE MEANING OF SENTENCES: A FIRST LOOK

Since the mid-1900s, many psychologists and linguists have turned to the investigation of how people learn their native language and how they produce and comprehend sentences.

This interest has led to the rise of a hybrid discipline, *psycholinguistics* (from **psyche,** meaning 'mind', and **linguistics,** meaning the study of language). Already psycholinguists have learned a number of things about sentence production and comprehension. Most of their investigations are too elaborate to be described in this book, but it is relatively easy to demonstrate that we do not simply combine the meanings of individual words in a sentence in order to arrive at the meaning of the whole.

Take, for example, the word **by** in the following sentences. In each case what does it mean, and *how do you know?*

1. That was prescribed by Dr. Lucy.
2. Charlie sat down by Dr. Lucy.
3. Woodstock went by plane.
4. Linus went by the airport.
5. By Snoopy's calculations, it ought to work.

In the first sentence, **by** indicates the agent, the doer of the action: Lucy. In the second sentence, **by** tells where Charlie sat down. In the third sentence, **by** indicates means: Woodstock went via airplane. In the fourth sentence, **by** indicates direction of movement: Linus went past the airport. And in the fifth sentence, **by** means something like 'according to': according to Snoopy's calculations, it ought to work. Instead of using the meaning of **by** to help determine the meaning of the entire sentence, we use the meaning of the entire sentence to determine the precise meaning of the word **by.**

Obviously the word **by** and other simple prepositions are extreme examples, for they have less meaning in isolation than do content words (nouns, verbs, adjectives, and adverbs). However, even the content words take much of their meaning from the context in which they are embedded. To determine this for yourself, try a brief experiment: quickly define the words **chair, run, white,** and **close.** Now read the following sentences and see which of your definitions are appropriate for these contexts:

Get Shirley to chair the meeting.

Marie has a run in her stocking.

Separate the egg white from the yolk.

That was a close call.

Chances are that at least one of your definitions was partially or completely inappropriate to the context. This is because context to a large extent determines the meanings of words.

We seem to be faced with the proverbial question of which comes first, the chicken or the egg. We have seen that the meaning of individual words is largely determined by context, yet what is context, if not a conglomeration of individual words?

One partial answer is that context includes various kinds of grammatical signals to clarify the meanings of words and the relations among them. The three major kinds of grammatical signals are word endings, function words, and word order. These will be briefly discussed in ascending order, from least useful to most useful. It is not necessary, however, to remember all the grammatical terms and details: just concentrate on getting an overview of how meaning is conveyed by word endings, function words, and word order.

WORD ENDINGS

There are various word endings which may signal a word's grammatical category (noun, verb, or whatever) and hence to some extent determine its meaning. Take, for example, the words **chaired, runner, whiten,** and **closely.** The **-ed** on **chaired** suggests that the word denotes an action rather than a place to sit; the **-er** on **runner** suggests that we are talking about a person; the **-en** on **whiten** suggests an action (as in **Clorox will whit**en **your clothes**); and the **-ly** on **closely** suggests the manner in which some action is carried out (as in **She examined it close**ly). Note, however, that most of these endings are not infallible or unambiguous signals: **-ed** can indicate a condition or state, as in **The exhaust**ed **doctor worked on through the night;** the **-er** can indicate either a condition or state or the manner of an action, as in **This one's funni**er (state) or **You'd better move fast**er (manner) ; the **-en** can indicate a condition or quality, as in **The melon's rotten** or **The toast is golden brown**; and **-ly** can indicate a quality or characteristic, as in **That's lovely** or **He's not very friendly**. Word endings help to determine the meanings of words, yet the interpretation of an ending often depends on its context, the base word to which the ending is attached and the way that word is used in a sentence.

FUNCTION WORDS

There are two basic kinds of words in our language, content words and function words. *Content words* are the nouns, verbs, adjectives, and adverbs, the words that indicate most of the specific meaning of the sentence. The *function words* or *signal words* are the ones that glue the content words together. The major kinds of function words are noun determiners, verb auxiliaries, prepositions, and conjunctions. Like word endings, these function words serve as useful but not infallible signals of what is coming next in a sentence. The word **this**, for example, usually works as a noun determiner, to signal that a noun is coming up in a sentence (as in **This problem is difficult**). However, the word **this** can also take the place of a noun, as in **I can't do this**. Somewhat similarly, the words **will** and **can** commonly work as verb auxiliaries, to signal that a verb is coming up (as in **Roger will do it** and **Maryellen can come**). However, both words sometimes function as nouns, as in **She has an iron will** and **He couldn't open the can**. Function words help to signal the relations among words, yet we do not always know whether something is even a function word or not until we see how it fits with other words in the sentence.

WORD ORDER

Word order is an important grammatical signal in modern English. Compare, for example, the following two sentences:

Snoopy kissed Lucy.

Lucy kissed Snoopy.

In the first sentence, Snoopy did the kissing and Lucy was the recipient of the kiss; in the second sentence, Lucy did the kissing and Snoopy received the kiss. The two sentences contain the same words, but the differing word orders signal different relations among the words. Clearly, word order in a sentence is an important clue to the relations among the words and hence to meaning.

So far, then, it should be clear that word endings, function words, and word order all help us determine the meanings of words and the relations among the words in a sentence. On the other hand, we have seen that word endings are often not infallible clues to word function, and that function words are not always identifiable out of context. That leaves us with word order as the best clue to word relationships. We shall see in the next section, however, that even word order is often not adequate to signal the basic relations among the words of a sentence.

SURFACE STRUCTURE AND DEEP STRUCTURE

In our attempt to understand "how sentences mean," we have so far looked primarily at what we might call *surface structure*, the grammatical relations signaled by word endings, function words, and word order. Often, however, these surface signals are not adequate to account for the word relationships that we intuitively perceive.

Take, for example, the sentence **The operation was performed by a new technique.** Looking just at the surface structure, we could analyze the sentence as follows:

Subject	*Predicate*	
Noun phrase	Verb phrase	Prepositional phrase
The operation	**was performed**	**by a new technique.**

We have used the signals of word endings, function words, and word order to cut the sentence and label its major grammatical parts. Let us perform the same procedure with a similar sentence:

Subject	*Predicate*	
Noun phrase	Verb phrase	Prepositional phrase
The operation	**was performed**	**by a new surgeon.**

As you can readily see, the grammatical analysis is exactly the same as before.

Intuitively, however, we know far more about the sentences than this surface analysis reveals. In the first sentence we do not know who performed the operation, but we know that it was performed by means of a new technique. In the second sentence we do not know how the operation was performed, but we know who performed it: a new surgeon. In the second sentence, **surgeon** is actually the underlying subject of the sentence, as we can prove by changing the sentence around: **A new surgeon performed the operation.** If we try this same change with the first sentence, we will produce a nonsensical result: **A new technique performed the operation.** This supports our intuition that **technique** is *not* the underlying subject of the sentence, not the agent who performed the operation.

The foregoing example suggests that we often know far more about word relations than is apparent just from the surface grammar, the signals provided by word endings, function words, and word order. Consider another example:

Snoopy was eager to see.

Snoopy was easy to see.

Once again, the surface signals would lead to the same grammatical description of both sentences. We can readily see, however, that the two sentences derive their meaning in different ways. In the first case, we know that Snoopy wanted to see someone or something; **Snoopy** is the underlying subject of the verb **see,** and an unidentified someone or something is the underlying object. The second sentence indicates essentially the opposite: that it was easy for someone to see Snoopy. An unidentified someone is the underlying subject of **see,** and Snoopy is the underlying object. We determine the underlying structure of the sentences not from any signals present in the surface, but from our knowledge of the words **eager** and **easy** and the kinds of relations they can enter into. In these cases, the nature of a certain key word determines the relations among the other words.

Ambiguous sentences provide still further evidence that the surface structure of a sentence is not always adequate to signal the underlying relations (see, for example, Brause 1977). Consider, for instance, the sentence **She was wearing a light dress.** Out of context, we do not know whether the dress was light in color or made of lightweight material, or both; the word **light** is semantically ambiguous. A somewhat different example is provided by the sentence **Young boys and girls shouldn't be exposed to pornography.** We cannot tell whether pornography should be kept from *young* boys and *young* girls, or from *young* boys and *all* girls (according to the double standard). The word **young** is syntactically ambiguous in the surface structure: we cannot tell for certain what word or words it is supposed to modify. Deep structure ambiguity is illustrated by sentences like **Mike is too young to hit.** We cannot tell whether Mike is too young for someone to hit him, whether he is too young to hit someone else, or both. Without reference to a larger context, we cannot even tell who is potentially doing what to whom.

It is no simple matter to explain how sentences derive their meanings. Although we use word endings, function words, and word order to determine the relations among words, this is by no means the whole story. We must bring to bear our understanding of the context, our internalized knowledge of words and meanings and grammar, and indeed our entire store of knowledge and experience. We cannot get meaning *from* the written page unless we can bring meaning *to* it, as you probably discovered with the paragraph on interpretive semantics (activity 1 in chapter 1).

Let us return to surface structure and deep structure, terms popularized in the early 1960s by Noam Chomsky, the father of transformational linguistics. Since their introduction, the terms have been defined in somewhat differing ways, depending on the definer's particular view of language and/or the purpose of the definition. For our purpose no single definition is entirely satisfactory.

We have defined *surface structure* as the relationships signaled by word endings, function words, and word order. Our cutting and labeling revealed the essential surface structure of the sentences **The operation was performed by a new technique** and **The operation was performed by a new surgeon.** This analysis did not reflect our understanding of the deep structure, our knowledge that the surgeon performed the operation but the technique did not. Despite the fact that there are no overt surface signals to tell us that the surgeon is the agent and the technique is the means, we intuitively understand these underlying relations. *Deep structure*, then, may be defined as the *underlying* relations among the words of a sentence.

Psycholinguists have scarcely begun to explore the question of how listeners and readers comprehend language. Yet it has become increasingly obvious that surface structure is not adequate to signal deep structure.

To further clarify this point, it may help to consider surface structure and deep structure as parts of a continuum. At the one extreme, we can think of surface structure as merely vibrations in the air, created by speaking, or marks on a page, created by writing. If you have ever listened to someone speak a language that you do not know, you may have found that you could not even tell when one word ended and the next word began; the spoken words may have seemed little more than noises. For someone who has no acquaintance with written language, written words probably look like little more than squiggles. Whether spoken or written, the words **I love you** will be meaningless to someone who knows no English, unless nonverbal communication makes them meaningful.

At the other extreme, we can think of deep structure as the personal interpretations one brings to a sentence, based on one's entire store of knowledge and experience. Under some circumstances you may interpret the words **I love you** to be an indirect request for sexual gratification, while under other circumstances you may interpret the same words as an expression of lifelong devotion.

——SURFACE STRUCTURE——			———DEEP STRUCTURE———		
vibrations		word endings,		relational	personal
or	words	function words,	word	meanings	interpre-
squiggles		word order	meanings	among	tation of
				the words in	propo-
				propositions	sitions

Surface–deep structure continuum

Figure 2.1   Figure 2.1 depicts, then, a surface–deep structure continuum. Among other possibilities, surface structure might be
defined as vibrations or squiggles; as words; or as the grammatical relations signaled by word endings, function words,
and word order. Deep structure might be defined as word
meanings; relational meanings among the words in propositions (the who-did-what-to-whom sort of thing); or the
personal interpretation of propositions. The term *proposition* is used here in a semitechnical sense: a proposition expresses a state or action and the entities involved in that
state or action. Thus in **I love you**, the state or action is
love, while **I** and **you** are the entities involved. However,
our precise interpretation of the relation(s) among the
entities in this sentence will depend upon the circumstances
and the meaning we bring *to* the sentence.

This again indicates what we have already seen: that
comprehension is *not* a one-way process from surface structure to deep structure. Indeed, as we interpret what we
hear or read, we in effect impose deep structure on surface
structure. Our prior knowledge and experience determine
our understanding of the relations among the words in a
proposition, as in **The operation was performed by a new
surgeon** and **The operation was performed by a new technique**. Also, our understanding of the possible relations
among words determines our interpretation of individual
words, as with the word **by** in **Charlie sat down** *by* **Dr. Lucy**
and in **Woodstock went** *by* **plane**. Perhaps more surprising,
however, is the fact that our entire system of knowledge
and belief can affect even our perception of individual words
and parts of words. While reading a story to my son, I made
the following miscue:

older
The other seals knew better.

My students insist that this miscue was caused not so much by the preceding context of the story as by my unwarranted belief that to be older is to be wiser. Their explanation is probably right.

It seems clear, then, that meaning is not in words but in us, the originators and users of language. Hence we must reject the simplistic notion that once words are identified, sentence meaning will take care of itself.

Unfortunately, however, this simplistic view seems to underlie most approaches to reading instruction. Even though the proponents of some approaches insist that meaning is of primary concern from the very outset, beginning reading instruction usually focuses upon the identification of words.

The next section deals with some of the major approaches to beginning reading instruction. Those who work mainly with older readers will doubtless recognize vestiges of one or more of these approaches in the materials designed for their students.

APPROACHES TO BEGINNING READING INSTRUCTION

Following are brief sketches of five approaches to reading instruction: a phonics approach, a sight word approach, a so-called linguistic approach, a language experience approach, and an eclectic approach. These descriptions are, of course, gross simplifications.

A PHONICS APPROACH

Advocates of a phonics approach are concerned about helping beginners become independent readers as soon as possible. They emphasize helping children learn letter-sound correspondences in order to sound out words. This approach was especially popular from about 1890 through the 1920s, when it was gradually superseded by a sight word approach.

The most extreme advocates of a phonics approach obviously believe that learning to read means learning to pronounce the words. As Rudolph Flesch put it, "Reading means getting meaning from certain combinations of letters. Teach the child what each letter stands for and he can read" (Flesch 1955, p. 10). Like Flesch, most proponents of a phonics approach seem to think that once words are identified, meaning will take care of itself.

A SIGHT WORD OR "LOOK-SAY" APPROACH

Those who advocate a sight word approach are concerned that meaning be emphasized from the very outset of reading instruction. They stress helping children develop a stock of words that the children can recognize on sight. Thus instead of stressing letter-sound correspondences and phonics "rules," teachers might use flash cards and other devices to help children learn to recognize basic words like **I, and**, and **the**. Advocates of a sight word approach argue that if children can begin with a stock of about one hundred basic sight words, they will be able to read about half the words in any text they might ordinarily encounter.

This approach was widely used from about 1930 until about the mid-1960s, when it became increasingly intertwined with (or infiltrated by) a phonics approach. Although advocates of the sight word approach have expressed concern with meaning, actual classroom instruction has tended to focus heavily on the recognition of words. Thus the sight word approach also seems to assume that once words are identified, meaning will take care of itself. It differs from a phonics approach mainly in focusing on whole words rather than on parts of words.

A LINGUISTIC APPROACH

The so-called linguistic approach is based upon the tenets of structural linguists, whose school of thought was prominent in the 1950s. Those who advocate a linguistic approach are generally concerned with helping children internalize regular patterns of spelling-sound correspondence. The emphasis is not upon teaching rules, but rather upon helping children read sets of words from which they can unconsciously infer regular spelling-sound correspondences; a a typical sentence from an early lesson would be something like **Nan can fan Dan**. The founder of this approach was Leonard Bloomfield, more widely known as the founder of structural linguistics. Although Bloomfield first advocated his "linguistic" approach in the early 1940s, it did not become embodied in a text of any kind until the early 1960s, when Bloomfield and Barnhart's *Let's Read* finally appeared. Their linguistic or spelling-pattern approach was embodied in several reading series of the late 1960s and early 1970s. The approach assumes that learning to read means learning to pronounce the words, and that once words are identified, meaning takes care of itself (see the "linguistic" definitions of reading in activity 3 of chapter 1).

A LANGUAGE EXPERIENCE APPROACH

Those who advocate a language experience approach are concerned with helping beginners learn to bring their own knowledge and experience to bear in getting meaning from the printed word. To do this, teachers start with the language and experiences of the children. Typically, the child dictates his or her story to the teacher, or the children compose a story or poem together and the teacher writes it on the board. Together they read and reread the story, until the children can begin to associate the written words with their own spoken words. This approach and related approaches have had several peaks of popularity: from about 1909 to 1918; in the late 1920s and early 1930s; and again from about the mid-1960s into the early 1970s. This approach seems to assume that learning to read means learning to glean meaning from a text, and that in order to get the meaning, we must bring meaning *to* what we read.

AN ECLECTIC APPROACH

Experienced teachers who have read the preceding descriptions may have concluded that they do not entirely agree with *any* of the approaches discussed. This is hardly surprising, since I have tried to present the various approaches very briefly and in their purest or most extreme form. Since the mid-1960s, textbooks and teachers have increasingly come to advocate what might be called an eclectic or smorgasbord approach. This approach may have been stimulated, at least in part, by the Cooperative Research studies sponsored by the U.S. Office of Education in the 1960s, which found no clear-cut superiority for any of the approaches just discussed. As a former president of the International Reading Association put it,

> In the First Grade Studies a few years ago, which compared different ways to teach beginning reading, greater variability was found among *teachers* in the results obtained, whatever the approach, than among *approaches*. A prevalent interpretation of this finding is that, since teachers (not approaches) make the greater difference, a teacher should choose and use a variety of approaches. This decision presupposes that if one approach which did not make so great a difference was somehow insufficient, several such insufficient approaches —end to end, simultaneous, stirred and served, or presented separately in an inviting smorgasbord—would create a sufficiency. (McCullough 1976, p. 6)

Obviously McCullough questions the wisdom of an eclectic or smorgasbord approach, but in the later 1960s and the 1970s it became increasingly common to draw from a variety of approaches: phonics, sight word, linguistic, language experience, and others not previously mentioned. With an eclectic approach as with most of its components, instructional attention tends to focus upon the identification of words, apparently on the assumption that once words are identified, meaning will take care of itself.

COMPARING THE APPROACHES

In actual practice there may be almost infinite variation upon the basic approaches sketched here. Oddly enough, however, many educators tend to reduce the approaches to two simple opposing alternatives: if you are not a phonics advocate, then you are assumed to be an advocate of a sight word approach, and vice versa. All the world seems to be divided into just these two parts (see figure 2.2).

In her influential book *Learning to Read: The Great Debate* (1967), Jeanne Chall divided beginning reading approaches into two similar but more inclusive categories: *code-emphasis approaches* and *meaning-emphasis approaches*. By a code-emphasis approach she meant an approach that initially emphasizes breaking the alphabetic code, that emphasizes learning correspondences between letters and sounds. The phonics approach and the linguistic or spelling-pattern approach are both code-emphasis approaches. By a meaning-emphasis approach Chall meant one which initially emphasizes getting meaning. In her scheme the sight word approach and the language experience approach are both meaning-emphasis approaches (see figure 2.3).

I would like to suggest, however, that Chall's categori-

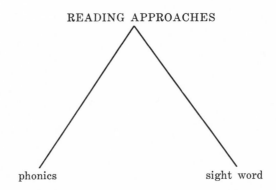

READING APPROACHES

phonics   sight word

Figure 2.2 *Simplistic categorization of reading approaches*

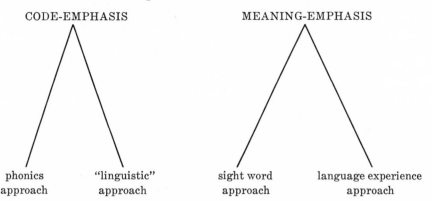

CODE-EMPHASIS   MEANING-EMPHASIS

phonics   "linguistic"   sight word   language experience
approach   approach   approach   approach

Figure 2.3   *Chall's categorization of reading approaches (a partial model). Based on Chall 1967. The eclectic approach is omitted because it does not fit into either category exclusively.*

zation overlooks an important similarity among the phonics, linguistic, sight word, and eclectic approaches: they are all word-centered, emphasizing surface structure rather than deep structure. More specifically, they all seem to assume that reading instruction should focus on the identification of words. Of the five approaches discussed here, only the language experience approach seems to be genuinely meaning-centered, emphasizing the getting of meaning and the fact that we must bring meaning *to* a text in order to get meaning from it. Figure 2.4 thus divides the major reading approaches into those which are word-centered and those which are meaning-centered—that is, those which focus on surface structure (identifying words in a sentence) and those which focus on deep structure (determining the meaningful relations among the words in a sentence).

Even a language experience approach can become a word-centered approach, of course, especially if adopted by someone who does not fully understand the underlying assumptions of the language experience approach. And it would surely be unfortunate to conclude that there can be no other approach which emphasizes learning to bring meaning *to* what we read in order to get meaning *from* it. In fact,

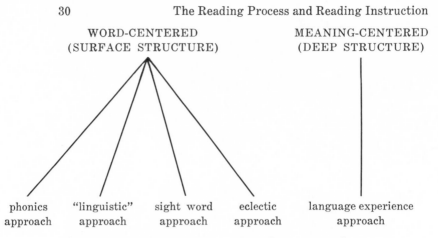

| WORD-CENTERED
(SURFACE STRUCTURE) | | | | MEANING-CENTERED
(DEEP STRUCTURE) |

| phonics
approach | "linguistic"
approach | sight word
approach | eclectic
approach | language experience
approach |

Figure 2.4 *Recategorization of reading approaches*

Part 2 outlines a much broader psycholinguistic approach for the school curriculum, an approach which includes language experience as only one of its components. At the present time, however, language experience seems to be the one widely known approach which implicitly recognizes what is known about the psycholinguistic nature of the reading process, the fact that effective reading involves a constant interaction between the mind of the reader and the language of the text.

Unless you already have some background in psycholinguistics, you have probably only begun to grasp the importance of the distinction between word-centered approaches and meaning-centered approaches. Indeed, you may wonder why anyone would even question the notion that beginning reading instruction should focus on the identification of words. Since this concern with word identification is so common, it seems wise to turn our attention next to the perception and identification of words, which we shall do in chapter 3.

ACTIVITIES AND PROJECTS FOR FURTHER EXPLORATION

1. Write a paragraph in which you explain, in your own words, why it is overly simple to say that we combine the meanings of the individual words in a sentence in order to arrive at the meaning of

the whole sentence. (You may first want to do one or both of the next two projects.) In your discussion, compare sentences such as those in the following pairs. But don't just deal with these particular sentences: try to draw generalizations about how we comprehend sentences.

    a. Alan rowed the boat with ease.
       Alan rowed the boat with Anne.

    b. Look at the minute hand.
       Look at the minute printing.

    c. Mary promised Ronnie to go.
       Mary asked Ronnie to go.

    d. John is happy to go.
       John is silly to go.

    e. It's a shame that Sally always wins.
       It's a game that Sally always wins.

2. Carol Chomsky was one of the first linguists to discover that many young schoolchildren could not understand certain kinds of syntactic constructions, apparently because the surface structure inadequately signals the deep structure (C. Chomsky 1969). You might try replicating some of her research with, say, four to six-year-olds. First, put the following objects (or reasonable substitutes) on a table: two different kinds of stuffed animals, such as a dog and a teddy bear; a doll; a blanket or towel; a handkerchief rolled up to make a blindfold. Next, try the following procedures:

a. Say to the child "The doll is easy to see. Would you please make her hard to see?" Observe whether the child puts the blindfold on the doll (making it hard for the doll to see), or whether the child correctly places the doll under the blanket or does something similar.

b. Say to the child "The teddy bear promised the dog to jump off the table. Please make him do it." Observe whether the child makes the dog jump off the table, or whether the child correctly makes the teddy bear jump off the table.

c. Say to the child "The dog asked the teddy bear to jump off the table. Please make him do it." Observe whether the child makes the dog jump off the table, or whether the child correctly makes the teddy bear jump off the table.
Discuss your results and the possible implications for reading instruction.

3. You might find it interesting to compare children's ability to read the words of a sentence with their ability to comprehend the sentence, using idiomatic or slang expressions. An excellent source of such expressions is Maxine Tull Boatner and John Edward Gates's *A Dictionary of American Idioms*, updated by Adam Makkai (Woodbury, N.Y.: Barron's Educational Series, 1975). Using your own ingenuity or some reference such as this, create a list of sentences which have words that early elementary children are likely to be able to read, but which have meanings that they may not understand. Then try out your list with some children, perhaps second or third graders. Find out whether they can read the words of the sentence and, if so, whether they can explain the idiomatic meaning. Here are some possible sentences, just to give you ideas:

> Bob really has it made.
>
> Jim has a lot on the ball.
>
> Mary pulled the rug out from under him.
>
> You're really out of step.
>
> She's really a ball of fire.
>
> Old Joe finally kicked the bucket.

4. Sometimes an approach to reading can be inferred from trade books. Particuarly interesting in this regard are the "Bright and Early" books published by Random House. Compare, for example, the following three books: Al Perkins's *Hand, Hand, Fingers, Thumb* (1969); Theo. LeSieg's *In a People House* (1972); and Stan and Jan Berenstain's *Bears in the Night* (1971). What reading approach or approaches seem to underlie each of these books?

5. In order to become better acquainted with some of the various reading approaches, you might examine and compare the reading series listed as the first four of the following suggested readings.

READINGS FOR FURTHER EXPLORATION

McCracken, Glenn, and Walcutt, Charles C. *Lippincott's Basic Reading,* 4th ed. Philadelphia: J. B. Lippincott, 1975. A complete basal reading series based on what its authors call a "phonic/linguistic" approach.

Durr, William K., et al. *Houghton Mifflin Readers.* Boston: Houghton Mifflin, 1974. If this eclectic basal reading series is not readily available, you might instead look at the Ginn *Reading 720* series (1976), or at the *Holt Basic Reading System* (1977).

Aaron, I. E., et al. *Reading Unlimited: Scott, Foresman Systems, Revised.* Glenview, Ill.: Scott, Foresman, 1976. Possibly the most psycholinguistically oriented basal reading series available in the late 1970s.

Martin, Bill, and Brogan, Peggy. *The Sounds of Language.* 2nd ed. New York: Holt, Rinehart and Winston, 1972–ff. A K-8 series that is sometimes considered supplemental, though it could well be used in place of a more ordinary basal reading series. It advocates a psycholinguistically sound approach which begins much like the language experience approach, by helping children associate aurally familiar songs and rhymes with their written counterparts. You should find it helpful to read the teacher's edition section, which is the same for each of the readers.

Smith, Frank. "Two Faces of Language." In his *Comprehension and Learning: A Conceptual Framework for Teachers.* New York: Holt, Rinehart and Winston, 1975, pp. 83–117. The first parts of the chapter (to the top of p. 95) are highly recommended as a complement to the discussion here.

Carton, Aaron S. *Orientation to Reading.* Rowley, Mass.: Newbury House Publishers, 1976. Presents a considerably more sophisticated treatment of many of the topics in the present text. Of particular interest at this point is chapter 6, "The Linguistics of Reading and Some Issues of Educational Psychology."

Hall, MaryAnne. *Teaching Reading as a Language Experience.* 2nd ed. Columbus, Ohio: Charles E. Merrill Publishing, 1976. An excellent introduction to the language experience approach. The first two chapters discuss the theoretical foundations of the approach and its relation to the total curriculum, while the remaining seven chapters provide a wealth of practical suggestions for the classroom.

Lee, Dorris M., and Rubin, Joseph B. *Children and Language: Reading and Writing, Talking and Listening.* Belmont, Calif.: Wadsworth, 1979. An outstanding introduction to the language experience approach, this text includes three excellent chapters on the reading process and reading instruction.

3

how are words perceived?

Words may be identified when their individual letters are separately indistinguishable.—Frank Smith

Questions for Study and Discussion

1   How do the eyes function in visual perception?

2   What does it mean to say that visual perception is more a function of the brain than of the eye?

3   Do we normally process words letter by letter, from left to right?

4   Which parts of words are more useful in word identification: the consonants, or the vowels? The beginnings, the middles, or the ends?

5   Why might the preoperational child find phonics instruction particularly difficult?

6   How useful are phonics rules? How necessary is it for children to learn phonics rules?

THE EYES AND THE BRAIN

When children have difficulty reading, it is common practice to have their eyes checked. This is wise, because various kinds of eye malfunction can indeed make reading more difficult. In most cases, however, appropriately prescribed glasses will be adequate to compensate for problems with the eyes themselves. There are few children whose reading problems can be attributed to irremediable difficulties with the eyes. This is because visual perception is only partly a function of the eyes. Perhaps your experience on the superhighways illustrates this point. Have you ever "seen" the words on a road sign, yet passed the sign before you were able to determine what the words were? Perhaps you were a little slow in looking at the sign, or perhaps you have nearsighted eyes that were a little slow in picking up the visual image. Nevertheless, the crucial problem was not in the eyes, but in the brain: your brain simply did not have enough time to process the visual image before it disappeared from sight.

The preceding illustration suggests that visual perception is not merely a function of the eyes, but a function of the brain. In this text we are concerned with one particular kind of visual perception, the perception of words. We will be concerned with *both* aspects of word perception: with ocular and sensory processing, and with the actual identification of words.[1] However, such division is merely a convenient fiction, as this and the next two chapters should make increasingly clear. Visual perception is an *active* process, and what the eye processes is in large part determined by what the brain directs it to look for, as well as the knowledge that the brain brings *to* the visual task. We use our prior knowledge and experience to guide even the most elementary aspects of visual processing.

After discussing the ocular and sensory processing of words, we will turn to several activities which should help you better understand how words are perceived.

OCULAR AND SENSORY PROCESSING

It was noted previously that the eye registers a visual image. Strictly speaking, however, this statement is not accurate. As the psycholinguist Frank Smith explains, "What goes into the open eyes is a diffuse and continual bombardment of electromagnetic radiation, minute waves of light energy that vary only in frequency, amplitude, and spatial and temporal patterning. The rays of light that

---

[1] It seems to me that the terms *perception, identification,* and *recognition* are nearly synonymous; hence I use them more or less interchangeably. My particular choice in any given instance is dictated by connotation rather than denotation: it seems to me that "perception" more readily includes the possibility of error, that "identification" and "recognition" imply *accurate* perception. Note, however, that all three of these words indicate a decision on the part of the *brain.*

impinge on the eye do not in themselves carry the color and form and texture and movement that we see." Rather, these are constructions of the brain (Smith 1978, pp. 26–27). So, too, in reading: the eye itself receives waves of light energy that are transmitted to the brain as a series of neural impulses. Initially, the written symbols may be perceived as sets of bars, slits, edges, curves, angles, and breaks (Gough 1972, p. 332; see also Smith 1978, chaps. 8 and 9). The brain may then construct the words of the text from these bars, curves, angles, or whatever.

How, then, do the eyes (the ocular part of the system) pick up these waves of light energy that are transformed into words? In 1879, the Frenchman Emile Javal discovered that the eyes move along a line of print with a series of jerky movements which he called *saccades*, meaning 'jerks.' It is difficult if not impossible to become aware of one's own saccades, for the eyes *seem* to move along a line of print with a smooth, continuous motion. Nevertheless, they do not: they move in a sequence of tiny leaps or jerks.

There is no useful vision during the eye movements themselves, as you can demonstrate by looking into a mirror with your head held still and moving your eyes from left to right between two imaginary points. As you will discover, you cannot see your eyes in motion. Neither can you read with your eyes in motion (Anderson and Dearborn 1952, p. 101).

The saccades, or eye movements, take up only a small fraction of total reading time—about 10 percent of the time in rapid reading and about 5 percent of the time in slow reading (Anderson and Dearborn 1952, p. 107). The rest of the time is taken up by eye *fixations*, or pauses. It is during these fixations that the eye receives the stimuli which are transformed into visual images in the brain.

Various aspects of visual processing have been studied in the laboratory, usually with the help of a *tachistoscope*. In simple terms, a tachistoscope is a device for presenting visual information for very short periods of time—say as little as 10 milliseconds (10 thousandths of a second, or 1 hundredth of a second). With the use of the tachistoscope, it has been found that successive letters or words can be perceived from a visual presentation as short as one-tenth of a second (see Huey 1908, p. 65). Further, it has been found that as many as four or five words can be perceived in a single fixation (see Smith 1971, p. 92). Such statistics represent the *maximal efficiency* of the ocular and sensory systems.

Usually, however, reading proceeds much more slowly. The average adult reader makes about four eye fixations per second and identifies about one word per fixation. This gives an average adult reading speed of 240 words per minute (see Carroll 1970, p. 292; Anderson and Dearborn 1952, p. 177; and Dechant 1970, p. 16). Many readers have a slightly higher rate, up to about 300 words per minute. This means either that they average slightly more than four fixations per second, or that they average slightly more than one word per fixation, or both.

These various measurements indicate that there is a considerable discrepancy between what the ocular and the sensory systems are capable of doing, and what they typically do in reading. The crucial differences are summarized in figure 3.1. From these comparisons it should be obvious that, for most people, the ocular and sensory systems do not operate at maximal efficiency in normal reading. The eyes can handle about 960 to 1200 words per minute, yet most of us read at an average speed of about 240 to 300 words per minute. Apparently most of us read at this slower rate because that is a comfortable speed for comprehending.

Of course, readers need to learn to vary their reading rate according to the material and their purpose for reading. To some extent we all do this, yet many of us could benefit from instruction and practice. We need to learn, for example, that it's okay to read a novel rapidly and without necessarily trying to remember all the details: there is no need to read a novel at a rate of only 240 to 300 words per minute unless we really want to. Then, too, we need to learn to skim and scan informational material, selecting only those parts of the text that are relevant to the par-

Maximal Ocular and Sensory Efficiency	Typical Ocular and Sensory Functioning in Reading
An eye fixation of 1/10 second is enough for identifying a letter or word.	Eye fixations are normally about 1/4 second long.
We can identify four or five words in a normal eye fixation of about 1/4 second.	Readers typically process about one word in a normal eye fixation of about 1/4 second.
We can visually process about 960 to 1200 words per minute.	Most of us read at an average rate of about 240 to 300 words per minute.

Figure 3.1   *Ocular and sensory processing*

ticular purpose at hand. In general, these seem to be the purposes of so-called speed reading courses.

While recognizing the widespread need for this kind of instruction, one should be wary of the simplistic notion that to improve a person's reading, all we have to do is improve his or her reading rate. If a person reads much slower than the average, this usually means that he or she has difficulty getting meaning from the text. The slow reading speed may be more a *symptom* of reading difficulty than a cause. In such cases, it may not help much to get readers to identify words faster; indeed, this may not even be possible.

What *will* help is various strategies for helping readers learn to bring meaning to a text in order to get meaning from it. This approach will actually make word identification faster and more accurate, as the next section begins to show.

HOW WE PERCEIVE WORDS

The brain does not just passively interpret the data relayed through the eyes. In fact, the brain is in large measure independent of the eye. In normal vision, the picture that the eye registers is upside down, but the brain rights it. And as Frank Smith observes,

In a number of perceptual experiments, many men and animals have been fitted with special spectacles which completely distort the information received by the eye, switching top to bottom, or left to right, or distorting form or color. But within a very short while the brain "adapts" and the perceived world reverts to its normal appearance. No further distortion is perceived until the trick spectacles are removed, whereupon the "normal" pattern of stimulation produces a topsy-turvy percept which persists until the brain readapts. (Smith 1971, p. 89)

For more details, see Kohler 1962. As you will probably conclude, the brain performs equally marvelous feats in normal reading.

Before investigating what cues within words are especially important in word perception, it seems wise to deal with the typical notion that words are processed in serial fashion, letter by letter, from left to right.

Activity 1. First, try the following exercise on formulating phonics rules. In each of the words below, one letter is printed in boldface type. Determine how each boldfaced letter should be pronounced, and what part of the word signals the pronunciation of the boldfaced letter. In other words, try to formulate a *rule* for producing the correct pronunciation of the boldfaced letters. You will need at least one rule for each of the three sets:

a. hat	hate
hatter	hater
pet	Pete
petted	Peter
bit	bite
bitter	biting
mop	mope
mopping	moping
cut	cute
cutter	cuter

b. wrap   war
   wren   wet
   wring   win
   wrong   won

c. car   cent
   care   cereal
   coat   cite
   cough   city
   cube   cyclone
   cut   cyst

Discussion. For the first column of words in set **a**, you may have formulated a rule something like this: a vowel is short when it is followed by just a single consonant, or when it is followed by a double consonant plus an ending of some sort. For the second column of words in set **a**, you may have formulated a rule something like the following: a vowel is long when it is followed by a silent **e**, or when it is followed by a single consonant plus an ending of some sort. Complicated, yes? The words in set **b** should have been easier to deal with, and you may have formulated a rather simple rule such as this: when a word begins with a **w** followed by an **r**, the **w** is not pronounced; otherwise, it is pronounced as a /w/. (The slashes indicate that we are talking about a sound rather than a letter.) For the words in set **c**, you might have formulated a rule something like this: when **c** is followed by **a**, **o**, or **u**, it is pronounced /k/; when **c** is followed by **e**, **i**, or **y**, it is pronounced /s/.

Doubtless these are not only rules possible, nor are they necessarily the best rules. But note that in each case *the pronunciation of the boldfaced letter is determined not by what precedes, but by what follows.* We could not possibly pronounce the listed words correctly if we processed and pronounced them merely letter by letter, from left to right. Furthermore, most of these words are not exotic words that we encounter only once or twice in a lifetime; most are relatively common words that we encounter fairly often. As Venezky put it in *The Structure of English Orthography*, "a person who attempts to scan left to right, letter by letter, pronouncing as he goes, could not correctly read most English words" (1970, p. 129).

Activity 2. Activity 1 leaves open the possibility that we might process each letter separately, even if not left to right. To test this possibility, try replicating the following experiment from p. 100 of Edmund Huey's *The Psychology and Pedagogy of Reading* (1968; first published in 1908). For this experiment, you will need either a stop watch or a watch or clock with a second hand. Figure 3.2 contains a column of letters, a column of four-letter words, and a column of eight-letter words. Time yourself or someone else reading the column of letters as rapidly as possible, either simply identifying each letter mentally or pronouncing it aloud. Repeat the same procedure for the column of four-letter words and the column of eight-letter words.

y	pool	analysis
w	rugs	habitual
u	mark	occupied
s	send	inherent
q	list	probable
o	more	summoned
m	pick	devotion
k	stab	remarked
i	neck	overcome
g	your	resolute
e	dice	elements
c	font	conclude
a	earl	numbered
z	whit	struggle
x	ants	division
v	role	research
t	sink	original
r	rust	involved
p	ware	obstacle
n	fuss	relative
l	tick	physical
j	rasp	pastness
h	mold	lacteals
f	hive	sameness
d	four	distract

Figure 3.2 *Huey's lists of letters and words*

Discussion. Even though you may have stumbled over some unfamiliar words, you probably found that it did not take nearly four times as long to read the column of four-letter words as it took to read the column of single letters. Nor, surely, did it take eight times as long to read the column of eight-letter words. Huey's four experimental subjects read the columns aloud, averaging 15.7 seconds for the isolated letters, 17.3 seconds for the four-letter words, and 19.6 seconds for the eight-letter words (Huey 1968, p. 101). When I first tried the experiment, I read the columns silently. It took me 7 seconds for the single letters, 7 seconds for the four-letter words, and almost 8 seconds for the eight-letter words. Clearly, fluent readers do not process words letter by letter. Just as we do not comprehend sentences merely by combining the meanings of individual words, so we do not perceive words merely by combining the perceptions of individual letters.

Activity 3. We have now demonstrated that we do not simply read words from left to right, and that we do not identify each of the letters in a word prior to identifying the word itself. This leaves open two major possibilities. On the one hand, we might process just part of the visual information from all or most of the letters in a word. On the other hand, we might process all or most of the visual information from just some of the letters in a word. To test the former possibility, try to identify the mutilated words in the list below:

couid

short

about

voice

trust

scarf

drank

ghost

which

stand

Discussion. You may have tried to determine individual letters in order to decide upon some of the words.[2] But for most, you were probably able to identify the word as a whole, without consciously identifying the separate letters, and by using only some of the visual information normally available from each letter.

WORD PERCEPTION IN REVIEW

From the foregoing activities we can draw several generalizations about word recognition in fluent reading:

1. We do not simply process a word from left to right.

2. We do not separately identify each of the letters in a word prior to identifying the word itself.

3. It may be that we process just part of the visual information from all or most of the letters in a word; certainly this *can* be done. On the other hand, it may be that we process all or most of the visual information from just some of the letters in a word.

The next section points out that certain letters and certain parts of letters are particularly useful in word identification. Hence it seems likely that neither of the extreme positions in the third of the preceding generalizations is entirely accurate. Rather, it appears that we identify words by processing just *part* of the visual information from *some* of the letters in a word. This is particularly likely when the word occurs in a context that narrows down the reasonable possibilities. Consider, for example, the following sentence:

Johnny put on his pajamas and jumped into b-d.

Surely we do not need to see the vowel letter or even all the parts of **b** and **d** to know that the last word is **bed**.

---

[2] The words, in order of occurrence, are: **could, short, about, voice, trust, scarf, drank, ghost, which, stand.** For a similar list of mutilated words, see Anderson and Dearborn 1952, p. 189; they reproduced the words by permission from a test constructed by L. L. Thurstone.

Given this example, it may not be surprising that words can be identified under conditions which make it impossible to identify individual letters. As long ago as the turn of the century, Erdmann and Dodge determined: 1) that words can be recognized when lying too far from the eyes' fixation point to permit recognition of individual letters; 2) that words can be recognized when they are constructed of letters so small that the letters cannot be singly identified; and 3) that words can be recognized from distances at which the letters, exposed singly, cannot be recognized (see Huey 1968, pp. 73–74). Similarly, it has been found that words can be identified at illuminations (lighting conditions) which do not permit the identification of single letters. In one experiment, it was found that even first graders could identify familiar three-letter words at lower light intensities than they needed for identifying single letters (see Smith 1971, p. 141).

To get an idea of what these experiments are like, suppose that two letters are flashed upon a screen in front of you and that you are told these letters form an English word. Suppose too that you cannot identify either of the letters with certainty, but you can see enough features to determine that the first letter must be **a** or **e**, and that the second letter must be **f** or **t**. Since this limits the possible combinations to **af**, **at**, **ef**, and **et**, you can readily identify the word as **at**. Because only one of the possible combinations forms a word in standard written English, you can identify the word without being able to identify either letter by itself (see Smith 1978, p. 125).

At this point we can begin to see what it means to say that we bring meaning *to* the written page in order to get meaning *from* it. We bring not only our knowledge of the world and our intuitive knowledge of grammar, but even an internalized knowledge of letter and sound patterns. Consider, for a moment, the following list of words. Which ones look like English words? Which ones do not?

glung	rpet	cratn	drepm
tsont	dremp	terp	stont
pret	lgung	crant	tepr

Without ever having been told, we know what is possible in English, and what is not. For example, we know that **glurck** and **blong** are possible, while **ckurgl** and **ngobl** are not (see Gibson, Shurcliff, and Yonas 1970, p. 59; Gibson 1972, p. 13). Just as we do not consciously think of how sentences are structured as we speak, so we do not consciously think of how words are structured as we listen or read. Nevertheless, even before learning to read, we have acquired an internalized knowledge of sound patterns, and we quickly begin to acquire a similar internalized knowledge of letter patterns. Thus our internalized knowledge of letter patterns enables us to identify words from only a fraction of the visual information available.

Edmund Huey's 1908 conclusion still serves to summarize much of what is known about word perception (1968, pp. 111–112):

> Even in the more pronounced cases of letter consciousness, . . . it is perfectly certain that words are not perceived by a successive recognition of letter after letter, or even by any simultaneous recognition of all the letters *as such*. By whatever cues the recognition may be set off, it is certainly a recognition of word-wholes, except when even these recognition units are subsumed under the recognition of a still larger unit. The only question is as to what parts are especially operative as cues in setting off this recognition.

It is to precisely this question that we will turn our attention in the next section.

PARTS OF WORDS AT WORK

The following three activities are designed to help you determine which parts of words are highly useful and which parts less useful in cueing the recognition of words. However, it must be admitted that the experiments are highly unscientific. There has been no strict control over vocabulary or sentence length and structure, and, most importantly, the words are presented in context rather than in isolation. But these experiments are more fun and easier to carry out than the more scientific kinds of experiments on isolated words, and in most cases your conclusions are likely to be the same.[3]

Activity 1. You will need a stop watch, or a watch or clock with a second hand, to time yourself or someone else reading the following two sets of sentences, which constitute the beginning of a little story:

  a. *Vowels absent*
    –nc– –p–n – t–m– th–r– w–s – h–nds–m– y––ng
    w–lf n–m–d L–b–. L–b– l–v–d w–th h–s m–th–r –nd
    f–th–r –t th– –dg– –f – d––p, d–rk w––ds. –v–r–
    d–– L–b– w–nt t– h–nt –t th– n–rth –dg– –f th–
    w––ds, n––r th– l–ttl– v–ll–g– –f C–l––s.

  b. *Consonants absent*
    –o–e–i–e– a–– –o–o –ou–– –i–– –a– a –i–e–e– o––
    –a––e– o– –i– –i–e, –o––i–– i– ––e –ie––s –ea–
    ––e –oo–– o– –i––i–– –e––ie– i– ––e ––i––e–. A–
    o––e– –i–e–, –o–o –i––– –e –u––y e–ou–– –o –i–– a
    ––u––, –ui–y ––i–– ––a– –a– –i–o–eye– i–– –a–e–––
    a–– –––aye– –oc –a– ––o– –o–e.

Discussion. After this experiment, it should be obvious that consonants are more important than vowels in cueing word recognition. This can be explained, at least in part, by two simple factors. First, there are considerably more consonants than vowels in English, and hence the consonants are more distinctive, more able to narrow

---

[3] One interesting example of such experiments involved the reversal of two letters at the beginning or the middle or the end of a word, as with **vaiation**, **avitaion**, and **aviatino** for the word **aviation**. The words were hardest to identify when the reversal occurred at the beginning, and easiest to identify when the reversal occurred in the middle; thus the experiment suggests that beginnings are most important in word perception and middles are least important (Bruner and O'Dowd 1958).

down the number of possible alternatives that any given word could be. Second, the consonants occur more frequently than the vowels; that is, in most cases there are more consonants per word. Given these factors, it is hardly surprising to find that consonants are more useful in cueing word recognition. Indeed, written Arabic omits the vowels altogether, except in beginners' books (Gibson and Levin 1975, p. 524).

Activity 2. This activity is related to the first. Again, time yourself or someone else reading the following two sets of sentences, a continuation of our ongoing story:

    a. *Bottoms absent*

       One day as Lobo was skirting the edge of the forest he came upon a little girl in a red hood. Her cheeks were so rosy and her arms so pudgy that Lobo knew she would be delicious. "Where are you going little girl?" he asked. "Oh," she replied. "I'm taking this basket of goodies to my grandmother on the other side of the woods. Grandma isn't feeling very well."

    b. *Tops absent*

       Lobo thought for a moment. He could hardly wait to devour this scrumptious child, but then again he was hungry enough to eat the grandmother too. "Which house does your grandmother live in?" asked the wolf. "In the house by the three big oak trees," said Red Riding Hood (for that is what she was called). "She lives there all by herself."

Discussion. Which paragraph took longer to read? Which part seems to be more important in cueing word recognition: the tops of words, or the bottoms? Most people conclude that the tops are more important, and this is indeed what research suggests. If you have not already figured out why, then look at the following list of the letters in our alphabet. How many ascend above the top line? How many descend below the bottom line?

a b c d e f g h i j k l m n o p q r s t u v w x y z

As you can readily see, almost twice as many ascend above the top line, making them visually more prominent. Note, too, that more than half of the consonants either ascend above the top line or descend below the bottom line, while none of the vowels do either (with the exception of y, which is only sometimes a vowel). Hence consonants are not only more numerous and more frequently occurring than vowels, but many are also visually more prominent.

Activity 3. Again, time yourself or someone else reading the following passages, in order to determine the relative importance of the beginnings, middles, and ends of words:

 a. *Middles absent*
  "W–at a mar–––ous oppo–––nity!" th–––ht L–bo.
  He t–ld t–e c––ld to s–op a–d p–ck fl–––rs f–r h–r
  gran–––ther on t–e w–y th–––gh t–e w––ds, t–en
  t–ok o–f on a s––rt c–t t–at o–ly t–e wo––es k–ow
  a––ut. S–on he ar–––ed at t–e grand–––her's
  co–––ge. "I–'s me, Gr–––ma," L–bo s–id in a t–ny
  v––ce, as he kn–––ed on t–e d–or. He pu––ed t–e
  d––r o–en a–d w–nt in.

 b. *Ends absent*
  Lob– wen– strai–––– to th– grandmoth––'– be–
  an– gobb–––– he– up. He donn––– he– ca– an– gow–
  an– clim–––– int– be–, feel–––– non– to– wel–
  hims––––. By th– tim– Litt–– Re– Ridi–– Hoo– ha–
  arri–––, howe–––, he ha– overc–––– hi– atta–– of
  indigest––– and wa– rea–– fo– dess–––. He
  answe––– Red'– kno–– in an ol–, crack–– voi––:
  "Com– in, dea–. Jus– com– on in."

 c. *Beginnings absent*
  –obo –as so –––enous –hat he ––dn't –ait –or
  ––ttle –ed ––ding –ood to –sk –er "–––ndma" –ow
  –he –as or –o ––ing –er –he ––sket of –––dies.
  He ––rew –ack –he ––vers, ––mped –ut of –ed,
  –nd –an –ver to –he ––ild. –he –––eamed –nd
  –an, –ut it –as –oo –ate. –obo –––bled –er up.
  –––erwards he –at by –he –––eside –––king
  –––ndma's –ipe, –––aming of ––icy ––ttle ––rls.

Discussion. Once again, which set of sentences took longest to read? Which took the shortest time to read? From this experiment, you have probably concluded that the beginnings of words are more important in word identification than the middles or the ends, and this is certainly what research suggests. Various kinds of research also indicate, quite clearly, that the ends are more important than the middles. If your results suggested otherwise, it was probably due to the flaws in the design of this particular experiment.

Again, we may ask the reasons for these common observations. First, it seems that the beginnings and ends of words are important just because they are visually prominent, being either preceded or followed by white space. Second, the beginnings of words are particularly important because we read the words of a text more or less from left to right. In addition, the beginnings of words are less predictable than the ends, and therefore more necessary. The ends are more predictable than the beginnings because they often consist of grammatical endings, many of which are predictable from context (see the "Crashe Helmutt" exercise, p. 206, and the first activity at the end of this chapter). Thus endings are less important cues to word recognition than beginnings, because endings are more predictable. On the other hand, endings are more important than middles, partly because they often do carry grammatical information. For a discussion of many of the experiments that give rise to such observations, see chapter 5 of Anderson and Dearborn 1952.

It is interesting to note that children pay increasing attention to the beginnings and ends of words as they become more proficient at reading. In one study, for example, the spaces between words were filled in with a symbol created by superimposing an x on a c (seexSpotxrun). Groups of children in the first and second grade read such a "filled" version of a story, as well as an "unfilled" or normal version of a story. The filled version took significantly longer to read, but the difference was most noticeable for the better readers. The poorer, slower readers were affected relatively little by the filled-in text (Hochberg 1970, pp. 87–88). Since the poorer and slower readers were not much affected by the lack of spaces between words, it seems that these readers had not yet learned to pay particular attention to the beginnings and ends of words (see Brown 1970, pp. 169–170). And this, in fact, might be one reason why these children *were* the less proficient readers.

PARTS OF WORDS IN REVIEW

Which parts of words are particularly important in cueing word recognition? We have found that:

1. Consonants are more important than vowels.
2. Beginnings of words are more important than middles and ends, and ends are more important than middles.
3. Some people may be relatively nonproficient readers at least in part because they have not yet learned to attend to the parts of words that provide the most useful information.

It seems evident that proficient readers do not identify words by first identifying the letters in the word; normal reading proceeds far too fast for this. Instead, we select some of the information from some of the letters in order to arrive at an identification of the whole word. And we do this by bringing to bear not only our unconscious knowledge of which parts of letters and words are particularly useful, but also our internalized knowledge of letter and sound patterns. We use a minimal amount of visual information and a maximal amount of nonvisual information. Thus the brain does not passively interpret data gathered by the eyes. On the contrary, the brain tells the eyes what data to gather, which parts of words to attend to. Visual perception is in fact more a function of the brain than of the eye.

THE IMPORTANCE OF PHONICS

In many phonics programs, about two-thirds of the rules taught are concerned with vowel letters and their sounds.

But since vowels are so much less important than consonants in word recognition, you may have wondered about the need for teaching such a number of vowel rules. Although the present discussion is somewhat incomplete, it at least begins to suggest that the teaching of a multiplicity of phonics rules (vowel *and* consonant rules) is not nearly as useful or necessary as is commonly thought.

PHONICS AND THE PREOPERATIONAL CHILD

It is important to note that many children in kindergarten and first grade (even second grade) may not yet be far enough along in their cognitive development to handle much phonics instruction. Though not complete or conclusive, research strongly suggests that children may have difficulty learning to read if they have not yet reached what the Swiss psychologist Jean Piaget calls the *concrete operational* stage of cognitive development, which is commonly attained somewhere around the age of 7.

The *preoperational* child is unable to do certain things that seem to be important in reading, perhaps particularly important when phonics is stressed. First, children in the preoperational stage are unable to *decenter*: they tend to center their attention on one aspect of something, and are unable to attend to more than one aspect at once. Second, children in the preoperational stage are unable to *reverse* in their thinking: they cannot think back to how something was before it was perceptually changed, because they do not understand the process of getting from one state to another. Third, and more specifically, children in the preoperational stage cannot *conserve:* they cannot understand that the number or amount of something remains the same regardless of any changes in appearance. These broad characteristics mean that the preoperational child does not understand certain kinds of things that seem obvious to us adults.

Since this general discussion is not primarily concerned with cognitive development but rather with phonics, we will merely list some of the more specific limitations of preoperational thought and briefly indicate how these limitations might hinder reading instruction in general and phonics instruction in particular:

1. Preoperational children do not understand *one-to-one correspondence*. Therefore, they may have difficulty matching written words with spoken words, and they are even more likely to have difficulty matching letters with letter names and/or sounds.

2. Preoperational children do not understand *class inclusion*, the relation between part and whole. Therefore, they may have difficulty understanding that a lowercase letter and an uppercase letter belong to the same category (that a and A are "the same"). Similarly, preoperational children may have even more difficulty understanding that a letter category can represent a whole class of sounds (for example, that there is a category of "a" sounds, a category which includes at least the six sounds illustrated in **at, ate, all, arm, above, any**). Furthermore, children who do not understand class inclusion may have difficulty understanding the relation between a sequence of individual sounds (parts) and the word which is constituted by these sounds (a whole). That is, children who do not understand part–whole relationships may have difficulty in analyzing a word into its constituent sounds, and also in blending sounds to form a word.

3. Preoperational children do not understand *seriation*: they cannot think both backward and forward at the same time. For example, they cannot alphabetize a list of words, because they cannot simultaneously think of a given letter as coming after something, but before something else (as **b** comes after **a**, but before **c**). An inability to seriate might contribute to children's difficulty in sounding out words, as well as to difficulty in using both preceding and following context to help identify a word.

To speak of "preoperational children" and "children in the preoperational stage" is a convenient oversimplification, since any given child may be preoperational with respect to one kind of cognitive ability, yet not with respect to another. The progress from preoperational thinking to concrete operational thinking is in fact gradual, and there are stages in the child's developing ability to understand each one of the concepts that characterize the more advanced stage of thought.

The concepts in the preceding list require either an ability to decenter, an ability to reverse in one's thinking, or both. An ability to decenter is important to reading in a variety of ways, including some global ones. Children who cannot focus their attention on more than one aspect of something are likely to have too limited an approach to reading; they may, for example, try to use phonics as the *only* method of tackling a word that they do not immediately recognize on sight. Indeed, as noted in chapter 1, such children may even have too limited a definition of reading; they may think reading simply means pronouncing the letters or putting sounds together. Such a view of reading obviously is inadequate and detrimental.

It seems reasonable, then, to hypothesize that the preoperational child may have more trouble with phonics instruction than the child who has mastered the cognitive abilities and concepts that characterize concrete operational thought. Teachers may find that children who are preoperational have trouble with phonics, and that children who have trouble with phonics are in at least some respects preoperational. It must be remembered, however, that these are only tendencies: research has not proven that concrete operational thought is absolutely necessary for reading in general or for phonics in particular (see Waller 1977, p. 23).

PHONICS KNOWLEDGE AND PHONICS INSTRUCTION

We have seen that phonics may be difficult for the preoperational child. But what about phonics for the child who understands one-to-one correspondence, class inclusion, and seriation, the child who can decenter and reverse in his or her thinking? In short, what about phonics for the concrete operational child, or even the adult? The following activities are designed to help you explore this question.

Activity 1.   First, pronounce the following lists of words:

a. longer   singer   finger   ranger
   longest   wringer   anger   stranger
   stronger   hanger   dangle   danger
   strongest   manger

b. phone   uphill   father   fathead
   sphere   uphold   other   outhouse
   graph

c. thesis   the   there
   theory   this   then
   theater   these   thence
   thinks   that   thenceforth
   thought   those   thus
   thin   they   therefore
   thick   them   though
   thirsty   their(s)   than

Presumably you had no difficulty pronouncing these words. But examine the words more carefully. How did you pronounce the **ng** in the words of set (a) above? Did your pronunciation differ somewhat from column to column? Try to formulate a phonics rule or set of related rules which would enable someone to pronounce correctly the **ng** in the **longer, singer, finger,** and **ranger** columns. Then do the same kinds of things with the **ph** and **th** in set (b), and with the **th** in set (c). In each case, try to formulate a phonics rule or set of rules that would enable someone to pronounce these letters correctly.

Discussion. Let us deal first with the words in set (a). You probably pronounced the **ng** in the **longer** column as an "ng" sound plus a "g" sound; together, these two sounds can be symbolized as /ŋg/. You probably pronounced the **ng** in the **singer** column simply as /ŋ/, unless your dialect happens to dictate an /ŋg/ pronunciation here too. In the **finger** column, you probably pronounced the **ng** as /ŋg/; and in the **ranger** column, you probably pronounced the **ng** as a "j" sound, which can be symbolized as /ǰ/. For convenience, these pronunciations might be recapitulated as follows:

/ŋg/	/ŋ/	/ŋg/	/ǰ/
longer	singer	finger	ranger

Now the question is, what rules govern these pronunciations? I myself am not completely certain, but the following rules are the best my students and I have been able to formulate:

1. When the base word is an adjective (like **long**), pronounce the **ng** as /ŋg/.
2. When the base word is a verb (like **sing**), pronounce the **ng** as /ŋ/, in most dialects.
3. When the base word is a noun of Germanic origin (as in **finger**), pronounce the **ng** as /ŋg/.
4. When the base word is a noun of Romance origin (like **ranger**), pronounce the **ng** as /ǰ/.

These rules will correctly account for the pronunciation of **ng** in most words that end in **nger**. Note, however, that **range** could be considered a verb as well as a noun, and could thus be assigned to category (2). Further specification of the rules would be necessary to avoid this consequence.

Now then, what about the rules for sets (b) and (c)? By comparison, these rules are relatively simple. The following will more or less take care of set (b):

1. When the word is a compound word divided between **p** and **h** (as in **uphill**), pronounce the **p** and **h** separately, as /p/ plus /h/. Otherwise, pronounce **ph** as /f/.
2. When the word is a compound word divided between **t** and **h** (as in **fathead**), pronounce the **t** and **h** separately as /t/ plus /h/. Otherwise, pronounce **th** as a single sound. (Actually this still does not tell us how

to pronounce the unit **th**, because there are two so-called "th" sounds, as in **thin** and **the**, respectively.)

In order to formulate any halfway simple rule for the **th** units in set (c), we would have to specify that we are talking about **th** in initial position, at the beginning of a word. Hence our rules might look something like this:

1. When a word begins with **th**, pronounce it as a "soft" **th** /θ/ if the word is a noun, a verb, or an adjective (as in the first column of set (c)).

2. When a word begins with **th**, pronounce it as a "hard" **th** /ð/ if the word is a pronoun, noun determiner, adverb, conjunctive adverb, or subordinating conjunction (as in the second and third columns of set (c)).

There are a few exceptions, like **through, throughout**, and **thither** (which, according to the rule, ought to be pronounced with a "hard" /ð/ sound). For the most part, however, these two rules will accurately predict the pronunciation of **th** at the beginnings of words.

If you are beginning to think that spelling-sound correspondences are very complicated, you are absolutely right. Imagine telling a child that you pronounce **ng** one way if the word is a noun of Germanic origin, but another way if the word is a noun of Romance origin. Or imagine telling a child that in order to decide on the pronunciation of **ph** and **th** within a word, you have to decide first whether it is a compound word or not. One hardly needs the phonics rule if one already knows whether or not the word is made up of two smaller words. And it is equally ridiculous to try to decide on a word's grammatical category in order to determine how to pronounce initial **th**; if one knows the word's grammatical category, one presumably knows the word itself and thus how to pronounce it.

Detailed investigations into the nature of our spelling system have disclosed that there are far more correspondences between spelling and sound than detractors of the spelling system have supposed. On the other hand, such investigations have also revealed what we have begun to see for ourselves: that the conditions governing such spelling-sound correspondences are often far more complex than is generally recognized (see Venezky 1970, both items, and Venezky 1967). Nor is this complexity confined to words that are used primarily by adults rather than children. In one of the more extensive studies, Berdiansky and her associates tried to establish a set of rules to account for the spelling-sound correspondences in over 6000 one-syllable and two-syllable words among 9000 different words in the comprehension vocabularies of six- to nine-year-old children. The researchers discovered that their 6092 words involved 211 separate spelling-sound correspondences, 211 correspondences between a letter or two letters functioning together (like **qu**) and a sound. Of these 211 correspondences, 166 occurred in at least 10 words out of the set of 6092 words; 45 correspondences occurred in fewer than 10 words (Berdiansky et al. 1969, p. 11; see Smith 1978, pp. 139–140).

The foregoing sets of words and rules should convince you that it is not possible to teach the more complex letter-sound correspondences or "rules" to children. But what of the simpler correspondences and rules, the kinds typically taught in phonics programs?

The fact is that many of these so-called rules do not work very well. There are too many exceptions (and the vowel rules are especially unreliable). These conclusions were made painfully obvious through a series of studies (Clymer 1963, Emans 1967, Bailey 1967, and Burmeister 1968). As Frank May and Susan Eliot suggest in *To Help Children Read* (1978), only a few phonics rules are consistent enough or cover enough words to make them worth teaching. May and Eliot suggest that the following seven rules are probably worth the effort (p. 38):

1) The "**c** rule." When **c** comes just before **a**, **o**, or **u**, it usually has the **hard** sound heard in **cat**, **cot**, and **cut**. Otherwise, it usually has the soft sound heard in **cent**, **city**, and **bicycle**.

2) The "**g** rule." (Similar to the "**c** rule.") When **g** comes at the end of words or just before **a**, **o**, or **u**, it usually has the **hard** sound heard in **tag**, **game**, **go**, and **gush**. Otherwise it usually has the soft sound heard in **gem**, **giant** and **gym**. (Some important exceptions are **get**, **give**, **begin** and **girl**.)

3) The VC pattern. This pattern is seen in words such as **an**, **can**, **candy** and **dinner**. As a verbal generalization it might be stated as follows: In either a word or a syllable, a single vowel letter followed by a consonant letter, digraph, or blend usually represents a short vowel sound. (Some teachers find it easier for children to remember the pattern rather than

the rule. Note that C stands for either a consonant letter, consonant digraph, or consonant blend, e.g., **bat, bath, bask.**)

4) The VV (vowel digraph) pattern. This pattern is seen in words such as **eat, beater, peach, see, feed, bait, float,** and **play.** As a verbal generalization it might be stated like this: In a word or syllable containing a vowel digraph, the first letter in the digraph usually represents the long vowel sound and the second letter is usually silent. ("When two vowel letters go walking, the first one does the talking.") According to Clymer (1963), this generalization is quite reliable for **ee, oa,** and **ay** (**fee, coat, tray**) and works about two-thirds of the time for **ea** and **ai** (**seat, bait**), but is not reliable for other vowel digraphs such as **ei, ie,** or **oo** (**eight, chief, boot**). And, of course, it is not valid for diphthongs represented by **oi, oy, ou,** and **ow** (**oil, boy, out, cow**).

5) The VCE (final **e**) pattern. This pattern is seen in words such as **ice, nice, ate, plate, paste, flute, vote,** and **clothe.** As a generalization it might be stated this way: In one-syllable words containing two vowel letters, one of which is a final **e,** the first vowel letter usually represents a long vowel sound, and the final **e** is silent.

6) The CV pattern. This pattern is seen in words or syllables such as **he, she, go, my, cry, hotel, going,** and **flying.** As a generalization it could be stated like this: When there is only one vowel letter in a word or syllable and it comes at the end of the word or syllable, it usually represents the long vowel sound.

7) The "**r** rule." This rule applies to words like **far, fare, girl, fur, her,** and **here.** As a generalization it might be stated as follows: The letter **r** usually modifies the short or long sound of the preceding vowel letter. For instance, the word **car** does *not* illustrate the VC pattern seen in the word **cat**; nor does **fir** represent the VC pattern seen in **fit.** The word **care** usually doesn't illustrate the VCE pattern seen in the word **cape** (although in some dialects it does). Likewise, the word **fair** usually doesn't illustrate the VV pattern seen in **wait.**

The following activity should help you consider whether children need to learn consciously even such generalizations and "rules" as the ones May has listed.

Activity 2. Read the following paragraph aloud, as smoothly as possible:

Corandic is an emurient grof with many fribs; it granks from corite, an olg which cargs like lange. Corite grinkles several other tarances, which garkers excarp by glarcking the corite and starping it in tranker-clarped storbs. The tarances starp a chark which is exparged with worters, branking a slorp. This slorp is garped through several other corusces, finally frasting a pragety, blickant crankle: coranda. Coranda is a cargurt, grinkling corandic and borigen. The corandic is nacerated from the borigen by means of loracity. Thus garkers finally thrap a glick, bracht, glupous grapant, corandic, which granks in many starps.

Discussion. You were no doubt able to pronounce most of the words in the paragraph. But did you *consciously* apply any phonics rules? If so, which ones? If not, how did you know or decide how to pronounce the words? Once having recovered from the shock of seeing so many nonwords, most people are able to read the paragraph rather well, and without consciously applying many phonics rules. They have simply internalized enough knowledge of spelling-sound correspondences to be able to pronounce most of the words with little trouble. In fact, I have found that most adult readers who once had phonics instruction cannot verbalize many if any of the rules, whereas most adult readers who never had phonics instruction can apply phonics rules anyway. Thus it is by no means clear that children should be expected consciously to learn and apply phonics rules, beyond perhaps the very basic correspondences typically taught in prereading programs. And these, it should be noted, are often taught prematurely, when the child may have difficulty mastering even the basic one-to-one correspondences between letters and letter names or between letters and sounds.

Since children can apply phonics rules without being able to verbalize them, much of the current phonics instruction probably goes beyond what is needed. Teachers can group words that reveal common spelling patterns and help children observe such patterns. However, it is not necessary for children consciously to learn phonics rules, just as you probably never learned the "rules" for pronouncing ng or th. With a little guided observation, children can internalize the more useful generalizations well enough to apply them, without conscious thought. We do not expect toddlers *consciously* to learn rules for putting sounds together in order to form words, and neither need we expect young schoolage children consciously to learn rules for taking words apart and putting them back together again.

To those steeped in phonics, it must be startling to think that we can learn spelling-sound correspondences without consciously studying phonics rules. Nevertheless, there is considerable evidence to substantiate this point. As indicated before, most adult readers can demonstrate such knowledge by reading words like those in the "corandic" passage in activity 2. Furthermore, children who learn to read before attending school usually demonstrate this kind of internalized knowledge, even if no one has called much attention to letter-sound correspondences and spelling-sound patterns. Although phonics *knowledge* is necessary, heavy phonics *instruction* is not.

PHONICS IN REVIEW

This introductory discussion of phonics began by questioning the need to teach a multiplicity of vowel rules, since vowels are much less important in word identification than consonants. Then it was noted that phonics may be particularly difficult for the preoperational child. Next we observed that: 1) spelling-sound correspondences are often very complex and not easily reducible to rules that can or should be taught; 2) only a few of the frequently taught rules are consistent enough or cover enough words to make them worth teaching; and 3) people can apply so-called phonics rules even though they may never have had phonics instruction. Finally, this discussion led to the suggestion that children may not consciously need to learn phonics rules, and that indeed they may not need nearly as much phonics instruction as has recently been thought.

This phenomenon of "overteach" became obvious to me when my seven-year-old son was working on a phonics exercise that involved words beginning with consonant clusters. Suspecting that he did not know several of the words on his worksheet, I asked him to read me the list. He proceeded to do so, with only a few hesitations. The ensuing conversation went essentially like this:

Me: "How did you read all those words?"

John: "Well, some I knew, and some I just tried."

Me: "On the ones you just tried, did you try to use any rule?"

John: "In school, the rule is just try to sound it out the best you can."

Me: "But did you try to use any specific rule you've been taught, like thinking 'That could be a silent **e**, so the **a** before it might be a long a'?"

John: "No, because sometimes the rules don't work anyway. I just tried saying the words."

The irony, of course, is that having taught the children certain phonics rules from the basal reading series, the teacher then had to teach the children not to apply the rules but just to "sound it out the best you can." And given the unreliability of many of the common phonics rules, and the difficulty of knowing *which* rule to apply, this was doubtless good advice.

Instead of teaching phonics "rules," we might better expose children to patterned sets of words like **ate, date, hate, late, mate, rate,** calling the children's attention to the consistent spelling-sound pattern. Such instruction will help children unconsciously formulate their own "rule" for pronouncing similarly patterned words.

ACTIVITIES AND PROJECTS FOR FURTHER EXPLORATION

1. To test for yourself the assertion that grammatical endings are often predictable when a word occurs in context, try to provide the endings missing from the following sentences (the same sentences from which the consonants were earlier omitted). As before, the dash indicates an omitted letter:

Sometime– all Lobo could find was a wizen–– old farm––
and his wife, work––– in the field– near the wood– or
pick––– berri–– in the thicket. At other time–, Lobo might
be luck– enough to find a plump, juic– child that had dis-
obey–– its parent– and stray–– too far from home.

Did you find it easy to provide the grammatical endings? What
do you think of the notion that we should teach grammatical
endings to children in order to help them identify words?

2. If you are not familiar with the symbols of the Initial Teaching Alphabet, try the following experiment (or try it with someone else
who is not familiar with the ITA). First, try to decide what
sounds are probably represented by the following symbols:

ae   ʊ   ω   ie   th   ʒ   ʃh   dʒ   ŋ

Now, simply read the paragraph below. This is an alternative
conclusion to our story about the wolf and Red Riding Hood:

þe littl girl taested deliʃhous
but loeboe hardly had tiem tω
enjoi þe flaevor befoer somwun
nakt at þe doer. þe wωlf
skrambld bak intω bed and sed,
"Cum on in. just oepen þe doer."
in stroed a big wωdsman. hee
recogniesd þe wωlf at wuns,
and loeboe berly had tiem tω
jump out ov bed and þrω a
windoe befoer þe wωdsman's aks
fel. tω þis dae, loeboe has never
gon bak tω þe south edʒ ov þe
wωds. hee staes nir hoem,
settliŋ for weezend oeld farmers
and þer wievs.

Were you able to read the preceding paragraph fairly easily, even
if you did not know what sound each of the symbols represents?
If so, how were you able to read the passage without knowing
all the letter-sound relationships?

3. To continue exploring the idea that the use of context can reduce our
need for visual information during normal reading, have someone

try to supply the words which are missing from the following, our story about the wolf and Red Riding Hood. The first letter of each missing word is provided as a clue, along with dashes to represent the missing letters:

Once upon a t--- there was a handsome y---- wolf named Lobo. Lobo l---- with his mother and f----- at the edge of a d---, dark woods. Every day L--- went to hunt at t-- north edge of the w----, near the little village o- Calais. Sometimes all Lobo c---- find was a wizened o-- farmer and his wife, w------- in the fields near t-- woods or picking berries i- the thicket. At other t----, Lobo might be lucky e----- to find a plump, j---- child that had disobeyed i-- parents and strayed too f-- from home.

One day a- Lobo was skirting the e--- of the forest, he c--- upon a little girl i- a red hood. Her c----- were so rosy and h-- arms so pudgy that L--- knew she would be d--------. "Where are you going, l----- girl?" he asked. "Oh," s-- replied, "I'm taking this b----- of goodies to my g----------- on the other side o- the woods. Grandma isn't f------ very well."

Lobo thought f-- a moment. He could h----- wait to devour this s---------- child, but then again h- was hungry enough to e-- the grandmother too. "Which h---- does your grandmother live i-?" asked the wolf. "In t-- house by the three b-- oak trees," said Red R----- Hood (for that is w--- she was called). "She l---- there all by herself."

"W--- a marvelous opportunity!" thought L---. He told the child t- stop and pick flowers f-- her grandmother on the w-- through the woods, then t--- off on a short c-- that only the wolves k--- about. Soon he arrived a- the grandmother's cottage. "It's m-, Grandma," Lobo said in a t--- voice, as he knocked o- the door. He pulled t-- door open and went i-.

Lobo went straight to t-- grandmother's bed and gobbled h-- up. He donned her c-- and gown and climbed i--- bed, feeling none too w--- himself. By the time L----- Red Riding Hood had a------, however, he had overcome h-- attack of indigestion and w-- ready for dessert. He a-------- Red's knock in an o--, cracked voice: "Come in, d---. Just come on in."

L––– was so ravenous that h– didn't wait for Little R–– Riding Hood to ask h–– "grandma" how she was o– to bring her the b––––– of goodies. He threw b––– the covers, jumped out o– bed, and ran over t– the child. She screamed a–– ran, but it was t–– late. Lobo gobbled her u–. Afterwards he sat b– the fireside smoking grandma's p–––, dreaming of juicy little g–––––.

Which kinds of missing words were easier to supply: content words, or function words? Was it possible to get the essential meaning, even without being able to supply all the words?

READINGS FOR FURTHER EXPLORATION

Cox, Mary B. "The Effect of Conservation Ability on Reading Competency." *The Reading Teacher* 30 (December 1976): 251–258. Provides an excellent introduction to research on the possible relation between preoperational thought and reading difficulty. Cox describes her research in enough detail that even the inexperienced can replicate her procedures, and her conclusions are interesting, perhaps even startling. My only quibble is with her suggestion that the phonics method may be easier than the sight word method for the preoperational child.

Smith, Frank. "The Efficiency of Phonics." In *Psycholinguistics and Reading,* edited by Frank Smith. New York: Holt, Rinehart and Winston, 1973, pp. 84–90. An article sufficient to convince almost anyone that it would be highly inefficient to rely on phonics as the sole method of teaching reading or the sole method of identifying words that are not immediately recognized on sight.

Artley, A. Sterl. "Phonics Revisited." *Language Arts* 54 (February 1977): 121–126. Convincingly puts phonics into an appropriate perspective.

McKee, Paul. *Primer for Parents.* 3rd ed. Boston: Houghton Mifflin, 1975. McKee's little booklet suggests that beginning reading instruction should stress the use of consonants and context as cues to word recognition.

Geissal, Mary Ann, and Knafle, June D. "A Linguistic View of Auditory Discrimination Tests and Exercises." *The Reading Teacher* 31 (November 1977): 134–140. An excellent argument against the use of auditory discrimination tests as a predictor of reading success.

Gibson, Eleanor J., and Levin, Harry. *The Psychology of Reading*. Cambridge, Mass.: MIT Press, 1975, pp. 119–125. As this summary reveals, there is considerable experimental evidence that many first graders may not be able to hear the separate sounds (phonemes) within words. The entire chapter on "Language Development" is very interesting, though much of it is too technical for the beginner.

4

how does context aid in word identification?

The art of becoming a fluent reader lies in learning to rely less and less on information from the eyes.—Frank Smith

Questions for Study and Discussion

1 What are the various kinds of context that can aid in word identification?

2 Are words easier to identify in isolation, or in context?

3 What does it mean to say that the more nonvisual information a reader can use, the less visual information he or she needs?

4 How do good and poor readers typically differ in their use of context?

5 How are the language cue systems (syntactic, semantic, grapho/phonic) related to reading strategies?

6 What characterizes the effective and efficient reader?

7 How much phonics should be taught? When, why, and how?

8 Given what is known about the reading process, what are some objections to the sight word, phonics, and eclectic approaches?

THE VARIETIES OF CONTEXT: AN OVERVIEW

In the preceding chapter, we saw that our knowledge of letter patterns aids in word identification. To convince yourself further, glance quickly at the column of pseudowords on the left below, then write down as many as you can remember. Next, do the same with the column of pseudowords on the right (Miller, Bruner, and Postman, 1954, p. 133):

RICANING	YRULPZOC
VERNALIT	OZHGPMTJ

MOISSANT	DLEGQMNW
POKERSON	GFUJXZAQ
FAVORIAL	WXPAUJVB

The pseudowords on the left are obviously much easier to perceive and recall, simply because their letter patterns are a much closer approximation to normal English.

Given our internalized knowledge of letter patterns, it should not be surprising that we can identify a word in about as much time as it takes to identify a single letter. Indeed, we have already seen this in the experiment with Huey's lists of letters and words. And we shall now see that just as we can identify a related group of letters in about the same length of time as it takes to identify a single letter, so we can identify a related group of words in about the same length of time as it takes to identify a single word. Research shows, in fact, that during a normal eye fixation of about one-fourth second, we can identify about four or five unrelated letters, or about ten or twelve letters organized into two or three unrelated words, or about twenty to twenty-five letters organized into a sequence of four or five related words (see, for example, Smith 1973, p. 56, and Smith 1975, p. 58). Hence during a normal eye fixation, we might be able to identify a sequence like **lgibh**, a sequence like **know boys that**, or a sequence like **that girl knew many boys**. Our perceptual span increases as does the relatedness of the units being identified:

4 or 5 unrelated letters	lgibh
10 to 12 letters, organized into 2 or 3 unrelated words	knew boys that
20 to 25 letters, organized into 4 or 5 related words	that girl knew many boys

We can identify more letters when they are organized into words, and more words when they are organized into a related phrase or sentence.

In phrases and sentences, we have basically two kinds of context to aid in word identification: syntactic context, and semantic context. *Syntactic context* consists of the signals provided by word endings, function words, and word order (see chapter 2). *Semantic context* consists of the meaningful relations among the words. In short, *syntax* means grammar, and *semantics* means meaning.

To see how grammar and meaning aid in the identification and recall of words, look for a moment at the following four strings of words. Which string would be easiest to process? Which would be hardest? Why?

Furry wildcats fight furious battles.

Furry jewelers create distressed stains.

Furry fight furious wildcats battles.

Furry create distressed jewelers stains.

As you might suspect, the first string is typically easiest to process, because it has both grammar and meaning: that is, it preserves normal word order, and it makes reasonable sense. The fourth string is typically hardest to process, because it has neither grammar nor meaning: the string does not preserve normal word order, and it does not make sense. Processing is easier when we have either normal word order (string 2) or some semblance of meaning (string 3). (For details, see Marks and Miller 1964, pp. 1–5).

Various laboratory experiments indicate that *both* grammar and meaning aid in the identification and recall of words. Both syntactic context and semantic context are important, as you probably concluded from some of the activities in the preceding chapter.

Another revealing activity is the so-called *cloze test*, a widely known and widely respected method for assessing a reader's comprehension and his or her use of reading strategies. The cloze test typically requires supplying every fifth word of a text, as in the following example from Bormuth (1975, p. 70). Try to fill each blank space with whatever you think was omitted from the original text (in some cases a number or a part of a hyphenated word has been omitted). As you fill in the blanks, try to be conscious of how you are using context, of what kinds of context you are using:

The Beaver

Indians call beavers the "little men of the woods."

But they (1)_____ really so very little.

(2)_____ beavers grow to be (3)_____ or four

feet long (4)_____ weigh from 30 to (5)_____

pounds. These "little men (6)_____ the woods" are

busy (7)_____ of the time. That (8)_____ why

we sometimes say, "(9)_____ busy as a beaver."

(10)_____ know how to build (11)_____ that

can hold water. (12)_____ use their two front

(13)_____ to do some of (14)_____ work. Cutting

down a (15)_____ with their four sharp-(16)_____

teeth is easy. A (17)_____ can cut down a (18)_____

four inches thick in (19)_____ 15 minutes.

At the outset you probably found that to fill in the blanks you had to use both the grammar and the meaning of the preceding part of the sentence. In the first sentence where a blank occurs, **But they**_____ . . . , the word **they** suggests that a verb will be coming next; this is grammatical context, or syntax. The word **but** suggests that this second sentence will in some way contradict the first, and that the verb should therefore contain a negative marker; this is meaning context, or semantics. Putting both kinds of information together (and some other information as well), we are likely to supply the word **aren't: But they** *aren't* **really so very little.** This word seems to fit syntactically and semantically with what comes after the blank as well as with what comes before.[1]

In some cases, following context is even more essential

---

[1] The omitted words are: (1) aren't, (2) Most, (3) three, (4) and, (5) 40, (6) of, (7) most, (8) is, (9) as, (10) Beavers, (11) dams, (12) They, (13) paws, (14) their, (15) tree, (16) pointed, (17) beaver, (18) tree, (19) about.

than in this first example. Look, for instance, at the sentence
**That _____ why we sometimes say, "_____ busy
as a beaver."** The word **that** can function as a noun determiner rather than a noun, as in **That fact explains why we
sometimes say, "as busy as a beaver."** If we did not look
ahead, we might supply the wrong kind of word in the blank
following the word **that.**

You may have found, also, that in some cases it helped to
use context provided by preceding sentences, or even by
following sentences. And you doubtless found that you had
to know something about beavers. Otherwise, how would you
know to supply **dams** in blank 11, or **tree** in blank 15?

"Context" is far more inclusive than people often realize.
Most comprehensively, we can and do use our entire "personal context" of knowledge and experience to help us identify words. Second, we use context before and after the sentence being read, but within the same reading selection.
Third, we use context before and after the word being identified, but within the same sentence. Figure 4.1 summarizes
these three major kinds of context.

You may be most aware of context within the sentence.
Yet even this kind of context has various aspects. On the
one hand, we use both syntactic context and semantic context, both grammar and meaning. On the other hand, we use
both preceding context and following context, both what
comes before and what comes after the word being identified.
Figure 4.2 summarizes these kinds of context in a grid,
showing how each kind helps us identify the word **water** in
The cruel giant fell into the water and drowned. The word
the indicates that the next word must be a noun or a noun

CONTEXT WITHIN THE SENTENCE	CONTEXT BEYOND THE SENTENCE	
	CONTEXT WITHIN THE SELECTION	PERSONAL CONTEXT
Context before and after the word being read	Context before and after the sentence being read	Entire store of knowledge and experience

Figure 4.1   *Contexts used in word identification*

	PRECEDING CONTEXT	FOLLOWING CONTEXT
SYNTACTIC CONTEXT	Preceding syntactic context indicates the word is a noun or a noun modifier.	Following syntactic context confirms that the word is a noun.

The cruel giant fell into the **water** and drowned.

SEMANTIC CONTEXT	Preceding semantic context suggests the word should indicate something into which one can fall.	Following semantic context shows that the word should indicate something in which one can drown.

Figure 4.2 *Context within the sentence*

modifier, while the word **fell** suggests that the word after **the** should indicate something into which one can fall. The word **drowned** confirms that the word in question must indeed be a noun; further, **drowned** shows that the word should indicate something in which one can drown. The word in question could be **water, lake, pond, river, ocean, well,** or **moat,** but there are not many other likely alternatives. The various kinds of context within the sentence have helped us narrow the alternatives to such a point that we need to use only a small amount of visual information to identify the word in question as **water.**

After further considering context within and beyond the sentence, we will look at the relation between language cues and reading strategies.

CONTEXT WITHIN THE SENTENCE

In looking at the sentence about the cruel giant (figure 4.2), you may have thought, "That's silly. I already know the word **water.** I don't need to use context in order to identify that word." And no doubt that is true. Nevertheless, the identification of words proceeds much faster and more efficiently when we are using the context provided by connected text. The fact is that fluent readers use context so automatically that they are rarely conscious of doing so. We become aware of our reliance on context mainly when we come to a word whose meaning we do not know, or when we make a miscue because of our reliance on preceding context.

To understand better this automatic use of context, read aloud the following sentences, without looking them over beforehand:

(1)   Can you read rapidly?

(2)   There was a strong wind blowing.

(3)   He wound the string up tightly.

(4)   I looked up and read the sign.

(5)   Her dress had a tear in it.

(6)   I saw a tear in her eye.

(7)   She looked at the minute printing on the label.

(8)   He made her a bow and arrow.

Each sentence contains a word that has, potentially, more than one pronunciation. In sentences (1–4), the preceding syntactic context was enough to signal the appropriate pronunciation of **read, wind, wound,** and **read.** In sentence (5), we needed the preceding semantic context to tell us that **tear** should rhyme with **dare** rather than with **dear.** In sentences (6–8), we needed following semantic context to signal the appropriate pronunciation of **tear, minute,** and **bow.** In short, we use preceding context to predict what is coming next, and we use following context to confirm or correct our predictions. This use of following context is facilitated by the fact that our eyes typically register about four words beyond the word we are focusing upon.[2] If we do not use following con-

---

[2] To see this for yourself, try a brief experiment with someone you know to be a reasonably proficient reader. First, locate a book that the person has not read, but that will not be especially difficult for him or her. Have the person begin reading a page aloud, and after a few lines stop the person's reading by suddenly turning out the light (if it is dark) or by putting your hand over the part being read. Then ask the person to tell you what words he or she saw beyond the word last focused upon. If you repeat this procedure several times, you will

text to help identify a word correctly in the first place, we use following context to tell us when we have made a miscue. Thus if you incorrectly pronounced **bow** to rhyme with **now** in sentence (8), you surely recognized the miscue when you noticed the word **arrow**.

Although such sentences as these are somewhat atypical, they do help us understand the nature of proficient reading. We do not normally rely just on *grapho/phonics*, our knowledge of letter-sound relations. Rather, we use context to reduce our reliance on grapho/phonic cues. Or, to rephrase the matter, we use nonvisual information to reduce our dependence on visual information.

It should come as no surprise, then, that beginning readers and nonproficient readers can often read words better in context than in isolation. Here are some examples from first and second graders. On the left is the word misread in isolation, with the miscue indicated above the word. On the right is a sentence in which the same child read the word correctly:

has
his . . . said his father.
hot
not His father said, "You are not old enough for that."
want
went The next day Hap and his mother and father went to the fair.
which
with "Hap can come with me."

---

probably find that the person can report, on the average, about four additional words. This is the person's *eye-voice span*, or *EVS*: the number of words the eye is ahead of the voice. In silent reading, of course, one has a similar *eye-memory span*, or *EMS*: the number of words the eye is ahead of the word being focused upon (Dechant 1970, p. 18; see Anderson and Dearborn 1952, pp. 127–136). The EVS and the EMS indicate the number of following words *seen* during one eye fixation, in addition to the word being identified. These additional words may, of course, be used in identifying the word being focused upon.

wig
wag   All morning Peter tried to make the turtle wag its tail.

now
know   "I know you would," said his mother . . . .

don't
didn't   But she didn't bring it back to Peter.

our
your   "Come on, Lassie," said Peter. "Wag your tail."

tail
tail   He wanted the turtle to wag its tail.

made
named   Peter named his fish Lassie.

Such examples are quite typical, as a study by Kenneth Goodman indicates. In context, his first grade group correctly read 62 percent of the words that they had missed in isolation; his second graders correctly read 75 percent of the words they had missed in isolation; and his third graders correctly read 82 percent of the words they had missed in isolation (K. Goodman 1965, p. 640).

A related study revealed that words are easier to recognize in familiar contexts than in relatively unfamiliar contexts. Even the function words tended to cause more recognition problems in the B sentences than in the A sentences following, for the less proficient beginning readers tested (Reid 1958, p. 297):

Group A	*Group B*
You must do your best work.	You must not go back on your word.
I can see his face in the darkness.	No man can do more than his best.
We went back to the deep mud.	Darkness was upon the face of the deep.
Can you give me more words to read?	We must not give up when work is hard.

The best readers had no trouble with either set of sentences, but the less proficient readers had difficulty with many of the words in what was, to them, an unfamiliar context.

Similarly, others have found that beginning readers may know color names like **brown** and **green**, but not be able to recognize these words when they are used in names like **Mr. Brown** and **Green Street**. Or the word **had** may be recognizable in a sentence where it indicates possession (as in **I had a dog**), but unrecognizable in a sentence where it indicates past perfect aspect (as in **He had left already**).

My favorite example of such difficulty comes from my son John. Early in his first grade year, we visited Chicago's Field Museum of Natural History. As we were looking at the bird exhibits, my husband excitedly called John's attention to a display of Weaver birds. "Look, John. What kind of bird is this?" he asked, pointing to the identifying label. But in such an unfamiliar and unexpected context, our son could not recognize his own last name.

We can now begin to assess the wisdom of a sight word approach to reading. It has sometimes been assumed that if only children had a large enough stock of sight words, they could read. But we have seen that children can often read in context words that they cannot read in isolation, and that they can often read in familiar context words that they cannot read in unfamiliar contexts. *Thus instead of helping children build up a stock of sight words in order to read, perhaps we should help children read in order to build up a stock of sight words.*

In effect, this is what is often called the language experience approach. By helping children relate familiar oral materials to their written counterparts, we can help them learn to use context (of all sorts) in identifying words. Thus a stock of sight words can be developed gradually, within the context of reading itself. And this approach would stress, from the very outset, those strategies which characterize the proficient reader.

CONTEXT BEYOND THE SENTENCE

As proficient adult readers, we are often conscious of using context to determine the *meaning* of words we do not know. One of my more recent experiences was with the word

desiccant. I could pronounce the word with no difficulty, but without context I would have had no idea what it meant. The word was printed on the outside of a little packet that came inside a bag of potato chips, and the manufacturers obligingly indicated that this packet of desiccant was included to absorb moisture and keep the chips fresh. Thanks to this explanation, I realized that the desiccant was not something to be thrown away as soon as the bag of chips was opened.

Writers are not always so obliging, yet often the preceding or following context gives a clue to the meaning of an unfamiliar word. Consider, for example, the context leading up to the word **fragile** and the word **melancholy,** below:

> The teacups were delicate, easily broken. So **fragile** that Ellen hardly dared grasp the handle.
>
> It was a gloomy day, more depressing than any that Margo had ever known. She lay motionless in bed, listless and **melancholy.**

Here, the preceding context indicates the meaning of **fragile** rather clearly, and at least supplies an appropriate connotation for **melancholy.** Note also that a reader would be able to get the essential meaning from these contexts, whether or not the words were pronounced "correctly." As a matter of fact, I knew the meaning of **melancholy** for years before I finally learned that my mental pronunciation of the word was incorrect (among other things, I incorrectly syllabicated and stressed the word: me · LAN · cho · **ly).**

If the context of preceding sentences is not enough to make the meaning of a word clear, often the context of following sentences will come to the rescue. Yetta Goodman cites as an interesting and instructionally useful example the concept of the word **krait** in Roald Dahl's short story "Poison" (1950). Goodman has excerpted the following sentences from the story (Y. Goodman 1976, p. 101). Stop after each sentence and ask yourself what mental picture you have of the krait:

"A krait! Oh, oh! Where'd it bite you?"

"It's on my stomach. Lying there asleep."

"Then out of the corner of my eye I saw this krait sliding over my pajamas. Small, about ten inches."

They hang around people's houses and they go for warm places.

The bite is quite deadly, except sometimes when you catch it at once; and they kill a fair number of people each year in Bengal, mostly in the villages.

I was going to be ready to cut the bitten place and try to suck the venom out.

"Shall we draw the sheet back quick and brush it off before it has time to strike?"

"It is not safe," he continued, "because a snake is cold-blooded and anesthetic does not work so well or so quick with such animals."

Obviously the author builds suspense by only gradually providing the information necessary to identify the krait as a snake. Note, too, that how quickly a person understands this fact will depend largely upon how much that person knows about snakes. If one knew nothing about snakes, one might have to read even the last of the sentences above to realize what a krait is. Context within the selection must be supplemented by personal context, the sum total of one's knowledge and experience.

So far we have talked about determining the *meaning* of words that one might not have understood without context. However, beginning and less proficient readers actually use context to identify (that is, to name) words that are in their speaking vocabulary but that they do not immediately recognize in print. We have already illustrated, with a wealth of examples, the fact that such readers use context within the sentence to identify words that they do not always identify correctly in isolation. However, it is also true that such readers use context in preceding and following sentences. Perhaps most remarkable is the fact that readers can use the context of following sentences to correct the miscues they themselves have made. Again, an example from my own son comes readily to mind. He was having unusual difficulty with a story I had asked him to read (there are certain disadvantages to being a professor's son). The boy in the story was named Hap. While at a local fair, he noticed someone who was jumping high as he walked along. The boy's father explained that the person was able to jump so high because of the pack on his back. Here are the following four sentences of the story, along with my son's miscues on the word **gas**:

gams
"The pack has a kind of gas in it.
gangs
The gas is very light.

It helps the boy to jump high."

gangs
"What kind of gas is it?" asked Hap.

As you might suspect, my son was getting little meaning from this passage. But on the next page of the story, Hap's father explained to him that the gas is called helium. This explanation apparently triggered my son's understanding, because the next time he came to the word **gas** his face lit up and he said "I got that wrong on the other page. It was **gas** all the time." In this case, the meaning of the word was familiar to the reader, but he did not recognize the word in print until the context of following sentences triggered his own personal context, his prior knowledge of helium and its effects.

Of course sometimes prior knowledge will lead us astray, as with the third grader who made the following miscue in a story about Henry Ford:

Henry felt that everyone should be able to own a car,

not just the wealthy people. In 1903 he started the Ford

more

Motor Company. His cars cost much less than other cars

had before.

Despite the context of preceding sentences, the child's real world experience led him to read "more" for the printed word **less**. He knows that prices normally go up rather than down.

Such miscues will not always be corrected, but if we are to help children learn to use *all* their resources in identifying words, we should at least give them the opportunity to correct their own miscues. With children who already read for meaning, about all we have to do is encourage them to detect and correct miscues that do not make sense, and then avoid correcting them ourselves or letting other children correct them. With children who do not already read for meaning, our task is of course more difficult: we must help them learn to read for meaning before we can expect them to detect and correct miscues that do not make sense. Or perhaps the two kinds of learning go hand in hand. In any case, such self-correction should be an important goal of reading instruction at every level. Otherwise, students may have difficulty becoming independent readers, able to read silently and without assistance. Instead of relying just on grapho/phonics and on us, children need to learn to make use of all the various kinds of context at their disposal. They must learn to use context within and beyond the sentence, in order to identify words and get meaning most effectively and efficiently.

LANGUAGE CUES AND READING STRATEGIES

The major *language cues* are syntactic, semantic, and grapho/phonic. Our intuitive knowledge of syntax enables us to use word endings, function words, and word order as cues to word identification. These syntactic cues are supplemented by semantic cues, the meaning relations among words and sentences in the text we are reading. In addition, we bring to bear our entire store of personal knowledge and experience. We use not only the syntactic and semantic cues available in the text, but also our entire experience with language and with life. Of course, reading could not exist without the grapho/phonic cues, the letters and words on the page and our intuitive knowledge of letter-sound relations and patterns. However, our reading would be both inefficient and ineffective if we relied just on grapho/phonic cues. As Paul Kolers has written, "reading is only incidentally visual" (Kolers 1969). At this point, such an outrageous statement should begin to make sense.

Figure 4.3 indicates how these language cues give rise to reading strategies. Of course during normal reading, all kinds of processes are going on simultaneously. But in order to understand some of this complexity it may help, temporarily, to think of reading as a matter of identifying words. In order to identify a word, proficient readers first use syntactic and semantic knowledge and cues to *predict* what is coming next. We do not necessarily predict a specific word, but at least we subconsciously narrow down the possibilities. Thus there is a limited number of words that might reasonably come after the second **the** in **The cruel giant fell into the** ———. After mentally restricting the possibilities, we normally look at the word itself—that is, we use grapho/phonic cues. But because prediction has narrowed down the number of reasonable alternatives, we need to use only a

		READING STRATEGIES		
		Predict	*Sample*	*Confirm/Correct*
LANGUAGE	*Syntactic*	✓		✓
CUES	*Semantic*	✓		✓
	Grapho/phonic		✓	

Figure 4.3 *Language cues and reading strategies*

minimum of visual information to tentatively identify the word. In the sentence about the giant, we would need to process only two or three consonant letters (or parts thereof) to decide that the word is **water** rather than one of the other reasonable possibilities. As proficient readers, we merely *sample* the grapho/phonic cues, even though we have the impression that we've "seen" the entire word. Finally, we use following syntactic and semantic cues to *confirm* our tentative identification of the word, or to *correct* if we have made a miscue that does not fit with the following context. The word **water** fits not only with the preceding context but with the following context in **The cruel giant fell into the water and drowned**; hence we would confirm our identification of the word in question. Figure 4.3 presents a slightly simplified version of this relation between language cues and reading strategies.

READING PROFICIENCY AND THE USE OF CONTEXT

Almost by definition, we can say that good readers are ones who use context efficiently, to reduce their reliance on visual cues and grapho/phonic knowledge. The following excerpt from a miscue analysis illustrates such use of context. The symbols have the same meaning as before: a carat points to an insertion, a circle indicates an omission, ⌒ indicates a reversal, and one or more words written above the text indicate a substitution. Each miscue or set of related miscues is numbered to facilitate discussion, but the reader's corrections are not marked. Try to read the text as this sixth grader did, complete with all his miscues. If your first reading tends to be jerky, read the paragraphs again, more smoothly. The passage is from an O. Henry story, "Jimmy Hayes and Muriel" (Porter 1936, p. 670).

①

around

After a hearty supper Hayes joined the smokers about

at all ②

the fire. His appearance did not settle all the questions in

^

③

the minds of his brother rangers. They saw simply a loose,

young ④
lank youth with tow-colored sunburned hair and a berry-
ingenious ⑤
brown, ingenuous face that wore a quizzical, good-

natured smile.

"Fellows," said the new ranger, "I'm goin' to interduce ⑦
⑥ much about
you to a lady friend of mine. Ain't ever heard anybody‸
⑦ call her a beauty,   a ⑧
but you'll all admit she's got some fine

points about her. Come along, Muriel!"
⑨
He held open the front of his blue flannel shirt. Out of
⑨   toad ⑩
it crawled a horned frog. A bright red ribbon was tied
the ⑪
jauntily around its spiky neck. It crawled to its owner's
it ⑫
knee and‸sat there motionless.
's ⑬
"This here Muriel," said Hayes, with an oratorical wave
‸ she's ⑬
of his hand, "has got qualities. She never talks back, she
⑭
always stays at home, and she's satisfied with one red

dress for everyday and Sunday, too."
d ⑮
"Look at that blame‸insect!" said one of the rangers
toads ⑯
with a grin. "I've seen plenty of them horny frogs, but I
⑰
never knew anybody to have one for a side partner. Does

the blame thing know you from anybody else?"
her ⑱
"Take it over there and see," said Hayes.

Almost all the boy's miscues fit the context: the preceding
syntactic and semantic context, and the following syntactic

and semantic context. The reader brought knowledge and meaning *to* the text, and got meaning *from* it.

Linguists generally agree that children have mastered the basic grammatical signals and patterns before entering school, so it should not be surprising that many beginners automatically make use of syntactic context as they read. In one study with first graders, Rose-Marie Weber sought to determine what percentage of miscues were acceptable with preceding syntax only, and what percentage were acceptable with following syntax as well. The following examples illustrate the two types of miscues:

Acceptable only with preceding   **and**
syntax   Spot can help Dick.

Acceptable with both preceding   **hear**
and following syntax   Spot can help Dick.

The miscue "and" for **can** is syntactically acceptable up to that point in the sentence, but not beyond it. However, "hear" for **help** is syntactically acceptable with the following context as well (though of course it does change the meaning).

Weber found that about 90 percent of these first graders' miscues were acceptable with the preceding syntax. This startling percentage was true for the low proficiency group as well as for the high proficiency group. Furthermore, 72 percent of the high group's miscues and 63 percent of the low group's miscues were acceptable with the following syntax as well. The major difference between groups was in the *correction* of miscues that did not fit with the following syntactic context (miscues like "and" for **can** in **Spot can help Dick**). The high group corrected 85 percent of these, while the low group corrected only 42 percent (Weber 1970, pp. 153, 160, and 161). Thus a major difference between proficient and nonproficient readers lies in the correction of miscues that are unacceptable with the following syntactic context.

We have focused just on the use of syntactic context. However, the broad conclusions are equally applicable to the use of semantic context as well. Beginning readers can indeed use context as a means of word identification, and many tend to do so, especially if they are already well acquainted with books and the joys of being read to. But we have seen that other readers make much less use of context, and that these readers tend to be among the less proficient, the least able either to identify words or to get meaning.

In many if not most cases, then, nonproficient readers are those who make inadequate use of context in identifying words and getting meaning. They overattend to grapho/phonic cues and underattend to syntactic and semantic cues. In his extensive study of reading miscues, Kenneth Goodman found that the miscues of low proficiency eighth and tenth graders frequently looked and sounded more like the text word than the miscues of high proficiency readers (K. S. Goodman 1973, *Theoretically Based Studies*, pp. 51, 53). But often this careful attention to grapho/phonic cues produced nonwords (like "souts" and "ramped") or words which did not fit the context. Such overreliance on grapho/phonics actually hindered word identification.

Doubtless an underreliance on context is not the only cause of reading difficulty, but it is certainly a major cause. In fact, I would go so far as to hypothesize the following as a typical continuum of reading proficiency (the term "interpretation" is used to suggest that the essence of a word may be understood, even when the word is not identified "correctly"):

1. Highly effective readers use preceding syntactic and semantic context to predict what is coming next (that is, to reduce the number of reasonable alternatives). In addition, they use following syntactic and semantic context to confirm their tentative interpretation of a word, or to correct this interpretation if it does not fit with the following context.
2. Moderately effective readers use preceding syntactic and semantic context to predict what is coming next, but they are less successful in using following context to correct inappropriate interpretations.

3. Somewhat effective readers use preceding syntactic context to predict, but they are not so successful in using preceding semantic context to predict a word that is appropriate to the meaning. Such readers make little or no use of following context to confirm or correct their tentative interpretation of a word.

4. Ineffective readers make little or no use of preceding context, much less of following context. They tend to deal with each word as if it stood in isolation.

Obviously such statements involve some degree of overgeneralization and oversimplification, but research suggests that they contain much truth. See, for example, Allen and Watson's *Findings of Research in Miscue Analysis: Classroom Implications* (1976), which reports on ten years of research into reading miscues.

We know now that reading does not proceed by grapho/phonics alone. Rather, proficient reading involves the use of context to predict what is coming next; the selective sampling of grapho/phonics to interpret tentatively the word in question; and the use of following context to confirm or correct this tentative interpretation. Thus reading involves the constant interplay of *all* the language cue systems: grapho/phonic, syntactic, and semantic. Let us reexamine phonics from this perspective.

PHONICS REVISITED

Without realizing it, teachers may unintentionally teach children to read as if each word stood isolated and alone, in a word list. This can happen if the teacher emphasizes just the use of phonics and structural analysis[3] to identify words that are not immediately recognized on sight.

We have already seen several other problems with phonics, in chapter 3: 1) that phonics may be particularly difficult for the preoperational child; 2) that spelling-sound cor-

___

[3] *Structural analysis* involves identifying prefixes, suffixes, and bases as cues to word recognition.

respondences are often very complex and not easily reducible to rules that can or should be taught; 3) that only a few of the frequently taught rules are consistent enough or relate to enough words to make them worth teaching; and 4) that people can develop and use an intuitive knowledge of letter-sound correspondences, even though they may never have had phonics instruction. In the long run, however, the most crucial problem with phonics instruction may be this: that a heavy instructional emphasis on phonics encourages readers to use just one language cue system, the grapho/phonic. And sole reliance on grapho/phonics makes the task of reading inordinately difficult, if not impossible.

At this point, we may well ask just how much phonics should be taught. There is no one answer appropriate to all situations, but many important observations and guidelines are provided in A. Sterl. Artley's "Phonics Revisited" (1977), from which the title of this section is borrowed. Artley makes several major points, including some which have already been touched upon in the preceding chapters of the present text. In particular, Artley makes the following observations about phonics:

1. First, phonics must be taught not as a method of reading, but as one cue system that is important in reading.
2. Context should be the first cue to word identification (or more properly, to meaning).
3. Where a choice must be made from among several words that would reasonably fit the given context, phonics knowledge becomes an invaluable aid.
4. However, "sounding out" a word is cumbersome, time-consuming, and unnecessary. By using context, we can identify words with only minimal attention to grapho/phonic cues.
5. Children should be taught the basic symbol-sound relations for consonants: the single consonants; consonant digraphs (**ch, th,** etc.) ; and consonant clusters (**st, bl,** etc.).
6. It is much less important to teach symbol-sound relations for vowels, since they are much less useful in

word identification. Furthermore, in about four out of
every five words met in early reading, a vowel letter
will indicate either the typical "long" or "short" vowel
sound, or the unstressed schwa (an "uh" sound). Therefore, "if a teacher feels impelled to deal with vowel
letters and sounds, the reader could be taught the long
and short vowel symbol-sound relations, and, on coming
to a new word, to try both sounds to discover which
pronunciation makes a known word, which fits, and
which makes sense in its contextual setting" (p. 125).

An example may help to clarify the latter point. Artley
suggests that instead of teaching children the silent **e** rule,
we should just teach them the long and short vowel sounds
and have children use context to decide which sound is appropriate in any given case. Thus if a child comes to the
visually unfamiliar word **tame** in normal reading, he or she
would not have to remember and apply the appropriate rule.
In a sentence like **The lion was very tame**, the correct pronunciation should be obvious from the preceding context,
assuming the reader is aurally familiar with the word **tame**.
   In concluding his fine article, Artley quotes from Heilman
(1972, p. 280): " 'In the final analysis, the *optimum* amount
of phonics instruction for every child is the *minimum* that
he needs to become an independent reader.' " And, as we
have suggested, this minimum is probably much less than
commonly supposed, because grapho/phonics is only one of
the three language cue systems available to the reader.
Instead of learning a multiplicity of letter-sound correspondences and phonics "rules," children need to learn to
minimize their use of grapho/phonic cues. Or as Frank
Smith puts it, "The art of becoming a fluent reader lies in
learning to rely less and less on information from the eyes"
(Smith 1975, p. 50).
   The message, then, seems clear: we should help children
learn to use context *first*.
   There are at least two important implications of this
statement. One is that we should use context to introduce
letter-sound relations and "new" words. Another implication

is that we should help children learn to use context to *predict* what is coming next, *before* sampling the available grapho/phonic cues. Such use of context will reduce their need for visual information.

In beginning reading instruction, both objectives can be approached almost at the same time. Suppose, for example, that you wanted to teach the letter s and its basic sound. You could begin by saying, "I'm going to put a sentence on the board: **Mary saw a snake.** Do you hear the "sssss" sound at the beginning of the word **snake**? Okay, can you think of another word that makes sense here and that also begins with a "sssss" sound? **Mary saw a . . .** what?" In the process of learning a specific letter-sound correspondence, the children are also learning to attend to syntactic context (the word must be a noun) and to semantic context (the word must designate something that can be observed), while at the same time bringing to bear the totality of their personal knowledge and experience (Weaver 1977, p. 883).

The following would be a more overt way of emphasizing the need to use context *first*. Before children can read anything at all, they can be asked to finish a sentence like **Rain came in when Sally opened the ———.** One obvious response is "window"; another is "door." Later, children can be asked to finish a sentence when the initial consonant of the last word narrows down the reasonable possibilities: **Rain came in when Sally opened the w———,** or **Rain came in when Sally opened the d———.** Activities such as this would help children learn to use a maximum of nonvisual information and a minimum of visual information as they read.

In trying such activities with young children, teachers should remember that it may be difficult if not impossible for some children to hear and identify the separate sounds in words, particularly if such children have not yet attained the concrete operational stage of cognitive development. Teaching such things may help many kindergarteners and first graders, but it is unrealistic and unreasonable to expect every child to master what has been taught. Some will simply not be ready to profit from such instruction.

There are at least two dangers of too much phonics too early. One is that we tend to expect children to master what we have taught, and this is an unrealistic expectation for at least some children. Second, we run the risk that the preoperational child will inappropriately center on grapho/phonic cues, assuming that reading means sounding out or pronouncing the words. Even if we were to be satisfied with mere word identification rather than the getting of meaning, it is quite clear that such word identification can best be accomplished through the use of *all three* kinds of language cues: syntactic, semantic, and grapho/phonic.

When they come to school, children are already experienced in using syntactic and semantic cues to understand what they hear: they bring a wealth of knowledge and experience to the task of reading. Perhaps it seems logical, then, to *teach* the one thing they do not know: letters and their sounds. As we have seen, however, many young schoolchildren may not be cognitively ready for phonics, and many others may fail to use their syntactic and semantic knowledge if they are not explicitly helped and encouraged to do so. Therefore, we must help children learn to use their prior knowledge to get meaning from the text.

Indeed, an emphasis on semantic cues to word identification is particularly appropriate for preoperational children, since they tend to center their attention on one cue system and strategy. Although beginning readers *can* use all the cue systems to some extent, they may have trouble using them simultaneously (see, for example, K. S. Goodman 1973, *Theoretically Based Studies*, p. 215). Canney makes a similar observation about poor readers: while proficient readers "seem to integrate, almost unconsciously, the various skills we teach into an effective method of reading, . . . the poor readers seem to learn the skills separately, yet do not integrate them into an effective strategy for processing print" (Canney 1977, p. 10). In effect, Canney's generalization is an indictment against the "eclectic" skills approach.

Teachers must help children coordinate the language

cue systems, to use simultaneously the productive reading strategies of predicting, sampling, and confirming/correcting their tentative identifications of words. But because there will be some children who necessarily center their attention on one cue system and strategy, we had better give careful thought to what should be emphasized. A heavy emphasis on letter-sound correspondences and "phonics" may produce readers who are not proficient either at identifying words or at getting meaning. Again, it seems wise to focus on context and meaning first, before giving much attention to grapho/phonics. Paradoxically, meaning is both an aid to word identification and the ultimate goal of reading itself.

CONTEXT IN REVIEW

Following is a brief summary of the major points covered in this chapter:

1. Proficient readers use three major kinds of context: context within a sentence, context within the selection, and their entire personal context of knowledge and experience.
2. Words are easier to identify in context than in isolation. In fact, beginning and less proficient readers can often identify words in context that they cannot identify in isolation.
3. Language cues are related to reading strategies. To identify words, we use preceding syntactic and semantic cues to predict what might be coming next (that is, to narrow down the reasonable alternatives); we sample grapho/phonic cues to make tentative identifications of words; and we use following syntactic and semantic context to confirm or correct these tentative identifications. Such strategies are essential to proficient reading.
4. The most effective and efficient readers are those who use a maximum of nonvisual information (context)

and a minimum of visual information (grapho/phonics).

In the course of the discussion, I mentioned objections to three of the major reading approaches presented in chapter 2. The *sight word approach* is objectionable because it puts the cart before the horse: it assumes that children cannot read until they know a number of words on sight. We have seen, however, that children can often read in context words that they cannot identify in isolation. Hence it may be more sensible to help children read aurally familiar material in order gradually to build up a stock of sight words, rather than vice versa. The *phonics approach* is objectionable for a variety of reasons discussed here and in chapter 3. The most compelling objection is that overreliance on grapho/phonics will lead to inefficient and ineffective reading: indeed, poor readers typically need to pay *less* attention to grapho/phonics, and more attention to context (see, for example, Tony's miscues in activity 2 of chapter 1).

On the face of it, an *eclectic approach* would seem much better, because it typically deals with sight words, phonics, *and* context. The problem, however, is that instruction all too often fails to emphasize the integration of the various skills that are taught. Many children will integrate the language cues more or less automatically, of course, but others may never learn that in order to read effectively they must predict, sample, and confirm/correct their tentative identification of words. It is these children who are shortchanged by an eclectic approach.

ACTIVITIES AND PROJECTS FOR FURTHER EXPLORATION

1. Look again at David's and Tony's miscues in activity 2 of chapter 1. What language cues and reading strategies does each child seem to have been using? Ask yourself the same question about the miscues recorded here. Examples (a) through (e) are from second graders; the others are from older readers (sixth, eighth, and tenth graders). The source is K. S. Goodman 1973, *Theoretically Based Studies*, pp. 210–211, 230–231, 250, 258, and 310).

to get down.

a. Here is something you can do.

I have not help the little kitten will we want little kitten to play?

b. I am not too little to help with little things, am I?

truck

c. "The little monkey had it."

him

d. . . . a voice calling , somewhere above.
^

up

e. . . . it was enough to wake the dead.
^

Know   fun   was   **sky**

f. Bil(ly) knew that fawns were always very shy.

liked   a crab potted

g. I leaned over the crib, pointing a finger. . .

proud

h. Billy was so pleased by the hunter's words.

afraid

i. . . . to see if there was any danger. He heard the . . .

j. . . . stop driving until we(can)see Los Angeles.

k. . . . I went(over)to his bed.

the

l. . . . when the children begin assuming control of the country.

to   bedroom ^

m. . . . the door of Harry's room . . . .

and   with

n. . . . a pair of pyjamas (with)blue, brown and white stripes.
^

2. To demonstrate that you, as a typical reader, use syntactic cues like word endings, function words, and word order, reread the "corandic" passage reprinted here, and then answer the comprehension questions that follow. How is it that you are able to answer such questions? And what does this experience suggest about the kinds of "comprehension" questions typical of standardized tests?

Corandic is an emurient grof with many fribs; it granks from corite, an olg which cargs like lange. Corite grinkles several other tarances, which garkers excarp by glarcking the corite and starping it in tranker-clarped storbs. The tarances starp a chark which is exparged with worters, branking a slorp. This slorp is garped through several other coruscus, finally frasting a pragety, blickant crankle: coranda. Coranda is a cargurt, grinkling corandic and borigen. The corandic is nacerated from the borigen by means of loracity. Thus garkers finally thrap a glick, bracht, glupous grapant, corandic, which granks in many starps.

What is corandic?
What does corandic grank from?
How do garkers excarp the tarances from the corite?
What does the slorp finally frast?
What is coranda?
How is the corandic nacerated from the borigen?
What do the garkers finally thrap?

3. If you have some understanding of basic grammatical terms like *noun*, *verb*, *adjective*, and *adverb*, you might try the following activity.

a. See if you can identify the grammatical category of any of the words in the following list. If so, how can you do this?

Bloopy	mult	zoll
corp	klom	ork
Glit	Sil	parfy
flof	naff	

b. What can you tell about the grammatical category of the words listed in (a) when they are presented in the following context? What can you tell about the meaning of the words? Finally, what does this exercise suggest about the normal functioning of syntactic and semantic context in reading?

The story is an adaptation of "Gloopy and Blit," from *Language and Thinking in School* (Smith, Goodman, and Meredith, 1976, p. 267).

Bloopy and Glit

Bloopy is a corp.
Glit is a flof.
Bloopy mults like Glit.
Bloopy and Glit are kloms.

Sil had naffed Glit to a zoll.
But he had not naffed Bloopy.

"The zoll is for flofs,"
Sil orked to Bloopy.
"You are a corp."

Bloopy was not parfy.
Then Glit was not parfy.

4. We can often get the meaning of a word from context (even though we may never pronounce the word correctly). Read the following list of words. What do you suppose each word means? Jot down your hypothesis. Then read the first chapter of Anthony Burgess's *A Clockwork Orange* (1963). In each case, how do you finally determine what the word means?

creech	malenky	skorry
deng	messel	spatted
droogs	millicents	veck
glazzies	poogly	viddy
goloss	razrez	zoobies

5. To determine for yourself whether words are easier to read in context or in isolation, first choose a reader to work with, either a beginning reader (late first grade, or second grade) or a poor reader of any age. Then choose a reading selection that should be appropriate for this reader: not easy, but not terribly difficult either. The selection should be about 250 words long or longer (except for the youngest readers, who may find this too much). It might be wise to photocopy the selection for your later convenience in analysis and discussion.

Once you have chosen the reading selection, type from this selection a list of about 50 words for the person to read (fewer, if the reader is a nonproficient beginner). One possibility would be to make a list of all the different function words in the selection. Another possibility is simply to choose every fifth word (avoiding duplications).

Have the reader read the list of words and then read the entire selection. Instead of trying to take notes on the reader's miscues as he or she reads, just tape record the session for later study.

To facilitate discussion, you will need to mark each of the miscues on the word list and each of the miscues the reader made on the reading selection itself. For the most part, the marking symbols introduced in this book should be adequate.

Consider such questions as the following:

a. On the whole, did the reader seem to be using context to predict what was coming next? What examples support your conclusion?

b. Did the person read in context any of the words that he or she missed in isolation? If so, what are some examples? How or why might the context have helped?

    c. Did the person read in isolation any words that he or she later missed in context? If so, what are some examples? Why do you suppose these words were read correctly in isolation but not in context?

    d. On the whole, would you conclude that words are easier to read in isolation, or in context?

READINGS FOR FURTHER EXPLORATION

Farnes, N.C. *Reading Purposes, Comprehension and the Use of Context.* Bletchley, Buckinghamshire, England: Open University Press, 1973. On pp. 47–64, Farnes provides a number of activities for exploring how words are identified in normal reading.

Goodman, Kenneth. "The Reading Process: A Psycholinguistic View." In E. Brooks Smith, Kenneth S. Goodman, and Robert Meredith, *Language and Thinking in School.* 2nd ed. New York: Holt, Rinehart and Winston, 1976. Goodman's chapter is an excellent follow-up to the present one. Also highly recommended is Goodman's subsequent chapter, "Teaching Reading: Developing Strategies for Comprehension."

Smith, Frank. "Between Eye and Brain." In his *Comprehension and Learning: A Conceptual Framework for Teachers.* New York: Holt, Rinehart and Winston, 1975, pp. 49–61. Though somewhat technical in places, this is a fine discussion of the role of visual and nonvisual information in reading.

Weaver, Constance. "Using Context: Before or After?" *Language Arts* 54 (November/December 1977): 880–886. Discusses the role of context in normal reading and provides some suggestions for helping children learn to use context more effectively.

Dahl, Patricia R., and Samuels, S. Jay, "Teaching Children to Read Using Hypothesis/Test Strategies." *The Reading Teacher* 30 (March 1977): 603–606. Reports on a program in which children were taught to use context first.

Bortnick, Robert, and Lopardo, Genevieve S. "An Instructional Application of the Cloze Procedure." *Journal of Reading* 16 (January 1973): 296–300. Presents some practical suggestions for using the cloze procedure to help readers make better use of context.

5

why is a word-identification view of reading inappropriate?

The major folklore of reading instruction relates to the "theory" that reading is considered an exact process. In other words, the reader is expected to read everything exactly as printed on the page in order to understand the message of the author. In general the consuming public, legislatures, courts and too many educators hold to this theory. It is like the theory of the world being flat during the time of Columbus.—Harper and Kilarr

Questions for Study and Discussion

1   Why is the quantity of a person's miscues not necessarily an adequate measure of his or her reading ability?

2   How do good readers' miscues typically differ from poor readers' miscues? That is, what are some of the qualitative differences?

3   About how long is surface structure held in short-term memory? What happens to information when it is "re-chunked" into long-term memory?

4   How can we demonstrate that proficient readers impose deep structure on surface structure?

5   Why are dialect miscues usually "good" miscues?

6   What good is it to get the surface structure (words) if you do not get the deep structure (meaning)? Conversely, what need is there to get every detail of the surface structure, if you do get the deep structure?

7   Why is a word identification view of reading inappropriate?

MISCUES AND READING PROFICIENCY

By focusing on word identification, the last two chapters demonstrated 1) that even in isolation, words can be identified from only a fraction of the visual information nor-

96

mally available to us; and 2) that in normal reading, we use syntactic and semantic context to reduce even further our need for visual information. Thus the focus upon word identification has shown the importance of the knowledge and information that the proficient reader brings *to* the written text. Now, however, it is time to reexamine the common notion that reading is first and foremost a matter of identifying words.

Let us begin by examining Anne's miscues on the following reading selection. Which miscues fit with the context? Which ones do not? The selection is from Jene Barr's *Little Circus Dog* (1949):

Now the band began to play. Then the lions roared.

about ①

Peter the pony ran around the ring. Bill the circus boy

ⓒ let ②　　　　　　　　　　　　　　　**Everyone ③**

led Penny the elephant into the circus ring. Everybody

forgot to eat popcorn. They forgot to drink soda pop.

A ④

They forgot to wave balloons. The circus man made a bow.

Trixie ran into the middle of the ring. She sat and

went ⑤

waited. Carlo the clown ran up to Trixie. Trixie jumped

on ⑥　　　　　　　　　　　　　　　　**the ⑦**

up and sat in his hand. Carlo put Trixie on a box. Trixie

stood on her hind legs. Then she jumped onto Carlo's head.

Every-

Trixie looked very funny sitting on Carlo's head. Every-

one ⑧

body laughed.

In every case, the miscue fits both the syntactic context and the semantic context. That is, the miscue results in a grammatical sentence that preserves the essential meaning of the original. Such miscues are typical of a good reader, one who ordinarily gets meaning from what is read. And in fact, Anne recalled almost every detail of the passage. She was a first grader.

Oddly enough, by some standards the foregoing passage might be considered too difficult for this particular child. In order to determine where to place a child within a given basal reading series, it is common to have the child read passages from several of the basal readers to determine the child's *independent*, *instructional*, and *frustration* levels within that series. Material at the independent level is supposed to be suitable for the child's unaided reading; material at the instructional level is supposed to be suitable for instructional use with that child; and material at the frustration level is considered simply too difficult for that child to read. The criteria for determining these levels are typically as follows (see, for example, May and Eliot 1978, p. 144):

Reading Level	Words Decoded without Error	Questions Answered without Error
Independent	about 98–100%	about 90–100%
Instructional	about 94–97%	about 70–89%
Frustration	usually below 94%	usually below 70%

Both word recognition and comprehension are taken into account in determining the reading level, but when there is a conflict between the two scores, it is common to rely upon just the word recognition score (see May and Eliot 1978, p. 144).

If we compute the word recognition score for the child whose miscues were just noted, we see that this passage from *Little Circus Dog* is too difficult for her to read, according to the preceding criteria. Anne pronounced only 92 percent of the words without error, which puts this selection at her frustration level.

Doubtless some children who read 8 percent of the words inaccurately in a given selection will consider that selection too frustrating, particularly if their miscues reflect a loss of meaning. But this is not the case with Anne's miscues. Each one suggests that she was making use of prior context to predict what was coming next; she was bringing meaning to the text in order to get meaning from it. Since following context confirmed the appropriateness of the miscues, she left most of them uncorrected. She was reading not to identify words, but to get meaning.

The same is true of Jay, the sixth grader whose miscues on the O. Henry passage we examined in chapter 4. Jay made 18 miscues but corrected only three of them: miscue numbers 4, 9, and 17. With the exception of miscue 4, all of Jay's miscues fit with both the preceding and the following grammar and meaning. Furthermore, both Anne and Jay read their respective passages fluently and confidently, and both recalled almost every detail of what they had read.

Is it reasonable, then, to conclude that Anne cannot read *Little Circus Dog* because she correctly identified only 92 percent of the words in a sample passage? Or that Jay cannot read "Jimmy Hayes and Muriel" because he correctly identified only 91 percent of the words in a sample passage?

These examples surely ought to make us question the notion that reading means identifying words. Over and over again, miscue analysis shows that the *crucial* difference between good readers and poor readers is not the quantity of their miscues, but the *quality*. The poorest readers tend to read almost one word at a time, as if each word stood in a list rather than in a sentence. They painfully sound words out, often producing a nonword or a real word that is inappropriate to the meaning of the text. Or they choose a grapho/phonically similar word from their stock of sight words, again often producing a word whose meaning is inappropriate. Because they concentrate too much on surface structure (the words), they are not very proficient at getting either the surface structure or the deep structure (the meaning). In contrast, the best readers tend to read for meaning rather than for words; they use only as much surface structure as necessary to get the deep structure.

GETTING THE WORDS

There are at least two basic objections to thinking of reading as involving the precise identification of words. One objection is that getting the words does not necessarily result in getting the meaning. The other is that getting the meaning is usually possible without getting all the words.

We have already seen some evidence for both of these objections. In chapter 2 we began to see the inadequacy of the notion that once words are identified, sentence meaning will take care of itself. In chapters 3 and 4 the various activities should have suggested that readers can get the essential meaning of a text without identifying all the words, an observation which is supported by our examination of Anne's and Jay's miscues. Examination of Anne's and Jay's miscues supports the notion that the meaning of a text can be understood without identifying all the words.

It was shown in chapter 4 that the use of context facilitates word identification, so that getting the meaning helps us to get the words. We also saw that less proficient readers may have difficulty recognizing familiar words in unfamiliar contexts, but even when they can recognize the individual words, both nonproficient and proficient readers may have difficulty getting the meaning of the whole sentence.

Comprehension can be thwarted by a variety of factors. Consider, for example, the following sentences. What might cause a problem with comprehension, even when the words are identified correctly?

(1)   She had a cramp in the calf of her leg.

(2)   Harley will chair the meeting.

(3)   Mom and Dad are playing bridge tonight.

(4)   He can't cut the mustard.

(5)   We should be proud of our flag.

(6)   They fed her dog biscuits.

(7)   The mayor asked the police to stop drinking.

The word **calf** may be a problem in sentence (1), if readers are familiar only with the animal type of calf. The word **chair** may be a problem in sentence (2), if readers are familiar only with its use as a noun. The word **bridge** may be a problem in sentence (3), if readers are not familiar with the card game: are Mom and Dad playing "London Bridge Is

Falling Down," or what?[1] In sentence (4), readers familiar with the word **mustard** may nevertheless fail to understand the idiomatic expression **cut the mustard**. And in sentence (5), readers may not understand that the sentence is supposed to be metaphorical rather than literal: it is not really the flag itself that we are to be proud of, but that for which the flag stands. In sentences (6) and (7), the problem is that the sentences are syntactically ambiguous. Did they feed biscuits to her dog, or did they feed dog biscuits to her? And are the police supposed to stop their own drinking, or are they supposed to stop others from drinking? (The last two examples are from Brause 1977, p. 41.)

When children are reading aloud, it is all too easy to assume that if they identify the words correctly, they are getting the meaning. This is often not the case. Some children do not read for meaning in the first place; they simply try to identify the words. Even good readers may fail to get the meaning if they lack experience with the words, the expressions, or the ideas. Consider your own experience reading technical literature like the generative semantics passage in chapter 1; you too may sometimes find it possible to identify the words of a sentence without getting the meaning.

Still other kinds of evidence support the point that getting the words does not necessarily result in getting the meaning. For example: given two synonymous sentences, one may be harder to comprehend than the other, and perhaps impossible for some readers to comprehend. This fact is obvious when the two sentences contain words of differing sophistication, as in **They have a high death rate** versus **They have a high mortality rate**. Different syntactic patterns can also be a factor. Consider the following pairs of sentences. In each pair, which sentence would be somewhat harder for most readers to comprehend? Why?

That Bob didn't know his way around was obvious.
It was obvious that Bob didn't know his way around.

[1] An amusing book capitalizing upon this kind of misconception is Fred Gwynne's *The King Who Rained* (New York: W'ndmill-Dutton, 1970).

He gave the son who lives in California all his stamps.
He gave all his stamps to the son who lives in California.

Jimmy, who plays with me every day, is my best friend.
Jimmy plays with me every day, and he is my best friend.

Various kinds of studies suggest that in each pair the first sentence would typically be harder to comprehend.[2] The first sentence places a greater burden upon short-term memory: it requires us to hold a fairly lengthy construction in mind while processing something else. Take, for example, the third sentence pair, about Jimmy. With the first sentence of the pair, we must hold the adjective clause in memory while trying to find out the main point about Jimmy: that he is my best friend. The second sentence about Jimmy is really two sentences, grammatically. It is easier to comprehend because we can process first one independent clause and then the other.

The following pairs of sentences also illustrate the fact that two sentences may not be equally easy to comprehend, even though they are synonymous and contain the same or nearly the same words. In each pair, which sentence would be somewhat harder to comprehend? Why?

They took a Thanksgiving turkey to the woman down the street.
They took a Thanksgiving turkey to the woman who lives down the street.

They thought Sam should know the truth.
They thought that Sam should know the truth.

He didn't remember having done it himself.
He didn't remember that he had done it himself.

Ask Mary what to feed the dog.
Ask Mary what you should feed the dog.

[2] Conclusions such as those discussed here are suggested by studies of perception, studies of language acquisition and use, and studies concerning the relation between the syntax children use and the syntax they can readily comprehend in reading. See, for example, Fodor, Bever, and Garrett 1974, pp. 326, 356–358; Menyuk 1969, pp. 16, 95,

In each pair, the first sentence would be harder for most people to comprehend because it is less explicit in signaling the underlying relations among the words. Note that the harder sentence in each pair is the shorter one, not the longer. The longer versions may be easier because they contain syntactic markers (like **who** and **that**) to help signal the deep structure, the meaning.

In a particular context, of course, a "difficult" sentence might be easy to comprehend, or an "easy" sentence might become difficult. But given two synonymous sentences in isolation, with the same or nearly the same words, one sentence may still be harder to comprehend than the other. Less proficient readers may have trouble even identifying the words, particularly in the structurally difficult sentences. But even those readers who have no trouble with word identification will find it somewhat more difficult to process sentences which place a considerable burden on short-term memory or which are not very explicit in signaling underlying relations. When structure is a deterrent rather than a help, even relatively proficient readers may sometimes get the words but not the meaning.

The difficulty of getting the meaning is perhaps most humorously illustrated by some of the early attempts at computer translation of sentences. In the mid to late 1950s and early 1960s, American scientists were trying to catch up with Russian space technology. In order to test the feasibility of translating Russian technical literature by computer, linguists first tried word-by-word translation of sentences into Russian and then back into English. But even when the computer was programmed to choose word meanings that were compatible with each other, the retranslations were unsatisfactory. Whether fictitious or real, the following examples illustrate the early difficulties with computer translation (taken from Malmstrom et al. 1965):

---

and 100–101; O'Donnell, Griffin, and Norris 1967, pp. 90–93; Coleman 1965, pp. 334–335; Ruddell 1965, pp. 272–273; Tatham 1970, p. 418; Reid 1958, p. 297; Wm. Smith 1971, p. 55; and Peltz 1973–74, esp. pp. 615 and 618.

Input sentence	*Output sentence*
Mary suspended for youthful prank.	Mary hung for juvenile delinquency.
The spirit is willing but the flesh is weak.	The liquor is good but the meat is rotten.

Even though not strictly translating word for word, the computer programs were not adequate to preserve the meaning of the original. Small wonder, then, that as early as 1956, "it became obvious that a mere word-for-word translation was so poor as to be nearly worthless" (Yngve 1962, p. 71).

So it is with reading: word-by-word reading and word identification are inadequate. And one of the reasons is that getting the words does not necessarily result in getting the meaning.

GETTING THE MEANING

Word-by-word reading is inappropriate as well as inadequate, in part because context aids in word identification and in part because getting the essential meaning of a sentence is usually possible without getting all the words. We will deal first with the latter observation, then discuss how surface structure is lost from short-term memory as deep structure is "chunked" into long-term memory.

Even proficient readers make miscues, because they are constantly trying to predict what will come next. It may help you realize how much the reader contributes to the task of reading if you think about how you read storybooks to children. If you are like most adults, you may often change the syntax and vocabulary to something more comprehensible and familiar to the child.

To further explore how proficient readers alter the surface structure of a text, you might try the following experiment with someone you consider to be a reasonably proficient reader. Without giving any hint of your purpose, have him or her read the following passage aloud, while you take careful note of any miscues that are made. The passage is from

Zachary Ball's *Bristle Face* (1962, p. 75), discussed in Rigg (1978, p. 287):

> He nodded. "Some good mud cats in there. That bluff you speak of, I denned me a bear in the rocks up there oncet."
> "A bear! When was that? Lately?"
> He chuckled. "Naw, that was way back yonder, when I was a boy, no older'n you. Ain't been no bear around here for sixty year, about. That was the last one ever I heard of hereabouts."

For those whose dialect is different from this rural mountain speech, "sixty years" for **sixty year** is a common miscue. As I checked this quote for accuracy, I first read "I ever" for **ever I**, changing the syntactic pattern to one more common in my speech. Your reader may have made other miscues that preserve the deep structure but change the surface structure to a more familiar pattern.

A second dialect passage may again help demonstrate the fact that we do not necessarily have to get all the words right in order to get the meaning. If possible, try this passage on yet another reader, someone who does not know your purpose. The passage is from Claude Brown's *Manchild in the Promised Land* (1965, p. 39):

> "Seem like nobody can't make him understand. I talk to him, I yell at him, I whip his ass, but it don't do no good. His daddy preach to him, he yell at him, he beat him so bad sometimes, I gotta run in the kitchen and git that big knife at him to stop him from killin' that boy. You think that might break him outta those devilish ways he got? Child, that scamp'll look Jesus dead in the eye when he standin' on a mountain of Bibles and swear to God in heaven he ain't gon do it no more. The next day, or even the next minute, that little lyin' Negro done gone and did it again—and got a mouthful-a lies when he git caught."

Among the numerous possible dialect miscues here, the more common are "he's got" for **he got**, and "he's standin' " for he **standin'**. Another is "gonna" for **gon**, which should be pronounced with a nasalized vowel and no final consonant. You may also find that your reader adds third person singular verb endings, saying, for example, "seems" for **seem**, "yells" for **yell**, and "beats" for **beat**. With miscues such as these, the reader has gotten the meaning without getting all the words entirely "right." Indeed, it is *because* the reader has gotten the meaning that he or she makes such miscues.

THE LOSS OF SURFACE STRUCTURE

As the dialect passages suggest, an author's surface structure can be partially lost through "translation." The reader grasps the author's meaning, but expresses it in his or her alternative surface structure.

What about the loss of surface structure when the passage conforms more closely to standard written English? The following exercise should help you answer that question. Read through the following passage twice, trying to fix it verbatim in your mind. Then write the sentences as you remember them, without looking back at the original. The passage is from Graham Greene's *The Power and the Glory* (1940, p. 139):

> The young men and women walked round and round the plaza in the hot electric night: the men one way, the girls another, never speaking to each other. In the northern sky the lightning flapped. It was like a religious ceremony which had lost all meaning, but at which they still wore their best clothes.

You may have found that you could not recall all of the passage after just two readings; this is indeed typical. But in trying to recall as much as possible, you probably preserved the essential meaning, making only or mostly superficial changes in surface structure. Among the more common changes are these:

"around" for **round**	"flashed" for **flapped**
"women" for **girls**	"that" for **which**
"the other" for **another**	"to which" for **at which**

In addition, it is common to find the first sentence divided into two sentences, or even three:

The young men and women walked round and round the plaza in the hot electric night. The men went one way and the girls another. They never spoke to each other.

Obviously the wording and sentence structure may be changed in several other ways while still preserving the essential meaning. Most of the deep structure is retained, but some of the surface structure is lost.

There is perhaps no definitive answer to the question of precisely how fast surface structure is lost, but an experiment by Sachs sheds some light on this question. The experimental subjects were told that as they listened to short passages, each passage would be interrupted and a sentence from somewhere in the passage would be more or less repeated. The subjects were to decide whether the sentence had been repeated word for word, whether it had been repeated with some change in meaning, or whether it had been repeated with some change in syntactic form. Sachs notes, for example, that after eighty syllables of interpolated material, seven of the eight subjects recognized the difference in **meaning** between the following two sentences:

Original
There he met an archaeologist, Howard Carter, who urged him to join in the search for the tomb of King Tut.

"Repeated"
There he met an archaeologist, Howard Carter, and urged him to join in the search for the tomb of King Tut.

Though signaled by only a one-word difference, the meaning change in the "repetition" was relatively easy to detect. But with a second "repetition," only one of the eight experimental subjects recognized the difference in syntactic *form* between the original sentence and the following:

"Repeated"
There he met an archaeologist, Howard Carter, who urged that he join in the search for the tomb of King Tut.

The change from **urged him to join in** to **urged that he join in** went relatively unnoticed. Slight differences from the original sentence tended to be recognized if they affected the meaning, but not if they affected the form alone. After about one-half second, the subjects' recall of surface structure was no longer reliable (Sachs 1967).

As deep structure is chunked into increasingly larger units for storage in long-term memory, surface structure is lost from short-term memory.

THE STORAGE OF DEEP STRUCTURE

Much of what we hear or read either is immediately forgotten or is integrated with our previous experiences and beliefs. We often forget what we have heard or read, or else remember only the broad gist, often in garbled and distorted form. I recently experienced this phenomenon in trying to cite an experiment in a letter I was writing to the editor of our local newspaper. At first I could not locate the source of my information, so I decided to take a chance and rely on memory. Here is what I wrote:

> I am reminded of an experiment in which a Russian investigator tried teaching a young child the word for "doll." The child still had not learned the word after the investigator had repeated it a thousand times. But when he introduced the word in the context of a game, the child learned the word within ten minutes.

About two weeks after my letter to the editor was published, I finally ran across the discussion of this experiment in a book I had read a year before. Sure enough, I had gotten most of the details wrong, yet reported the general gist of the discussion.[3]

---

[3] Here is the discussion I originally read, from Carton 1976, pp. 61–62:

Russian investigators (Mallitskaya cited by Slobin, 1966) have done some fascinating studies of how children learn names of things when an experimenter attempts to teach them. It seems reasonable to conclude from some of these studies that sheer repetition is not very effective, particularly if the child is paying attention to some-

How is it that we move from a specific surface structure to a generalized and often distorted representation of deep structure? There is no simple answer, but psycholinguistic research does suggest certain interesting possibilities.

We know that surface structure is stored in what is called *short-term memory* and that this working memory can hold only about five to nine chunks of information at a time. With verbal information, the upper limit seems to be around five chunks: we can hold in memory about five unrelated letters, or four or five related words, or even three or four related and familiar phrases or short sentences (see Miller 1956, pp. 90–95). Short-term memory accepts a new chunk of information about every quarter second; this may explain why our eye fixations are normally about one-quarter second long. As short-term memory accepts more chunks of information, the information is either lost or rechunked into larger units for processing into long-term memory. Our so-called *long-term memory* accepts a new chunk of information about every three to five seconds.

There is a fair amount of evidence to suggest that the clause is the major syntactic unit into which verbal material is initially rechunked, and the major unit from which meaning is initially determined. Some of the evidence comes from laboratory experiments, while other evidence comes from studies of reading miscues.

One of the more interesting experiments involved pairs of sentences like this:

Now that artists are working in oil, prints are rare.

Now that artists are working fewer hours, oil prints are rare.

---

thing else. Children who were allowed to hold dolls and toys and were free to play with them and move them about during the study did not learn the names of objects in their hands even if the name was repeated 1500 times! On the other hand, children who had been trained to play a game where the experimenter showed them pictures on the sides of blocks and told them the names for the pictures, showed a kind of "orienting behavior" (that is, a readiness to look and listen) when they later encountered pictures on these blocks for which they did not know the name. Under these circumstances names were learned in one to three trials.

Each subject listened to one or the other of these sentences and was then asked whether or not the word **oil** occurred in the sentence heard. Those who heard the first sentence took longer to respond. Note that the word **oil** was four words from the end of the sentence in each case. But with the first sentence, the word **oil** occurred not in the clause just heard, but in the preceding one. Those who heard the first sentence seem to have mentally closed off that first clause, making it harder for them to acknowledge that they had indeed heard the word **oil** (Caplan 1972). Though the experiment is hardly conclusive, it at least suggests that verbal material is re-chunked into clausal units as it is processed into long-term memory.

Further evidence comes from the accumulation of ten years' research into reading miscues. As Kenneth Goodman notes, the clause seems to be a more significant unit than the sentence. Readers sometimes change sentence boundaries, making one sentence into two, two sentences into one, or shifting a dependent clause from one sentence to another. In virtually all cases, however, the clause boundaries remain intact. Consider the following examples (from K. S. Goodman 1973, *Theoretically Based Studies*, pp. 141 and 236, and K. S. Goodman 1976, "What We Know about Reading," pp. 60–61):

Text	*Reader*
It must have been around midnight when I drove home, and as I approached the gates of the bungalow I switched off the headlamps of the car . . .	It must have been around midnight when I drove home. As I approached the gates of the bungalow I switched off the headlamps of the car . . .
The boys fished. Then they cooked their catch.	The boys fished and then they cooked their catch.
Then Billy and his father built a summer house. They covered it . . .	When Billy and his father built a summer house, they covered it . . .

It must have been around
midnight when I drove
home . . .

It must have been around
midnight. When I drove
home . . .

It was fun to go to school.
When he wasn't in school
he skated with his friends.

It was fun to go to school
when he wasn't in school.
He skated with his friends.

Such shifts in sentence organization usually cause no change
in meaning, but even where there is a meaning change, the
clause boundaries remain intact. Such examples suggest that
the clause is a significant unit in the rechunking of verbal
information into increasingly larger and more global units.

As we process clauses, we apparently extract the underlying propositions for storage in long-term memory. Consider the following example:

The ants in the kitchen ate the sweet jelly which was on
the table.

The sentence contains two clauses and four underlying
propositions:

The ants were in the kitchen.
The jelly was on the table.
The jelly was sweet.
The ants ate the jelly.

As you might suspect, the proposition we are most likely to
retain in memory is the major one, expressed by the main
surface structure subject, verb, and direct object: **The ants
ate the jelly**. It is possible to retain more propositions from
the original sentence, however, and Bransford and his associates have discovered some interesting things about the
way we combine related propositions when we store them in
memory.

Bransford and Franks first took the four propositions just
cited and incorporated them in a set of six sentences: two
sentences which included only one of the propositions above,
two which included two of the propositions, and two which

included three of the propositions. The following are examples:

The ants were in the kitchen.   (one proposition)
The ants ate the sweet jelly.   (two propositions)
The ants ate the sweet jelly which was on the table. (three propositions)

After listening to the set of six sentences (and to three other similar sets), subjects were presented with additional sentences and asked which ones they had heard before. The additional set contained some of the sentences actually heard, as well as some other sentences embodying one, two, or three of the original propositions. In addition, subjects were presented with a sentence embodying all four of the original propositions: **The ants in the kitchen ate the sweet jelly which was on the table.** People were most confident that they had heard the sentence including all four of the propositions, even though they had never heard this sentence at all. They were less confident of having heard the three-proposition sentences, still less confident of the two-proposition sentences, and least confident of the one-proposition sentences (Bransford and Franks 1971). From the six sentences they had actually heard, these people seem to have determined the four underlying propositions and integrated them into a coherent whole.

This and subsequent experiments are powerful evidence for the view that the mind actively constructs meaning from what is heard and read (see, for example, the summaries in Palermo 1978, pp. 161–167).

At first, such experiments were undertaken with adults. More recent studies show much the same results with children (for example, Blachowicz 1977–78 and Pearson 1977–78). Blachowicz worked with children ranging from second grade through seventh grade, as well as with adults. She presented her subjects with ten short, written paragraphs, such as:

The birds sat on the branch.
A hawk flew over it.
The birds were robins.

Less than five minutes after the original paragraphs were taken away from the readers, they were given a set of forty sentences, with four related to each of the original ten paragraphs. The task was to indicate whether the sentence had or had not been read before. There was a strong tendency for all subjects to "recognize" not only sentences they had actually read, but also sentences which reflected a reasonable inference from what was actually read. In the preceding example, subjects claimed to have read not only **The birds sat on the branch**, but also **A hawk flew over the birds** (Blachowicz 1977–78). The readers' mental construct of the paragraph included more than what they had read. They used their real world knowledge to supplement and interpret the information actually presented.

COMPUTERS AND MEANING

We have come a long way from the starting point of this section, the observation that it is usually possible to get the essential meaning of a sentence without getting all the words. This suggests, of course, that it may be inappropriate for teachers to insist that precise identification of every word is necessary if one is to get the meaning. And this suggestion is further supported, somewhat indirectly, by the fact that we lose the details of surface structure within about one-half second anyway; our memory for the precise words and constructions is no longer very reliable. We have determined the underlying propositions and chunked the information into a more global mental representation, losing at least some of the surface structure in the process.

Again, we may learn from work with computers. Since word-by-word reading (and translation) does not work, recent investigators have been programming machines to interpret meanings by much the same processes as humans use. Roger Schank has built into his computer programs a long-term memory of sorts. The information stored in this long-term memory enables his programs to read and summarize (as well as to translate) a variety of materials, from simple stories to newspaper articles. Here is one such newspaper article, along with the summary provided by the computer program SAM (from Nelson 1978, p. 74):

Story

A New Jersey man was killed Friday evening when the car in which he was riding swerved off Route 69 and struck a tree. David Hall, 27, was pronounced dead at the scene by Dr. Dana Blauchard, medical examiner. Frank Miller, 16, of 593 Foxon Road, operator of the vehicle, was taken by Flanagan Ambulance to Yale-New Haven Hospital. He was treated and released. The Branford Fire Department extricated the passenger from the vehicle. No charges were made. Patrolman Robert Onofrio is continuing the investigation.

Summary

An automobile hit a tree near highway 69 four days ago. David Hall, age 27, residence in New Jersey, the passenger, died. Frank Miller, age 16, residence at 593 Foxon Road in New Haven, Connecticut, the driver, was slightly injured. The police department did not file charges.

Like a human mind, the computer program has extracted the most basic underlying propositions. In fact, this summary looks a lot like the kind of summary we might store in our own long-term memories, except that it is probably somewhat more detailed.

Also like humans, a computer can even be programmed to interpret and potentially distort the information from its original source. Consider the program POLITICS, which Schank has developed in collaboration with social psychologist Robert Abelson. POLITICS is a computer program with a point of view. Here, for example, are two of the headlines fed into the computer, along with the program's interpretation (Nelson 1978, p. 80):

Headline	Interpretation
Russia Masses Troops on the Czech Border	Russia May Order Its Troops into Czechoslovakia
Russia Sent Massive Arms Shipments to the MPLA in Angola	Russia Wants to Control Angola through the MPLA

Again, the computer output looks remarkably like what a person might store in his or her long-term memory, particularly if the person assimilated America's political stance in the 1950s. We tend to remember our interpretation of something rather than what we have actually heard or read.

Schank's views on computer translation seem applicable to the kind of "translation" we call reading. As Schank points out, the early programmers hoped to avoid the issue of understanding. But "Human beings do not match words" as they translate (Nelson 1978, p. 74). Neither do they do so in reading: proficient readers do not merely try to match each and every written word with its oral counterpart. Indeed, in their quest for meaning, they may even change some of the details of the author's surface structure.

THE IMPORTANCE OF WORD IDENTIFICATION

In the commonsense view, words stand for things. It is rare for a "thing" to be designated by one and only one word, however. Look, for example, at the boldfaced words and phrases in the following sentences:

"Here, **Daisy**."
"Don't let **the dog** in."
"Look at **'er** go!"
"**She's a handsome animal**."

All of these expressions and more could be used to designate a particular dog. Usually more than one word or expression can be used to designate an entity; more than one word can be used to express an action; and so forth. As speakers and writers, we choose whichever word best suits our immediate purpose. And as listeners and readers, we may well substitute a contextually equivalent word or expression for that of the original.

One example is Jay's substitution of "toad" for **frog** in the O. Henry story "Jimmy Hayes and Muriel":

toad
Out of it crawled a horned frog.
toads
I've seen plenty of them horny frogs . . .

Though Jay's term was different, it still designated the same entity: Muriel. Like me, Jay had probably heard of horned toads but not of horned frogs. Instead of reflecting a loss of meaning, his substitution showed that he got the essential meaning of the author but translated it into something that made more sense to him.[4]

Especially common is the substitution of an appropriate pronoun for the noun to which it refers, as was done by a second-grader reading the following passage from Bernard Wiseman's *Morris Has a Cold* (1978):

Boris said,

"Beds do not jump.

Beds do not run.

Beds just stand still."

"Why?" asked Morris.
they
"Are beds lazy?"

[4] When I tried to locate "Jimmy Hayes and Muriel" through a short story index, the entry under "Frogs, horned" referred me to an entry for horned *toads*. I have since discovered that so-called horned frogs do exist, though.

In this context, it was perfectly reasonable to substitute the pronoun "they" for the repeated noun **beds**. Jay made a similar miscue, substituting one pronoun for another:

her
"Take it over there and see," said Hayes.

In context, "her" made perfectly good sense, because Muriel was female.

It is mainly proficient readers who make substitutions like these. The percentage of miscues involving pronouns and function words tends to *increase* as one becomes a more proficient reader (see K. S. Goodman 1973, *Theoretically Based Studies*, pp. 165–166 and p. 184). Insofar as they serve to signal relations between words, pronouns are like function words. And we can often supply many of the function words ourselves, if we are getting the essential meaning. That is, the content words, word order, and the total context are often adequate to signal many of the relations among the words in a sentence. To test this, try to fill in the function words missing from the following paragraph (the original is from the *New York Times*, May 5, 1970, p. 17):

███ crack ██ ███ rifle volley cut ███ suddenly still air. It appeared ██ go on, ██ █ solid volley, ███ perhaps █ full minute ██ █ little longer.

Some ██ ███ students dived ██ ███ ground, crawling ██ ███ grass █ terror. Others stood shocked ██ half crouched, apparently believing ███ troops were firing ████ ███ air. Some ██ ███ rifle barrels ████ pointed upward.

████ ███ top ██ ███ hill ██ ███ corner ██ Taylor Hall, █ student crumpled over, spun sideways ███ fell ██ ███ ground, shot ██ ███ head.

████ ███ firing stopped, █ slim girl, wearing █ cowboy shirt ███ faded jeans, ███ lying face down ██ ███ road ██ ███ edge ██ ███ parking lot, blood pouring ███ ███ the macadam, ████ 10 feet ████ ███ reporter.

People usually find they can supply reasonable function words, often the precise one that was omitted from the original.[5] Just as words can often be identified from only part of the visual information normally available, sentences can often be understood from fewer than the total number of words normally available. We are able to recreate part of the surface structure from our understanding of the deep structure.

If meaning is the goal of reading, we hardly need to insist that every word be identified accurately. Instead of demanding an accurate rendition of the surface structure, we might better call for a reasonable interpretation of the deep structure.

Some will argue that there are times when it is vital to read every word accurately, and this is probably true. Surface accuracy may be important, for example, when we are reading warranties and guarantees, application forms, recipes and other directions, or legal contracts. But even with such materials, surface accuracy is not as important or as helpful as commonly supposed. The proof of this is in our everyday experience. Many of us have had the frustrating experience of being able to read all the words in a set of directions or a contract, yet been unable to determine precisely what was meant. We are often able to get the surface structure, yet unable to get the deep structure—the intended meaning.

An experience of my own seems pertinent: a few years ago I was asked to render an expert linguistic opinion in a court case involving a life insurance claim. The deceased had

---

[5] Here is the original passage:

The crack of the rifle volley cut the suddenly still air. It appeared to go on, as a solid volley, for perhaps a full minute or a little longer.

Some of the students dived to the ground, crawling on the grass in terror. Others stood shocked or half crouched, apparently believing the troops were firing into the air. Some of the rifle barrels were pointing upward.

Near the top of the hill at the corner of Taylor Hall, a student crumpled over, spun sideways and fell to the ground, shot in the head.

When the firing stopped, a slim girl, wearing a cowboy shirt and faded jeans, was lying face down on the road at the edge of the parking lot, blood pouring out onto the macadam, about 10 feet from this reporter.

died piloting his own plane. The linguistic question involved the following exclusion clause in the insurance policy, and in particular the word **passenger**. The insured person was not covered by the policy

> While engaged in or taking part in aeronautics and/or aviation of any description or resulting from being in any aircraft except while a passenger in an aircraft previously tried, tested, and approved.

The insurance company claimed that the word **passenger** excluded the pilot of a plane, and hence the man was not covered by the policy at the time of his death. The family claimed that the man *was* covered at the time of his death, because the pilot of a plane is also one of its passengers. Both parties agreed on the word, but not on the meaning of the word. And it was a crucial $50,000 difference.[6]

Once again the conclusion seems clear: what is important is not necessarily the surface structure, but the deep structure. The proficient reader reads more for meaning than for surface detail.

MISCUES REVISITED

It is true, of course, that many proficient readers make relatively few miscues of any sort. However, the most *crucial* difference between good readers and poor readers is not the quantity of their miscues, but the *quality*.

Good readers' miscues typically preserve meaning, fitting both the preceding and the following syntactic and semantic context. For another example, try to read the next passage as the sixth-grader Billy originally did, complete with all his miscues. After one or two attempts, you will probably find

---

[6] My opinion supported the position of the family. The definitions in some of our major dictionaries suggested that the word **passenger** at least *could* be taken to include the operator of a vehicle. Ultimately, however, the Michigan Supreme Court ruled in support of the insurance company's interpretation, arguing that the "ordinary man" would not consider the operator of a vehicle to be one of its passengers (Kinnavy v. Traill, 1976).

that you can read the passage fluently and with expression, since most of the miscues fit in the given context. The passage is from Joanne Williamson's *The Glorious Conspiracy* (1961, pp. 17–18):

Tully ①

Life went on as usual. Mr. Tully beat me more often

and more cruelly than Mr. Coffin had (done.) But I was
        ②

used to that now. And there were ways a poor boy could

find of having a bit of fun once in a while—like daring
                                        © of ③

the other apprentices to steal a bit from the shops and

watching to see if they got caught. If they did get

caught, they would be hanged at Gallows Mill, so that was

a real dare. Or one could throw bits of garbage in the way

of gentlemen in wigs and hide around the corner to see
                                    ④

them slip and fall (down.) There wasn't much time for
        though ⑤

such sports, so we made the most of what time we had.

My granddad had become pretty sick about this time.
                                        ⑥

He had the lung fever. He (had) had it a long while, but

now it was beginning to be bad, and Aunt Bet was begin-

ning to look frightened. I began to be scared, too, hearing

him cough so much and seeing him look so pale and ill.
                                        o'clock ⑦

And when I got through work at eight or nine of the

clock, I took to hanging about the streets, tired and hungry as I was, hiding out of the way of (the) watchmen, so [8]

as not to go home till I had to. I knew this made Aunt Bet

even more frightened; and that made me ashamed and

even more anxious not to go home. **to** [9]

One night after I had scrubbed down Mr. Tully's fish

house and come (out) into the street, I saw a man come out [10]

of a chandler's shop. I knew (who) he was—Mr. Watson, [11]

a ropemaker and an excellent workman, so everyone said.

I didn't want him to see me, for I meant to tell Aunt Bet **to see him** [12]

that I had been kept late, and go (looking) for mischief. [13]

So I hid in a doorway and watched for him to go by. **him go by.** [14]

It is interesting that most of these miscues involve the
omission, insertion, or substitution of function words. Since
function words are the most predictable part of a sentence,
good readers are especially likely to make miscues involving
them.

More generally, good readers tend to predict what is
coming next. The good reader's miscues usually preserve the
essential meaning of the text, and hence they often go uncorrected. However, good readers generally do correct those
miscues which are not confirmed by the following context.
In contrast, the poorest readers tend to deal with each word
almost as if it existed in isolation. Often they are not even
reading for meaning, and hence there is nothing which
prompts them to correct their miscues.

Even beginning readers can be good readers, proficient
at predicting what is coming next and correcting those miscues which do not make sense in context. The following
miscues were made by a boy with only two months of read-

ing instruction. In context each miscue preserves the sense of the original. The sentences are from Mae Knight Clark's *Opening Books* and *A Magic Box* (1965):

the
Get a ball, Mary.

Who rides with Mike?
can ride
Mary rides with Mike.

Mary said, "Play ball, Jeff.
ball
Mike and I want to play."

Mike said, "I can't ride.
Mary and Jeff
I can't play with Jeff and Mary.
but
I can play ball."

Velvet will go (on) up the tree.

Though the child has departed somewhat from the surface structure of the original sentences, he has retained the deep structure. In some cases his surface structure is even more explicit in reflecting the deep structure.

All of these examples suggest that having understood the deep structure of a sentence, proficient readers sometimes express it partially in their own words and language patterns. This is demonstrated particularly by miscues that reflect immature language patterns, such as the following one:

sticked
Morris stuck out his tongue.

Fortunately, many teachers are more amused than distressed by such miscues, realizing that the child has understood the meaning of the original.

On the other hand, dialect miscues are seldom treated with such indulgence. We tend to think that the words on a page must be reproduced in the sound patterns and grammatical patterns of standard English as we know it. Your experience with the dialect passages earlier in this chapter should have helped you see the fallacy of this assumption, though. We saw that in reading a passage like that from *Manchild in the Promised Land*, speakers of a so-called standard dialect will often *add* some of the surface grammatical markers that would be normal for their dialect. Similarly, speakers of other dialects may read a passage written in standard English and *omit* some of the surface grammatical markers that are not always present in their dialect. What we often fail to realize is that such dialect translation would not be possible unless the reader had understood the deep structure of the author's sentence.

Teachers are most disturbed by miscues that reflect a partially different grammatical system: "we was" for **we were**, "he don't have none" for **he doesn't have any**, and so forth. But such miscues as these are relatively rare. The more common grammatical miscues involve just pieces of words, the grammatical endings. Kenneth Goodman and his associates have found, for example, that among inner city black children, the following are the most common dialect-related miscues that appear to involve grammar. Most of these miscues involve grammatical elements (adapted from K. S. Goodman and C. Buck 1973, p. 9).

1. *Absence of past tense marker*
   look for **looked, call** for **called, wreck** for **wrecked, love** for **loved, pound** for **pounded, help** for **helped, use** for **used, run** for **ran, have** for **had, keep** for **kept, do** for **did**

2. *Absence of plural noun marker*
   thing for **things, work** for **works, story** for **stories, prize** for **prizes**

3. *Absence of third person singular verb marker*
   look for **looks, work** for **works, hide** for **hides**

4. *Absence of possessive noun or pronoun marker*

Freddie for **Freddie's, Mr. Vine** for **Mr. Vine's, one** for **one's, it** for **its**

5. *Substitution and omission of forms of* to be

was for **were, is** for **are, we** for **we're, he be** talking for **he'd been** talking

6. *Hypercorrections (the use of two grammatical markers of the same type)*

likeded for **liked, helpeded** for **helped, stoppeded** for **stopped**

One important point about such "grammatical" miscues is that they are not all grammatical in nature. Their origin may be phonological, as is the apparent omission of the past tense marker by speakers of Black English. The past tense marker is absent from Black English primarily when the base word is a regular verb ending in a consonant other than /t/ or /d/. In such cases, addition of the past tense ending results in a consonant cluster (the examples are mostly from Fasold and Wolfram 1970, p. 45):

stopped	/pt/	rubbed	/bd/
looked	/kt/	hugged	/gd/
laughed	/ft/	loved	/vd/
unearthed	/θt/	seethed	/ðd/
missed	/st/	raised	/zd/
watched	/čt/	judged	/jd/
finished	/št/	named	/md/
		rained	/nd/
		hanged	/ŋd/
		called	/ld/
		cured	/rd/

In each case, the past tense ending is represented by /t/ or /d/. Word-final consonant clusters are especially likely to be simplified when they end in a /t/ or /d/, and virtually all speakers of English show some tendency to omit the final /t/ or /d/ when it does not represent a tense marker. Such omission is particularly common when the word in question is followed by a word that begins with a consonant, as in **She** *just* **left** or **I'll** *find* **the book.** Speakers of so-called standard English occasionally omit even a past tense /t/ or /d/ when the following word begins with a consonant, as in **I** *missed* **Mike** and **He** *lived* **near me.** Speakers of Black English simply carry this tendency somewhat further, so that they are often perceived as consistently omitting past tense markers although in reality their usage varies, as it does for all of us. The same is true for other dialect features.

With oral reading, then, we do not ordinarily need to be concerned about the absence or use of such features as those cited by Goodman and Buck. Such miscues typically reflect not a lack of understanding, but only an alternative surface structure common in the reader's everyday speech. Having understood the deep structure, the reader simply expresses it in an alternative oral form. Such a process is reflected in Figure 5.1.

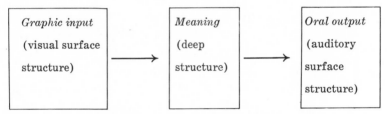

Figure 5.1   *A simplified model of proficient oral reading*

This model indicates that when reading aloud, our understanding is usually ahead of our voice, as was suggested in chapter 4. Unless we are having unusual difficulty, we get the meaning *before* speaking the words, rather than vice versa.

This fact suggests that many teachers may need to rethink their attitudes and their approach to dialect miscues, those miscues which reflect a mismatch between the language of the text and the dialect of the reader. In his excellent book on the Black English dialect, Robbins Burling offers some particularly pertinent remarks (1973, pp. 158–159):

What should a teacher do when her children make such "mistakes"? She may be willing to accept the idea that children should be permitted to read aloud in their own natural pronunciation, but grammatical changes [or apparent grammatical changes] seem far more dramatic. To most teachers they look like out-and-out errors and they seem to warrant correction. Nevertheless, these "errors" give far better evidence of comprehension than would more literal and "accurate" recitation of the words. Word-for-word recitation may amount to no more than parroting. It may be no different from reading a word list in which the words have no relation to one another. Conversion to nonstandard forms, so long as the meaning is preserved, amounts to a kind of translation that would be quite impossible if the child did not understand. If reading with comprehension is our goal, then these "errors" prove that we have been successful.

At least some research indicates that it is the *best* readers who produce the most dialect-based miscues (B. Hunt 1974–75), supporting the observation that good readers tend to express the author's deep structure in a surface structure which is partially their own. They are less concerned with surface detail than with meaning.

THE READING PROCESS IN REVIEW

Reading is commonly viewed as first and foremost a matter of identifying words. In this chapter, however, we have seen a number of reasons for challenging that view:

Getting the words of a sentence does not necessarily result in getting the meaning.

Within about half a second or less, we have already begun to forget some of the details of sentence surface structure. What we "remember" is not necessarily the words or their grammatical organization, but the meaning. We determine the underlying propositions from the clauses of the text and construct a global representation of the meaning. This mental representation is influenced and even distorted by our prior knowledge, beliefs, and experiences.

All readers make some miscues, but good and poor readers differ in the quality of their miscues. The miscues of poor readers often suggest that they are attending mainly to surface structure, although even poor readers usually show some concern for meaning. The miscues of good readers usually suggest that they are attending mainly to deep structure.

Getting the meaning is usually possible without identifying all the words.

There seems to be little justification for the common view that precise word identification is a necessary prerequisite to understanding. As Harper and Kilaar have so incisively put it, this view "is like the theory of the world being flat during the time of Columbus" (1977, p. 918).

The common view of reading may soon involve our schools in lawsuits, if it has not done so already. The increasing move toward competency-based diplomas is almost certain to bring us to this crisis, if we continue to measure reading ability as if precise word identification were necessary to understanding. Many of our schoolchildren read far better than they are given credit for. And if parents know that their child can read with a reasonable degree of understanding, they may not be willing to see their son or daughter denied a high school diploma simply because of so-called problems with word identification. Sooner or later someone will sue the schools, this time not for failing to teach their child to read, but for determining their child's reading ability by inappropriate means. True, many proficient readers will make no more than one or two miscues per hundred words, at most. Nevertheless, accurate word identification is not an appropriate criterion for measuring reading ability. For one thing, many nonproficient readers can reproduce surface structure (identify the words) with reasonable accuracy, even though they get little meaning from what they read. More importantly, though, reading is not an exact process, and we should not define or measure it as if it were. The proficient *and efficient* reader uses only as much surface structure as necessary to get to deep structure.

ACTIVITIES AND PROJECTS FOR FURTHER EXPLORATION

1. The passage below is from Joan Baratz and William Stewart's dialect reader *Friends* (1970, pp. 24–30).[7]

> One morning Ollie and Leroy was getting ready to go to school. Leroy he put on one of Ollie sock 'cause he lost his. Ollie say, "Boy give me my sock" but Leroy wouldn't give it to him. Leroy say, "It's my sock." But Ollie know it wasn't 'cause it wasn't even the same color as Leroy other sock. Ollie kept on begging and begging Leroy for the sock. But Leroy still wouldn't give it to him. Ollie hit Leroy. And they got to fighting. Leroy hit Ollie in the nose and it start to bleeding. Then, Ollie got real mad and hit Leroy on his arm as hard as he could. Leroy hollered real loud. Big Momma must of heard them fighting 'cause she come running in the room and she stop the fight. She say, "All right, who start this mess?" Ollie say Leroy start it and Leroy say Ollie start it. Big Momma say, "I done told you about fighting before. Since don't nobody know who start this mess I'm just going to whip both of you."

It might be interesting to try one or both of the following activities with this passage:

a. Have one or more persons read the first four sentences of the passage twice, then try to write down exactly what they have read. Look to see what changes they have made in the authors' surface structure. Have they translated some of the patterns of the text into the patterns of their own dialect?

b. Have one or more persons read the passage aloud; if possible, try it with both children and adults. Listen to hear what dialect miscues they make. Again, have they translated some of the patterns of the text into the patterns of their own dialect?

2. To compare proficient reading with nonproficient reading, try our blacked out *New York Times* passage (p. 117) with both good and poor readers of about junior high age or beyond. First, be cer-

---

[7] Note that in this approximation of Black English, pastness is not always indicated by the verb form itself, even for verbs which express pastness by some means other than the mere addition of /t/ or /d/.

tain that each person can identify all of the content words in the selection; if necessary, read these words to the person one or more times. Then ask the person to write in the missing function words (you may want to use a photocopy of the passage for this purpose). Are the good and poor readers equally able to supply reasonable possibilities for the missing words? If not, what does this suggest about their differing approaches to the task of reading?

3. If you know of any teachers with widely differing instructional approaches and/or definitions of reading, it might be interesting to compare their reactions to Anne's miscues (p. 97) or Jay's (pp. 81–82) or Billy's (pp. 120–121), or all of them. Does the teacher think most of these miscues are "serious," a matter for concern? If not, why not? If so, what kind of instructional help would the teacher recommend? Compare the responses from the different teachers.

4. This group activity emphasizes that the same ideas can be expressed in different ways. Working separately, each participant should first follow the directions below. The sentence-combining activity is from R. O'Donnell and K. Hunt, as printed in Fagan et al. 1975, p. 201; see also Hunt's 1970 monograph, pp. 64–65. Once you have all completed this part of the activity, compare your results. Did you indeed find different ways to express the same ideas? What are some of the possible implications for reading? Though the relevant research is by no means conclusive, there is at least some evidence that extensive practice in sentence-combining can help improve reading comprehension. See, for example, Hughes 1975. A useful introduction to sentence-combining is provided in Weaver 1979, *Grammar for Teachers* (see full reference in the following list of readings).

Aluminum

Directions: Read the passage all the way through. You will notice that the sentences are short and choppy. Study the passage, and then rewrite it in a better way. You may combine sentences, change the order of words, and omit words that are repeated too many times. But try not to leave out any of the information.

Aluminum is a metal. It is abundant. It has many uses. It comes from bauxite. Bauxite is an ore. Bauxite looks like clay. Bauxite contains aluminum. It contains several other substances. Workmen extract these other substances from the bauxite. They grind the bauxite. They put it in tanks. Pressure is in the tanks. The other substances form a mass. They remove the mass. They use filters. A liquid remains. They put it through several other processes. It finally yields a chemical. The chemical is powdery. It is white. The chemical is alumina. It is a mixture. It contains aluminum. It contains oxygen. Workmen separate the aluminum from the oxygen. They use electricity. They finally produce a metal. The metal is light. It has a luster. The luster is bright. The luster is silvery. This metal comes in many forms.

READINGS FOR FURTHER EXPLORATION

Goodman, Yetta. "I Never Read Such a Long Story Before." *English Journal* 63 (November 1974): 65–71. Highly recommended by my students, this is "must" reading for teachers at all levels.

Allen, P. David. "Implications for Reading Instruction." In *Findings of Research in Miscue Analysis: Classroom Implications*, edited by P. David Allen and Dorothy J. Watson. Urbana, Ill.: ERIC Clearinghouse on Reading and Communication Skills, and the National Council of Teachers of English, 1976, pp. 107–112. More "must" reading. In only a few pages, Allen has provided a number of valuable suggestions for teachers.

Adams, Marilyn Jager. "Beginning Reading: Theory and Practice." *Language Arts* 55 (January 1978): 19–25. A discussion of the difficulty of determining the underlying syntax and hence the meaning of word groups and phrases.

Standal, Timothy C. "Readability Formulas: What's Out, What's In?" *The Reading Teacher* 31 (March 1978): 642–646. A useful summary of recent views and research on readability.

Gibson, Eleanor J., and Levin, Harry. "Do Variations in Dialect Affect Learning to Read?" *The Psychology of Reading*. Cambridge, Mass.: MIT Press, 1975, pp. 505–518. An excellent summary on dialect and reading.

Weaver, Constance. *Grammar for Teachers: Perspectives and Definitions*. Urbana, Ill.: National Council of Teachers of English, 1979. Provides a useful introduction to sentence-combining.

6

how is a psycholinguistic view of reading relevant to reading instruction?

A viable theory of reading instruction has to be based on an articulated theory of the reading process.—Kenneth Goodman

Questions for Study and Discussion

1   How do psycholinguistic definitions of reading typically differ from other definitions?

2   How can we demonstrate that for the proficient reader comprehension is usually ahead of the voice in reading aloud, and that it is not necessary to decode either to overt sound or to "silent speech" in order to get meaning?

3   What are some of the problems with a word-centered approach to reading instruction?

4   What is the difference between reading *skills* and reading *strategies*?

5   What are some of the parallels between the acquisition of speech and the acquisition of reading? What are some of the instructional implications?

6   In general, how do proficient readers read? What are some of the implications for reading instruction?

READING DEFINITIONS REVISITED

The most successful reading instruction is likely to be that which is based on a solid understanding of the reading process itself, and which promotes rather than thwarts the acquisition of good reading strategies. Therefore, this chapter will review the nature of the reading process and some of the possible implications for reading instruction.

131

Just as there is no single definition of deep and surface structure, so there is no single psycholinguistic definition of reading. However, it may help to review the major differences between a psycholinguistic view of reading and some of the other common views. Here, then, are three different characterizations of the reading process:

Reading means pronouncing words. That is, reading means going from visible surface structure (written words) to audible surface structure (spoken words).

Reading means identifying words and getting their meaning. That is, reading means going from visible surface structure to deep structure (meaning).

Reading means bringing meaning *to* a text in order to get meaning from it. That is, reading means using deep structure to interpret surface structure.

The first definition is clearly incompatible with a psycholinguistic view, since it emphasizes the recognition of words rather than the getting of meaning; indeed, it says nothing whatsoever about meaning. The second definition mentions getting meaning but is also inadequate. It implies that sentence meaning can be gotten from individual word meanings, whereas the reverse is more often the case: our general understanding of the whole sentence, the context, helps us determine the meaning of the individual words (see chapters 2 and 5). Further, the definition would remain unsatisfactory even if we were to eliminate this problem by saying "Reading means identifying words *and getting the meaning of the sentence.*" There are two basic problems with this reformulated definition. First, it implies that precise word identification is necessary in order to get meaning, which is ordinarily not so. Second, this definition says nothing about what readers bring *to* a text. It gives no hint of the fact that proficient readers use contexts of all sorts, including their entire store of knowledge and experience, in order to get meaning as they read.

The first two definitions reflect what I call an *ink blotter* or *sponge* view of reading. They imply that readers are essentially passive, and that reading is entirely a one-way process, originating in the text and ending in the reader. The reader merely soaks up the words and meanings signaled by the marks on the page. A psycholinguistic view of reading contrasts sharply with this view (see figure 6.1). Most psycholinguists emphasize the fact that meaning lies not in words themselves but in people, the users of words. If we are to *get* meaning from a text, we must actively search for meaning, we must actually bring meaning *to* what we read. Hence reading is not a one-way process, but a two-way interaction between the mind of the reader and the language of the text. *The proficient and efficient reader uses nonvisual information (context of all sorts) plus the fewest, most productive visual cues to get deep structure.*

Some of the major tenets of a psycholinguistic view of reading are as follows:

Getting meaning is more important than identifying words. Indeed, precise identification of all the words is not usually necessary for getting the meaning.

Reading involves the use of all three language cue systems: syntactic, semantic, and grapho/phonic. It is both inefficient and ineffective to rely just on the grapho/phonic system, to deal with each word as if it stood in isolation. Indeed, readers who make effective use of nonvisual information can greatly reduce their need for visual information.

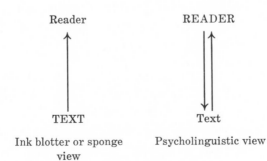

Figure 6.1   *Contrasting views of reading*

Reading is an active process, a deliberate search for meaning. And indeed, readers cannot get meaning from a text unless they bring meaning to it.

Most psycholinguistic definitions of reading emphasize one or more of these points.

THE IMPORTANCE OF SOUND

This section is especially for those who have always thought that as readers, we must not only identify all the words, but pronounce them—either aloud or in our heads. The word identification view of reading seems to have gained support from the theory that we necessarily go from the written word to the spoken word and *then* to meaning as we read, a view promulgated by certain structural linguists and by various educators who have followed in their footsteps. Consider, for example, the following statement (Strickland 1964, p. 10):

> The linguist conceives the reading act as that of turning the stimulus of the graphic shapes on a surface back into speech. The shapes represent speech; meaning is not found in the marks but in the speech which the marks represent.

Similar definitions can be found in Soffietti 1955 (p. 69), Bloomfield and Barnhart 1961 (p. 31), and McCracken and Walcutt 1970 (p. xiv). Of course these theorists recognize that there is such a thing as silent reading, but they argue that even in silent reading we to some degree say the words to ourselves. That is, we go from the written word to "silent speech" and then to meaning.

This view has lent credence to the idea that we must identify all the words in order to get meaning. Although for most of us some form of silent speech does often accompany silent reading, the getting of meaning usually *precedes* overt speech and presumably silent speech as well, when we are reading. Hence there is no need to turn written words into spoken words.

Obviously there are varying degrees of silent speech. At one extreme, we have speech which is nearly audible or semi-audible. At the other extreme, we have some sort of articulatory or auditory imagery—perhaps some sort of mental "echo" of the spoken word (Edfeldt 1960, p. 77; Conrad 1972, p. 207).

Before we look at some of the relevant laboratory experiments, you may want to investigate the role of silent speech for yourself. Here is an easy experiment. Read the following words: **wound, lead,** and **tears.** Did you mentally pronounce the words? Most people do, even though there is no way to predict a "correct" pronunciation out of context. Such evidence is informal, of course, but it does strongly suggest that reading is usually accompanied by some form of silent speech.

Another experiment you might try is to ask someone to cross out all the **e**'s in a paragraph or two of prose. Do not tell the person what you are investigating, but have him or her cross out the **e**'s as rapidly as possible. When your subject is done, look carefully for the **e**'s that have been missed. Has the person missed more silent **e**'s (as in **hope**) than pronounced **e**'s (as in **seat**)? If so, what does this suggest about the role of silent speech in visual processing?

In a similar laboratory experiment, silent **e**'s were missed nearly four times as often as pronounced **e**'s (Corcoran 1966, p. 658). In a second experiment, **e**'s were systematically omitted from a text and the subject was asked to detect the absence of **e**. Once again, significantly more silent **e**'s were undetected (Corcoran 1967, pp. 851–852). This seems to be fairly strong evidence, then, that most of us commonly "hear," in some sense, the words that we are reading.

An interesting experiment with deaf subjects suggests that reading is often accompanied by some degree of activity in the speech muscles. Though such activity may be invisible to the eye, it can be measured by determining the electrical charge of the muscles: the greater the muscle activity, the greater the electrical charge. Because the deaf people in this experiment communicated through sign language, the experimenter measured the electrical charge in the muscles of the *hands*, rather than in the speech muscles. A control group, people who had no hearing difficulty, showed hand muscle activity in only 31 percent of the tests of abstract thinking, including reading. The deaf subjects showed hand muscle activity in 84 percent of these tests. That is, reading seemed to be accompanied by movement in their speech muscles (Max 1937, p. 335). People who speak "normally" also show a tendency toward some speech muscle activity while reading (Edfeldt 1960, pp. 151–152).

Both common experience and laboratory research suggest, then, that silent reading is often accompanied by some form of silent speech. Silent speech appears to be most evident when our attention is called to individual words and parts of words, as in most of the experiments just mentioned (and in most instructional programs). But the crucial question is whether or not silent speech is a *necessary* prelude to understanding.

The evidence suggests the contrary, that understanding normally precedes vocalization as we are reading aloud. And it seems only logical that the same would be true for silent reading.

Some of the evidence comes from reading miscues. We have seen, for example, that good readers may translate the language of a text into alternative dialect patterns as they read aloud. Similarly the reader's understanding seems to have been ahead of his voice in the following examples:

not getting anything
I'm getting nothing for Christmas.   [a line from a song]

mean inside
"No, no," said Boris. "I don't mean outside."

ⓔ didn't do
Boris growled, "That's because you did it the wrong way."

[The reader started to say, "You didn't do it right."]

In each example, the reader got the meaning of the original and "translated" it into his own words. Clearly, understanding preceded the overt act of speech.

Such translation is possible in part because our eyes are typically ahead of the word we are focusing on. We can measure this phenomenon by seeing how far the eyes are ahead of the voice when someone is reading aloud. Simply obscure the person's sight of the page (say, by putting your hand over it), and then ask the person what additional words he or she can report. Here are the additional words reported from five trials with a person who was reading a science fiction story:

but rather because of

from the galactic rim

none completely satisfactory

of the universe

but as the ship leaves

The shortest stretch of words is **of the universe,** a grammatically complete unit. These examples suggest what research in fact shows: that a reader's **eye-voice span** (EVS) is influenced not only by the difficulty of the material being read, but also by the syntactic structure of whatever follows the word focused upon. The EVS ordinarily extends to the end of the largest grammatical unit possible. On the average, the eyes are about four words ahead of the voice. This helps explain how our understanding can precede overt or silent speech.

Evidence from earlier chapters also suggests that understanding normally comes before vocalization, not after. We have seen, for example, that it is not until we know the word or the structure of the word that we know how to pronounce the **t** and **h** in **father** and **fathead,** or the **p** and **h** in **graph** and **uphill.** With the boldfaced words in the sentences below, the situation is similar. To see this for yourself, read the sentences aloud:

She had an ugly **wound** on her cheek.

The elephant can **lead** the parade.

Big **tears** rolled down her cheeks.

Have you **wound** up the string?

It's made of **lead.**

Did you see the **tears** in his pants?

We do not know how to pronounce these words until we know something about their meaning. In the case of **wound** and **lead**, we must know their grammatical category; in the case of **tears**, we must know even more specific information about the word. Comprehension must come **before** overt or silent speech.

We have seen, then, that silent reading is often accompanied by some form of silent speech. But we have also seen that silent speech does not seem to be necessary for comprehension, since understanding normally precedes overt speech and presumably covert speech as well. Furthermore, it has been discovered that good readers show less use of silent speech than poorer readers (see, for example, Edfeldt 1960, pp. 153–154; Cleland 1971, pp. 139–140; Bever and Bower 1966, pp. 13–14, 23–24).

It is mostly when we are having difficulty comprehending what we are reading that we engage in silent speech, particularly in the more obvious kinds (like forming the words with our lips or even mumbling them semi-audibly). So instead of being necessary to comprehension, silent speech seems to be a sign of comprehension difficulty. The fastest and best readers seem to make the least use of silent speech.

This is not to suggest, of course, that we should avoid associating written words with their spoken counterparts as we help children learn to read. Can you imagine trying to teach a child the meaning of **the, of, pretty, enjoy,** and thousands of other words, without speaking the words aloud? This would be an unnecessarily difficult task. No, of course I am not suggesting that the spoken word has no place in reading instruction. Indeed, I would argue precisely the opposite: that beginning reading instruction should help children associate familiar aural materials with their spoken counterparts. But once they know some of the written words, even beginners can go directly from print to meaning. It is not *necessary* to pronounce the words, even mentally, as we read.

APPROACHES TO READING INSTRUCTION REVISITED

Most of the major approaches to beginning reading instruction have one basic element in common: they typically focus
on the identification of words. This is true of 1) the sight
word approach, which emphasizes the development of a
stock of words that can be immediately recognized; 2) the
phonics approach, which emphasizes the sounding-out of
words; 3) the so-called linguistic approach, which emphasizes the internalizing of regular patterns of spelling-sound
correspondence; and 4) the eclectic or smorgasbord approach, which emphasizes a variety of skills for identifying
words. Few if any major approaches initially emphasize the
getting of meaning rather than the precise identification of
words.

Even if reading *did* necessarily involve the precise identification of all the words, there would be a major problem
with these word-centered approaches. Although supposedly
recognizing the importance of context, even the sight word
approach and the eclectic approach often encourage children
initially to "attack" words as if they stood in isolation.[1]
When they cannot recognize a word immediately on sight,
children are encouraged to try to pronounce the word, using
their knowledge of letter-sound correspondences and, if relevant, their knowledge of bases and affixes (their "structural
analysis" skills). Often, they are encouraged to use context
only if this procedure has failed, or only as a check on their
tentative identification of the word. For identifying words,
then, the following sequence is often recommended:

1. Memory for word form: see if you can recognize the
   word.
2. Word analysis skills: try to pronounce the word, using

---

[1] A historical note may be of interest. In the 1948 edition of *On
Their Own in Reading*, William Gray suggested five major aids to
word perception. "Meaning clues from the context" was listed first
(p. 41). In the 1960 edition of his book, "memory of word form" came
first, and "context clues" came second (p. 16). Now, context seems to
have fallen to third position, after memory for word form and the use
of phonic and structural analysis skills.

your knowledge of letter-sound correspondences, plus your knowledge of bases and affixes (if relevant).

3. Context: if the word analysis skills have not worked, use context to get at least the gist of the word, if not the word itself.

Since the resurge of interest in phonics during the late 1960s, context has often been recommended only as a last resort.[2] We have seen, however, that using context as a last resort is neither efficient nor effective. The proficient reader uses context *first*, to predict what is coming next. By using both preceding syntactic and preceding semantic context, the reader is able to reduce his or her dependence upon visual information. On the whole, this makes word identification not only easier but more accurate. Thus to make reading more efficient and effective, we should recommend the following sequence instead of the one just listed:

1. Context: use your entire store of knowledge and experience plus the preceding context in order to predict what might be coming next.
2. The word itself: using only as many visual cues as necessary to confirm or modify your prediction, make a tentative identification of the word.
3. Context: use the following context to confirm or correct your tentative identification of the word.

Such a procedure would certainly help children become proficient readers. Proficient readers predict what is coming next and then confirm or correct their predictions in accordance with what follows.

But remember that proficient reading does not necessarily involve the precise identification of every word in a text, and proficient readers do not necessarily correct those miscues which fit with the context. Hence the second major problem with the various word-centered or word-identification models

---

[2] Of the cues available in the text itself, context seems to have become a last resort. However, the dictionary is often recommended, when even context proves insufficient.

of reading: they focus on the identification of words, rather than the getting of meaning. Though supposedly a means to an end, word-identification becomes an end in itself. And, as we have seen, this is inappropriate for several reasons:

1. Getting the words does not necessarily result in getting the meaning.
2. Within a very short time, we no longer remember surface structure anyway. We "remember" not the precise words or even necessarily the exact ideas of the author, but our own mental construct of what we have read.
3. Good readers read for meaning rather than for the precise identification of all the words.
4. Getting the meaning is usually possible without identifying all the words.

These facts suggest, then, the inadequacy of a word-centered approach to reading instruction. For one thing, such approaches are inefficient: they make reading as difficult as possible, by encouraging children to deal with each word as if it stood in isolation. As a result, even word identification suffers. Further, a word-identification approach distorts the nature of the reading process, inaccurately implying that precise identification of all the words is necessary for getting meaning. As a result, all too many children come to assume that reading means simply identifying words. The supposed means to comprehension becomes an end in itself, and in fact *the* end, for some children.

We may well wonder, then, why word identification approaches are so popular. One reason is that they are so in tune with the popular conception of reading: most people seem to think that in order to read, one *obviously* has to identify all the words. A second reason results from the movement toward competency-based education and the use of minimal performance objectives. To assess a person's competence at some task we have to have some way of measuring it, and it is much easier to assess a person's ability to identify words or master phonics rules than it is to assess that person's ability to comprehend what he or she reads. At least it is much easier to be *objective* in measuring someone's sight vocabulary and word attack skills.

A third reason is that in the late 1960s and early 1970s, a considerable body of research was interpreted as favoring ι phonics approach to reading (see, for example, Chall 1967, pp. 113–114). The following quote is from Walcutt, Lamport, and McCracken (1974, p. 397):

> The evidence clearly demonstrates that children who receive early intensive instruction in phonics develop superior word recognition skills in the early stages of reading and tend to maintain their superiority at least through the third grade. These same pupils tend to do somewhat better than pupils enrolled in meaning-emphasis (delayed gradual phonics) programs in reading comprehension at the end of the first grade.

The authors go on to say that through grade three, children who have received early intensive instruction in phonics are "at least as capable" in reading comprehension as those whose instruction has been characterized by a delayed and more gradual introduction to phonics.

Most such summaries purport to compare phonics or code-emphasis approaches with so-called "meaning-emphasis" approaches. But as we saw in chapter 2, most of these "meaning-emphasis" approaches merely focus on whole words rather than on parts of words. With the exception of the language experience approach and perhaps a few others, most approaches focus instructional attention not on getting meaning as one reads, but on identifying individual words.

As yet, there is no massive body of research comparing word-centered approaches with a psycholinguistic meaning-centered approach. However, one of the pioneering studies is particularly interesting and significant. In 1970, the Cajon Valley Union School District in El Cajon, California, investigated the reading progress of its students and discovered that "a significant number were failing in reading." Subsequently, the school district instituted a program that apparently involved over 1600 students from kindergarten through grade eight.[3] The target students were identified as those who were at least 1.2 years below grade level, as measured by standardized reading tests at the end of grade three. It was found that these students relied on the grapho/phonic cueing system to the exclusion of the semantic and syntactic cueing systems (Cajon Valley 1974, p. 2). Therefore, the target students received individually prescribed strategy lessons to help them use all three cueing systems in order to get meaning.

The results were both statistically and educationally significant. As expected, the most dramatic growth occurred during the first year of a student's exposure to the program. On the average, the experimental students showed one or more years of reading growth, as compared with an average yearly growth rate of less than one-half year when they were in grades one through three. Overall, the experimental group showed considerably greater gains than the control group, which presumably was taught by a more conventional approach (Cajon Valley, pp. 3–4).

Perhaps most interesting, however, are the specific ways in which the experimental group exhibited reading growth. The following are the major conclusions about the children in the experimental group:

1. They improved in their use of reading strategies, apparently in their ability to predict what might be coming next and to correct those miscues which do not make sense in context.
2. They improved in their ability to comprehend what they read. (Comprehension was measured in two ways: by determining the percentage of miscues which resulted in no loss of comprehension, and by having the child retell the story or other selection that was read.)
3. They improved in their ability to use syntactic cues as they read.

[3] A brief summary of this project is included in *Effective Reading Programs: Summaries of 222 Selected Programs*, prepared under the auspices of the National Right to Read Effort and the ERIC Clearinghouse on Reading and Communication Skills, 1975. The book is available from the National Council of Teachers of English.

4. They became less dependent upon grapho/phonic cues.

In the first two areas of improvement the experimental group showed more than twice the growth of the control group.

The next chapter will present some possible ways of measuring these aspects of reading growth. And in chapter 8, we will examine some kinds of strategy lessons that can be used to help readers improve their use of syntactic and semantic cues. For the present, it seems wise to elaborate upon the difference between reading strategies and reading skills.

Most approaches to reading emphasize the development of reading *skills*. Though some of these are "comprehension skills," a great deal of attention is paid to skills for pronouncing and/or identifying words. In contrast, most psycholinguists emphasize the development of *strategies* for getting meaning from connected text. Figure 6.2 illustrates this difference. In the word-centered skills approaches, children are taught to use their stock of sight words, their phonics and structural analysis skills, and (often last) their understanding of context in order to identify words. Concern with comprehension typically comes later, after the selection has been read. But in a meaning-centered strategies approach, children are actually taught to use their comprehension of a text to help them identify the words. They are taught to use context of all sorts to *predict* what will come next; to *sample* the visual display, using a minimum

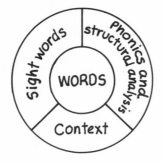
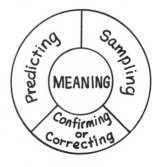

SKILLS   STRATEGIES

Figure 6.2 *Skills versus strategies*

of grapho/phonic cues to confirm or modify their prediction and to tentatively interpret a word; and to use following context to *confirm* or *correct* this tentative interpretation. As the term "interpretation" suggests, getting the meaning is more important than precise word identification. It is assumed that readers will translate the deep structure of the author into a surface structure which is partially their own. Meaning is the beginning and the end of reading.

An example (adapted from Weaver 1977) may help to clarify the distinction between the two approaches. Suppose that while reading a story about Jane's father fixing their TV antenna, a child comes to the sentence **Jane's father was on the house.** Now what if the child says "horse" for **house**? Given a sight word approach, a teacher might say "Look at that word again. You know that word." Given a phonics approach, the teacher might say "Look at that word again. There isn't any **r** in it, is there? And what sound does the **ou** make?" Given a psycholinguistic approach, the teacher might say "Think for a moment. Where was Jane's father, anyway? Where did he climb to?" That is, a psycholinguistically oriented teacher would begin by helping the child use preceding context to predict what will come next. If the child had read "roof" for house, such a teacher would not expect the child to correct the miscue.

We have seen, then, that proficient readers predict, sample, and confirm/correct as they read. But how can we help beginning readers develop facility in using such strategies? More generally, how can we design a beginning reading program which reflects our knowledge of the reading process and the way reading ability is acquired? Let us address these questions in the following section.

BEGINNING READERS AND READING INSTRUCTION

Many beginning readers tend, more or less intuitively, to predict what is coming next and to correct or try to correct those miscues which do not make sense in context. Still, we know that there are some important differences between mature readers and five- to seven-year-old children who are beginning readers. First, beginning readers may have trouble hearing the separate sounds in a word. And second, like older nonproficient readers, beginners may have trouble using all three language cue systems simultaneously. Indeed, they may center their attention on one cue system and strategy, to the virtual exclusion of everything else. In beginning reading instruction we would do well to build upon children's strengths instead of attacking such problems head-on at a time when at least some children may be cognitively unable to deal with separate sounds or to read for both meaning and surface accuracy simultaneously.

Children bring tremendous resources to school. They bring a considerable wealth of experience (even though not all such experience has always been welcomed by middle class schools and teachers). Children also bring considerable unconscious knowledge of language, as well as considerable experience in using language. Because most children entering school have had at least five years' experience in listening to the speech of others, they are accustomed to using all sorts of knowledge and context to interpret what they hear. This already learned strategy only needs to be transferred to the reading process. Beginning reading instruction would be more universally successful if we began by emphasizing what children *do* know and *can* do.

Instead, we tend to begin with what many children do not already know: the basic correspondences between letters and sounds. And we often ask children to do what many of them cannot do: determine the sounds in words, and blend sounds together to form words. With such an approach, we may quickly convince some children that they can never learn to read.

Imagine a mother following a similar procedure in teaching her child to talk. Her little girl has reached the magical age of two, and mother decides it is time for beginning instruction in speaking. Methodically, she strips the room bare of any possibly distracting influences, including Daddy. Then, on Monday, she teaches the child the /d/ sound—which unfortunately sounds more like "duh" when said in isolation. On Tuesday, she teaches the child the /æ/ sound, the vowel sound in **cat** and **bat**. On Wednesday, she teaches the child to blend the two sounds and say /dæ/. On Thursday, she teaches the child to repeat the syllable and say /dædæ/. And on Friday, she teaches the child to say the word whenever Daddy is allowed into the room.

Surely *no one* ever followed quite such an absurd procedure, either in teaching a child to talk or in teaching a child to read. But this imaginary situation does indicate, albeit in exaggerated form, one of the problems with focusing early reading or prereading instruction on letters and their sounds. Such an approach confronts the child with meaningless units that he or she is not always accustomed to dealing with, and it implicitly denies the considerable store of knowledge and experience that the child can and should bring to the task of reading.

Actually, there are a number of parallels between learning to talk and learning to read, between natural language acquisition and the more or less natural acquisition of reading. Such parallels are seen most clearly, of course, when children learn to read before entering school. In order to make learning to read as painless and as natural as possible, we might do well to examine some of these parallels and determine some of the implications for reading instruction.

First, we do not and cannot ordinarily *teach* children to talk. Think, for example, of the "rule" for pronouncing the past tense of regular verbs (as in **laughed, loved,** and **waited**). Could you teach that rule to young children? Indeed, do you even know what the rule is?[4] Children must learn for themselves the basic rules for putting words and sentences together. We help provide the opportunities, but we do not and cannot teach them to talk. Nor can we really *teach* them to read. Children must learn for themselves such things as the basic spelling-sound correspondences.

---

[4] The most economical "rule" has three *ordered* parts: a) if the verb ends in /t/ or /d/ add /id/, as in **waited** or **waded**; b) if the verb ends in a voiceless consonant sound other than /t/, add /t/, as in **laughed**; c) if the verb ends in any other sound, add /d/, as in **loved** and **agreed**. The first part of the rule, for verbs ending in /t/ or /d/, is normally the last part mastered by children.

Instruction can facilitate such learning, but cannot bring it about. On the other hand, such learning is in fact possible with very little, if any, direct instruction. Consider this example of a girl who began to read at the age of 3 (Forester 1977, p. 164):

> She began by looking at storybooks (*The Wizard of Oz* was her first) and listening to the record which accompanied the book. The record signalled when she should turn the page and by listening over and over again she learned the story by heart while following the words in the book with her finger. From that beginning she learned to recognize words and by the time she was observed [at the age of four], it was apparent that she had derived the sound values of letters and used that knowledge to sound out unfamiliar words.

This type of learning is typical of children who have learned to read (not merely to identify some words) before they enter school.

A second parallel between learning to talk and learning to read is that both are facilitated by a language-rich environment. Children progress best when they are innundated by language and when they have myriad opportunities to use language themselves. One way to stimulate reading acquisition is to encourage children to read the signs and labels in their environment: the octagonal red sign at an intersection, the labels on soup cans and toothpaste tubes, and so forth. If the child reads "soup" for **Chicken Noodle** and "toothpaste" for **Colgate**, this is powerful evidence that he or she knows what reading is all about. Furthermore, such miscues demonstrate the child's natural tendency to use context, to predict what something is likely to mean. This use of the environmental context is an important first step in the acquisition of good reading strategies.

It is particularly important to read to children, at first just in order for them to learn the purpose of books and the joys of reading. Also, children need to have someone to stimulate their curiosity about language, and to answer their questions. Again, both initial language acquisition and later reading acquisition can be stimulated through books. As adult and child share favorite books again and again, the child will gradually learn to associate the spoken word with the written word. In fact, the child may soon insist upon "reading" the book to anyone available, as I used to do with *The Night before Christmas.* And at this point if not before, children typically begin to ask questions about the relation between the spoken language and the written language.

A third parallel between learning to talk and learning to read involves the relationship between deep structure and surface structure. In learning to talk, children at first express their deep structures in a relatively limited surface structure. The meaning of simple utterances like "Mommy sock" and "Sweater chair" is usually made clear through context and other nonverbal cues. So it is with the natural acquisition of reading. When they first depart from familiar, memorized texts, children are better able to get the meaning than to reproduce the author's exact words. Just as children's utterances become increasingly closer to adult models, their renditions of a written text will become increasingly closer to the surface structure of that text—at least up to a point. Among other things, this suggests that children naturally develop a stock of sight words through reading, by concentrating upon meaning.

Another parallel between the two processes has to do with errors. In learning to talk, certain errors can be signs of progress. For example: if instead of saying "ate" and "bought" and "went" the child suddenly begins saying "eated" and "buyed" and "goed," we know that he or she has learned the regular past tense endings; such errors are actually a sign of progress in learning the system of English. Similarly, children will show changing patterns of miscues as they learn not only to read for meaning, but to render the surface structure more accurately (see Y. Goodman 1976, "Developing Reading Proficiency"). At least for a short while, even "natural" readers may show some tendency to overrely on grapho/phonics, as they try to coordinate all three language cue systems.

Finally, we know that language acquisition proceeds more or less from whole to part, rather than vice versa. This seems to be true in all aspects of development. A baby, for example, learns to recognize the mother's face before learning to recognize her hair, eyes, and nose. Of course we do try to help our children learn language by teaching them the names for things. Nevertheless, they basically learn language by hearing it in natural and meaningful contexts and by trying to use language themselves. We do not teach them isolated letters, then words, and last sentences. So in reading: when a child learns to read more or less naturally, he or she learns by working from whole to part: from memorized stories to words, and from words to the letters and their sounds. Even those children who "know their letters" before learning to read do not learn to read from the bottom up, beginning with the bits and pieces of words and sentences (see, for example, Huey 1908, pp. 348–350).

Contrary to what one might think, it is possible to preserve most if not all of these features of natural reading acquisition in the classroom. Many teachers in Great Britain and New Zealand are doing this, and so are many teachers in the United States. Indeed, this is essentially the aim of the language experience approach: to make the acquisition of literacy (reading and writing) a natural extension of the acquisition of oracy (listening and speaking).

Anne Forester describes one program that practices this philosophy, in an article entitled "What Teachers Can Learn from 'Natural Readers.' " As we have seen, studies of natural reading acquisition show that just as children learn to talk not from direct instruction but mainly from hearing language and using it themselves, so children can learn to read in much the same way (see, for example, Durkin 1961 and Durkin 1966, pp. 133–139). Accordingly, the classroom teacher whose technique Forester describes decided not to teach any lessons *about* reading. Instead, she would emphasize the modeling of fluent reading and give extensive practice in actual reading. As Forester describes it (1977, p. 165),

In Mrs. Reinhard's [first grade] class, children listen to stories and read familiar nursery rhymes from large wall charts. They hear and say the sentences and stories they themselves dictated and listen to tape recordings of books while following along page-by-page. They read to each other and put on plays. They quickly learn what it means to read and how useful and pleasureable it can be.

At the end of the school year that Forester investigated, all of the children in this first grade class had learned to read. Even the slowest students succeeded and were promoted to grade two. Furthermore, the children learned to read fluently and expressively, with pleasure.

I think one of the lessons teachers can learn from such classrooms is that we should have faith in children's ability to learn to read, just as we have faith in their ability to learn to talk. We cannot really "teach them to read" any more than we can teach them to talk. But we *can* provide appropriate stimulation and guidance, and we can do children the credit of assuming that they can learn to read.

READING INSTRUCTION REVISITED

Fortunately, many teachers are far more effective than the approach suggested in their basal reading series. They let intuition and experience guide them in helping children learn to predict, sample, and confirm or correct as they read. And they realize that getting the author's meaning is more important than accurately identifying each and every word of a text.

But even these teachers may be more effective, and certainly more comfortable in what they are doing, if they realize that their practices are supported by what is known about the reading process itself, by what proficient readers do as they read. Ideally, such teachers may also find support from professional organizations and even from various governmental agencies.

Given the typical concern with word attack skills and the bits and pieces of language, I find the following definition and list of assumptions very encouraging (despite the fact that I would quibble with certain points). The statement was developed jointly by representatives from the Michigan Reading Association and the Michigan Department of Education. It is intended that the state's efforts at reading improvement and assessment will be guided by this definition and its accompanying set of assumptions (from a "Reading Position" document of the Michigan Department of Education;[5] essentially the same statement appears in "News from the Professional Studies and Standards Committee" 1977):

A Department of Education Definition of Reading

The Department's definition of reading is based upon the assumption that the only legitimate, final outcome of reading instruction is comprehension. That is, although certain enabling word attack skills may be related to comprehension skills, mastery of these skills, in and of themselves and in the absence of comprehension, is not a sufficient terminal objective for reading instruction.

Thus, reading must be defined not as the process of transforming visual configurations into sound, which is a widely held conventional view of reading, but the *process of transforming the visual representation of language into meaning*. Thus, if one is reading, an idea is being transferred from the written page to the reader's mind.

This definition assumes that 1) Virtually everyone *can* learn to read, given the appropriate reading instruction. 2) From the earliest levels, the various *uses* and application of reading, which range from the purely functional to the broadly humanistic (reading to enhance one's human understandings), including reading for work-related pur-

---

[5] Michigan Department of Education, "Reading Position," no date. A draft copy was obtained in 1978 from Robert Trezise, Coordinator for Communication Skills. Used by permission.

poses, should be stressed within reading programs. It is not sufficient that pupils merely recognize the words of a passage and comprehend and interpret their meaning. They must also learn to apply the ideas gained from the printed page. Reading, as conceived here, not only includes comprehension and interpretation, but the application of the meaning of words to one's own life. 3) Students learn to read most successfully *within the context of a total language arts experience,* which includes speaking and listening activities, writing, reading for enjoyment, and reading within a variety of content areas, such as the sciences, vocational education, social studies, mathematics, and so on. 4) The most appropriate type of reading instruction varies from person to person. Some students learn to read most successfully with one approach, others with a quite different approach. *Determining the most appropriate approach for a particular student is one of the keys to successful reading instruction.* 5) Instructional objectives in the area of word attack skills should be integrated with objectives that focus on comprehension. 6) Instruction in comprehension can and should occur *at the earliest instructional levels* and with all students, including those who appear to be having difficulty with learning skills. 7) *Comprehension and word attack skills are complementary and mutually dependent;* that is, word attack skills help students to attain comprehension skills, while comprehension skills help them with decoding. If a reader understands the context of the words he/she is attempting to decode, the decoding process is greatly facilitated. 8) By the time students who have had instruction in comprehension skills from the earliest levels have reached their upper-elementary and secondary school experiences, fewer of them will be "word callers"; that is, fewer of them will be persons who can say the words, but cannot interpret what they read, cannot make inferences on the basis of what they have read, cannot distinguish between main ideas and subordinate ideas, cannot identify authors' themes and purposes—in short, cannot comprehend what they read. Indeed, *a person who can only say the words without understanding them, or can merely demonstrate a cer-*

tain proficiency in terms of word attack skills, cannot really be said to be reading at all.

Perhaps Michigan's definition and characterization of reading, an almost revolutionary statement, can serve as a help and a guide for teachers in other states as well.

ACTIVITIES AND PROJECTS FOR FURTHER EXPLORATION

1. To solidify your understanding of the reading process, write a letter in which you deal with the issues raised by the questions below. Assume that you are writing to a principal who has interviewed you for a job and who has asked you to explain and defend your philosophy of reading instruction in detail. If you already have a teaching job, you might write to someone within your school system, suggesting certain curriculum changes. Whomever you choose as your audience, remember that this person probably does not know nearly as much about the reading process as you do. Therefore, you will have to illustrate your points with *specific* and *convincing* examples. Whenever possible, *use not only your own words but your own examples as well.* Naturally you may want to cover additional points that are particularly relevant to your real or imagined situation. But deal with at least the following questions, combining and organizing your points however you wish:

   a. Why is it overly simple to say that we combine the meanings of the individual words in a sentence in order to arrive at the meaning of the whole?

   b. How might we define surface structure and deep structure? What does it mean to say that readers bring meaning *to* sentences instead of getting meaning *from* them?

   c. Do we normally process words letter by letter, from left to right? Which parts of words are most useful in word identification?

   d. How useful are phonics rules? How necessary is it for children to learn phonics rules?

   e. Are words easier to identify in isolation, or in context? What does it mean to say that the more nonvisual information a reader can use, the less visual information he or she needs? What are the various kinds of context that can aid in identifying words and getting meaning?

    f. How do good readers typically differ from poor readers in their use of context? How do the miscues of good readers typically differ from the miscues of poor readers?

    g. What is the difference between reading *skills* and reading *strategies*? What strategies do good readers typically use?

    h. Why is a word-centered approach to reading inappropriate?

    i. How does a psycholinguistic view of reading typically differ from other views?

    j. In general, how do proficient readers read? *What are some of the implications for reading instruction?*

2. Read at least two of the following three articles. Then make up your own list of eight or more rules for making learning to read difficult and distasteful, together with a companion list of eight or so rules for making learning to read easy and pleasurable. You may want to complete this activity before writing the letter suggested in the activity above.

Allen, P. David. "Implications for Reading Instruction." In *Findings of Research in Miscue Analysis: Classroom Implications,* edited by P. David Allen and Dorothy J. Watson. Urbana, Ill.: ERIC Clearinghouse on Reading and Communication Skills and the National Council of Teachers of English, 1976, pp. 107–112.

Smith, Frank. "Twelve Easy Ways to Make Learning to Read Difficult, and One Difficult Way to Make It Easy." In *Psycholinguistics and Reading,* edited by Frank Smith. New York: Holt, Rinehart and Winston, 1973, pp. 183–196.

Estes, Thomas H., and Johnstone, Julie P. "Twelve Easy Ways to Make Readers Hate Reading (and One Difficult Way to Make Them Love It)." *Language Arts* 54 (November/December 1977): 891–897.

3. Return to the questionnaire that was presented in activity 3 of chapter 1. Try it again, then compare the results with your original results. Have you changed your opinions in any significant ways?

READINGS FOR FURTHER EXPLORATION

I highly recommend the three readings just cited in activity 2. All three are of importance for teachers of reading.

Goodman, Yetta, and Watson, Dorothy J. "A Reading Program to Live With: Focus on Comprehension." *Language Arts* 54 (November/

December 1977) : 868–879. Suggests how to implement a psycholinguistic understanding of reading in the elementary classroom.

Cooper, Charles R., and Petrosky, Anthony R. "A Psycholinguistic View of the Fluent Reading Process." *Journal of Reading* (December 1976) : 184–207. Summarizes the nature of fluent reading, showing how our understanding of the reading process can be implemented in a developmental reading program for secondary students.

Forester, Anne D. "What Teachers Can Learn from 'Natural Readers.'" *The Reading Teacher* 31 (November 1977) : 160–166. Reviews some of the research on children who have learned to read before entering school, showing how an understanding of such "natural" readers has been used to structure beginning reading instruction in a particular first grade classroom.

Smith, Frank. "Decoding: The Great Fallacy." In *Psycholinguistics and Reading*, edited by Frank Smith. New York: Holt, Rinehart and Winston, 1973, pp. 70–83. Provides good follow-up to our discussion of whether people decode written words to spoken words and then to meaning.

part two

reading in the classroom

Now that we have examined the nature of the reading process and seen some of the implications for reading instruction, it is time to consider in more detail how a psycholinguistic understanding of reading can be applied in the classroom. Chapter 7 explains some methods for assessing a reader's strategies and comprehension. Chapter 8 indicates how we can help readers develop good reading strategies. Chapter 9 suggests a design for a comprehensive reading program suitable for a wide range of instructional levels. The book closes by emphasizing the integration of reading with the total curriculum.

7

how can we assess readers' strengths and determine their instructional needs?

Only two basic uses of reading tests are legitimate. They are as follows: (1) To measure the effectiveness with which any person uses reading to comprehend written language. . . . (2) To diagnose the strengths and weaknesses of readers as an aid to planning instruction which will help to make them more effective.—Kenneth Goodman

Questions for Study and Discussion

1   Why isn't an informal reading inventory appropriate for assessing a reader's strengths and weaknesses?
2   How can we assess a reader's strategies and comprehension in some detail?
3   How can we assess reading quickly and informally?
4   How can we determine a child's readiness for reading and reading instruction?

ASSESSING THE INFORMAL READING INVENTORY

As everyone knows, reading can be assessed in a variety of ways, and for a variety of purposes. Perhaps most common is the *standardized test,* commercially prepared and machine scored. Most standardized tests measure people not against their own ability or against a desired outcome, but against other people. This, indeed, is the major purpose of such tests. Hence the results are often not used to pinpoint specific areas of strength or weakness. Furthermore, standardized reading tests cannot tell us what strategies a person uses as he or she reads. In order to make such an assessment, we

158

must observe the reading process in action. We must listen to the person read aloud.

Recognizing this necessity, many teachers and reading specialists have come to use what is often called an *informal reading inventory* (*IRI*). The examiner actually listens to a person read and analyzes the reader's miscues or "errors," as they are more often called.

Used flexibly, the informal reading inventory can be a good way to decide where to place a child within a basal reading series. The teacher begins by having the child read from a basal reader that is likely to be quite easy for him or her, and ends when the child has progressed through other readers to one that is obviously too difficult. The wise teacher determines the child's placement through a variety of factors, such as the quality of the child's miscues, the child's comprehension, and the child's fluency and confidence. Often these factors cannot (or at least should not) be weighted in any simple, numerical way. For example, suppose that Mary and Sally both read from the same text and both make good miscues, about the same number overall. Suppose further that they both show good comprehension of what they have read. Does this mean that they should both be placed at the same level of reading materials? Not necessarily. One child may read the text fluently and with confidence, while the other may read the same text slowly, choppily, and with obvious discomfort and frustration. The wise teacher will take such differences into account in deciding what instructional materials to use with a given child.

Unfortunately, teachers' good judgment tends to be thwarted by the more rigid procedures often recommended for administering and scoring an informal reading inventory. The word "administering" is itself a key to the current state of affairs, for the teacher may merely be using any of several informal reading inventories now commercially available either separately or as part of a basal reading package (see, for example, Johns et al. 1977, p. 36). Even in textbooks for prospective teachers, the recommended procedure tends to be excessively rigid. Remember,

for example, the offtimes misleading recommendation that
when a person miscues on more than six words out of one
hundred, the reading selection is probably too difficult for instructional use with that person (see chapter 5, p. 98).

In addition to rigidity, there are other problems with the
informal reading inventory as it is often advocated and
structured. One problem is presented by the various word
recognition and word analysis tests that often accompany an
informal reading inventory. Another problem is that even in
analyzing the reader's miscues, teachers are subtly encouraged to consider quantity rather than quality.

Let us consider the tests which assess a reader's sight
vocabulary or ability to apply phonics rules and other skills
for analyzing words. By now the reason for worry about
such tests should be obvious. Some readers are good at recognizing words on sight, but not very good at getting meaning
from connected text. Other readers are good at getting
meaning, but not particularly good at recognizing or analyzing isolated words. In either case, such tests do not tell us
very much about a reader's ability to comprehend a written
text. This is perhaps most distressing when as a result of
such tests, we underestimate someone's reading ability.

Indeed, this is true for most methods of assessing an
individual's reading "errors": they generally assume that
reading is an exact process, requiring word-for-word accuracy. When readers make miscues, it is assumed that they
need instructional help. The only question is, what kind of
help? To answer this question, teachers are encouraged to
determine the kind(s) of miscues that the reader commonly
makes.

Typically, the teacher is directed to tabulate the number
of insertions, omissions, substitutions, reversals, and so
forth, as if these were obviously and always a sign of reading weakness. Even repetitions and regressions are sometimes counted against the reader, though we know that *good*
readers tend to regress and repeat words to correct any
miscue that does not make sense in context. Most methods

of analysis actually penalize the use of good reading strategies.

Although those who advocate an informal reading inventory are often aware that miscues should be analyzed in context rather than as if they occurred in isolation, the various charts and schemes tend to take on a life and character quite distinct from that originally intended. Let us look at one version of the informal reading inventory and see what kinds of inappropriate conclusions might easily be drawn. In *To Help Children Read* (1978, p. 156), May and Eliot provide a checklist for analyzing a child's oral reading. The checklist itself invites teachers to make various kinds of observations, as the child reads from increasingly higher level basals. That is, the teacher is directed to look for such things as whole-word omissions, whole-word insertions, acceptable substitutions, nonsemantic substitutions, and nongrammatical substitutions (a considerable improvement over the 1973 version, which had just one "substitution" category). After recording whatever observations seem appropriate, the teacher is directed to make inferences about the reader's problems. The checklist suggests these areas of possible difficulty:

1. Basic irregular sight words not known
2. Weak in phonic analysis skills
3. Weak in structural analysis skills
4. Nonstandard dialect
5. Weak in contextual analysis: semantic clues
6. Weak in contextual analysis: grammatical clues
7. Comprehension poor
8. Punctuation not understood
9. Needs help on phrasing

Obviously the checklist is directed toward helping teachers pinpoint children's reading weaknesses, rather than both their strengths and their weaknesses. And that, indeed, is one serious objection to such a scheme. A further objection is that such a scheme can all too easily encourage teachers to find weaknesses that do not exist.

To see how this might happen, let us focus upon some of the inferences that an examiner is invited to make. Much of the discussion is from Weaver and Smith (1979).

Basic Irregular Sight Words Not Known

Observing a child sometimes substitute one basic sight word for another or omit basic sight words, one might conclude that the child does not know these words. But the child may simply be reading for deep structure rather than for surface structure. Function words and pronouns are often among the "basic sight words," and we have already seen that good readers are likely to make miscues involving such words. They tend to substitute one pronoun or function word for another, and to omit or insert optional function words. The following are examples (some from K. S. Goodman 1973, *Theoretically Based Studies*):

their
White men came from the cities.
It
That took us about an hour.
might
"You may be right."

She made her own paints from (the) roots.

. . . but after a month we saw (that) nothing was growing.

Mr. Tully beat me more often and more cruelly than Mr. Coffin had (done.)

the
Billy feasted on ∧ roast corn . . . .

up
. . . it was enough to wake ∧ the dead.

that
They told him ∧ he had been foolish to plant sesame . . . .

In each of the foregoing examples, the meaning is preserved even though the surface structure is altered. The child made *good* miscues, and we are not justified in assuming that the child did not know the word printed in the text. Instead, we should assume that the child is reading for meaning rather than for accurate reproduction of all the words. And since the getting of meaning is supposedly the goal of reading and of reading instruction, we would do well not to lead the child away from this goal by insisting that every detail of the text be rigorously preserved.

In the 1973 edition of *To Help Children Read*, one possibility the teacher was to consider is that the reader might be "guessing at words" (May 1973, p. 130). Observing that a child sometimes replaces the text word with a word that looks and sounds radically different, one might indeed conclude that the child is guessing at words. Again, however, we must look at the quality of the "guess." We know that the good reader makes educated guesses or *predictions* about what is to come next, and that such predictions sometimes result in miscues. But if these resulting miscues preserve the essential meaning of the text, or if they fail to fit with following context but are subsequently corrected by the reader, then the teacher has little or no reason for concern. Examples of such good miscues might be "roof" for **house**, "baby" for **child**, and "bird" for **canary** (depending, of course, on the context). Note also the following example, where the child made a miscue at the end of a line, then corrected her miscue when the next line revealed the error of her prediction:

saw
I first saw Claribel when I was

working in my office.

The miscue "saw" for **was** is not a habitual association for this girl, nor was it merely a random guess: it was a logical prediction, given the preceding grammar and meaning, and it reflected minimal attention to grapho/phonic cues. When the following line failed to confirm the appropriateness of "saw," the girl corrected it to "was." A similar miscue from the same student is the following (both are from Goodman and Burke's *RMI Practice Analysis Manual,* 1972):

Instead, there was a
                                    heard
lovely song. I looked up and had

my first view of Claribel.

The miscue "heard" was again logical, given the preceding grammar and meaning. And it too reflected minimal attention to grapho/phonic cues. Such miscues suggest that this reader does not merely guess at words; rather, she makes good use of predicting and sampling strategies.

Note that if we were to look at these last substitutions without reference to context, we might indeed assume that the child was guessing—or, in the case of "saw" for **was,** that the child might have a tendency to confuse the two words or to reverse letters. By examining these words in context, however, we can see that they are good quality miscues, stemming from productive reading strategies.

Weak in Phonic Analysis Skills

Observing a child sometimes sound out words but end up with the wrong word or a nonword, one might conclude that the child is weak in phonic analysis skills. Examples we have seen which might lead to such a conclusion are the following miscues made by one child:

                                    beaches
the children sat on little benches in front of the teacher
        expert
Every day except Friday,
                                    souts
The sandy shore rang with the happy shouts and cries of the village boys and girls.
        ramped
the boys repeated everything the teacher said

Seeing such miscues, one might be tempted to conclude that the child needs more work with phonics. Examining the words in context, however, we see that the problem may be *too much* phonics, or rather phonics with too little else. The miscue "beaches" made reasonable sense in the total context, but the miscue "expert" for **except** does not. The nonwords "souts" and "ramped" show that the child is attending to grammar (the plural -s and the past tense -**ed**), but they show no concern for meaning.

As we saw in chapter 3, an extensive study revealed 211 letter–sound correspondences in just the one-syllable and two-syllable words typically understood by six- to nine-year-olds. Of this total, 166 were considered "rules" because they occurred in ten or more words (Berdiansky et al. 1959, as reported in Smith 1973). Thus even if it were possible for beginning readers to master all 166 rules, how would they know whether any given case represented a rule or an exception? Clearly phonics can supply only a clue, an approximation to how the word is pronounced. The child who made the foregoing miscues needs to learn to predict what is coming next, then use his knowledge of letter–sound correspondences to produce a word that makes sense in context. *More* phonics instruction will simply make the child an even poorer reader than he already is, because it will force him to pay even closer attention to small details and lead him away from a concern for meaning. Indeed, at the junior high and high school levels, the poorest readers are often those whose miscues show the *closest* letter-sound correspondence to the text word (K. S. Goodman 1973, *Theoretically Based Studies*, pp. 51, 53). Such readers come close to sounding out the word, but because they are using grapho/phonics almost exclusively, they get neither the word itself nor the essential meaning of the material being read.

We must be cautious, then, about concluding that a reader does not know basic sight words, or that a reader merely guesses at words, or that a reader is weak in phonic analysis skills. If inappropriately drawn, such conclusions could lead to instruction that is not merely unnecessary, but damaging. The reader may be led to focus too much upon words and parts of words, and too little upon meaning.

What are we to do instead to determine a reader's strengths, weaknesses, and instructional needs? I would suggest that instead of struggling to use an informal reading inventory wisely and well, we should adopt a procedure that more adequately reflects what is known about proficient reading. Such a procedure should have the following characteristics:

1. It should implicitly recognize that getting meaning is more important than reproducing surface detail.
2. It should help us determine a reader's strengths as well as his or her weaknesses.
3. It should examine miscues in context, distinguishing between those which are appropriate in context and those which are not.
4. It should in effect reward the correction of miscues that are not appropriate in context.
5. It should provide insight into a reader's strategies, particularly into how well the reader uses context to predict what is coming next and to correct those miscues that do not make sense with what follows.
6. It should enable us to determine, in general terms, what kind(s) of strategy lessons the reader needs, if any.

Such characteristics could be embodied in a variety of schemes for analyzing a reader's miscues, as demonstrated in the next sections.

ASSESSING READING STRATEGIES AND COMPREHENSION

Kenneth Goodman inaugurated not only a new way of thinking about reading "errors," but also an insightful way of analyzing them. His Taxonomy of Reading Miscues has been widely used in research. The 1973 version is readily available in Allen and Watson's *Findings of Research in Miscue Analysis: Classroom Implications* (1976), but this taxonomy is far too complicated for the day-to-day needs of classroom teachers and reading specialists.

To meet the ordinary needs of teacher and specialist,

Yetta Goodman and Carolyn Burke prepared a *Reading Miscue Inventory Manual* (1972), which explains their simpler procedure for analyzing a reader's strengths and weaknesses.[1] I regularly have my students practice using the Goodman-Burke forms and procedure, because this training provides valuable insights into the reading process. Furthermore, their miscue analysis forms may be helpful with students whose miscues are particularly puzzling. An even simpler form should be adequate for most needs, however.

In the following pages, then, I will suggest a simpler but still fairly detailed procedure and form for analyzing a reader's miscues. The procedure is essentially that recommended in Goodman and Burke's manual (henceforth usually called just the *RMI Manual*). The form is my own, but it also draws heavily upon the *RMI Manual* and my experience with it. As you become more familiar with miscue analysis, you too may find yourself experimenting with variations in procedure and form.

It is important to have the reader read aloud, so we can analyze his or her strategies for dealing with print. We also need another way of measuring the reader's comprehension. Therefore, we not only analyze a reader's miscues, but also evaluate his or her retelling of what has been read. The retelling provides an important check on our miscue analysis. Some readers are good at reproducing surface structure, but not very good at getting meaning. Others get most of the meaning, even though they have made a number of miscues that did not seem to preserve meaning and that they did not overtly correct. Besides providing a balanced view, an examination of both the miscues and the retelling provides us with two different measures of comprehension: a measure of how well the reader seemed to comprehend while in the process of reading, and a measure of what the reader remembered after reading the selection.

---

[1] This manual is available not only as a separate item, but as part of a complete kit for helping teachers learn how to analyze a reader's strengths and weaknesses. See Yetta M. Goodman and Carolyn L. Burke, *Reading Miscue Inventory Complete Kit: Procedure for Diagnosis and Evaluation* (New York: Macmillan, 1972).

When you try the following procedure for yourself, you will doubtless have some questions that are not answered by this brief discussion. Do not be afraid to use your own good judgment in deciding what to do. However, it would also be wise to consult someone more experienced in such matters or to consult the *RMI Manual*, which, although it need not be regarded as the ultimate authority, does provide some useful guidelines not repeated here.

PREPARING FOR THE READING SESSION

You will need to choose material to be read by the individual whose reading ability you are analyzing. The material must be difficult enough to cause the reader to make miscues, but not so difficult as to cause extreme frustration and distress. You will need to collect about twenty-five or more consecutive miscues for analysis, preferably on the same reading material. It is even better if you can collect thirty-five or more miscues and discard approximately the first ten, those made when the reader is just starting to read the selection. Here are some specific suggestions and guidelines:

1. A good rule of thumb is to begin with material one grade level above what the reader usually deals with in class. However, it is helpful to have two or three selections of different difficulty available for use, because you will need to try another selection if the reader is not making many miscues or if the selection is producing extreme distress (causing the child to cry, for example). You may find it convenient to use the reading selections that are part of Goodman and Burke's *Reading Miscue Inventory Complete Kit* (1972).

2. It is important for the retelling that the selection be read in its entirety. Hence you should choose something which is complete in itself—a story, a chapter in a book, an article, or whatever. If you select a story, it should ordinarily have a plot (usually centering around some problem or conflict), as well as a theme (an underlying idea). If you select an informational piece, it should in-

volve concepts which are clearly stated and not too complex. *The selection must be entirely new to the reader*, but the content should be something that he or she can understand.

3. You will probably need to select about fifteen to twenty minutes worth of reading. Some students may need to read two or three related selections in order to produce at least twenty-five miscues. In any case, *the entire selection(s) must be read* in order for the retelling to have much significance.

4. The student should read from the original printed material (book, or whatever). You will also need a copy of the selection(s) for marking the reader's miscues. It is a good idea to have this copy ready in advance of the reading session, so that you can make notes concerning any behavior that will not be apparent from the tape recording. If there is enough room to write between the lines of the text, you can simply make a photocopy of the original. Otherwise, you will need to prepare a typed copy for marking the reader's miscues. This typed copy should a) be double- or triple-spaced, so that there is enough room to indicate the reader's miscues above the lines; b) retain the exact line divisions of the original, and indicate the page divisions; and c) be entirely accurate.

Once you have chosen material for the individual to read, you will need to prepare yourself for the retelling session. It is important that you be prepared to help the reader tell you as much as possible about what he or she has read. Hence you should make an outline or list of the things you think the reader ought to be able to remember and explain. For me, this is sometimes difficult because I am not at all convinced that we have either the right or any good reason to expect a reader to recall most of the details of what has been read. We adults often read an article or other informational piece just to find out certain things; we pass over the details that are not especially important to us. We read a story to identify with the characters, or to appreciate the plot and theme—but not usually to remember every detail of the characterization, scene, and events. Thus I do not feel comfortable about expecting a child to remember most of the details of what he or she has read. Even if we are willing to ask only for the "significant" details, we should remember that what is significant to us may not be significant to someone else. Hence I think we must be very cautious in deciding what a reader "ought" to be able to tell us about a selection.

Nevertheless, it is important that you be prepared to help the reader tell you as much as possible about what he or she has read. You should prepare careful notes on the selection(s) you have chosen. If it is a story, for example, prepare an outline or list dealing with characters, events, plot, and theme:

> *Characters*: Which characters should the reader be able to recall? What should the reader remember about each of these characters? (This could include such aspects as physical appearance, attitudes and feelings, behavior, relationship with other characters, problems or conflicts, and so forth.)

> *Events*: What events should the reader be able to recall? What should the reader remember about the sequence of events?

> *Plot*: What should the reader be able to tell you about the central conflict or problem of the story?

> *Theme*: What should the reader be able to tell you about the theme, the underlying idea that the story seems to convey?

It is also wise to note along with your outline the kinds of questions you might ask to elicit more information from the reader (see p. 172).

CONDUCTING THE READING SESSION

You will need to make certain that you have all the necessary materials. You will need 1) the reader's copy of whatever is to be read; 2) your own copy of the material; 3) your outline or list of what you think the reader should be able to tell about the reading selection; and 4) a tape recorder. It is vital that you tape record the session for later study. Here are some additional guidelines:

1. The reader should be told that he or she is expected to read the entire selection aloud and then retell the story (or whatever) when the reading is finished.

2. The reader should be told that he or she will not be given any help during the reading, because one of the purposes of the session is to see how the reader deals with reading problems. The reader should be told to handle problem words as best he or she can, using any reading strategies possible and "guessing" if need be. Tell the reader that, if all else fails, he or she should simply skip the word (at least temporarily) and go on. (During the actual reading, remember that you are not to supply any words. But if necessary, you can reassure and encourage the reader by repeating some of this initial information and advice.)

3. The reader should be told that the entire session (reading and retelling) will be tape recorded for later review. It is often wise to let the reader "play" with the tape recorder before beginning the session, to lessen his or her nervousness about being recorded.

GUIDING THE RETELLING

After the reader has finished the selection, ask him or her to close the book and tell you everything he or she can about the material read. Do not interrupt or ask any questions during this initial retelling.

Some readers will tell you absolutely everything about what they have read. Others will volunteer very little, even though they may remember a great deal. Therefore, you must be prepared to ask questions that will help the reader expand upon the retelling. These questions should focus on elements of your retelling outline that were neglected or insufficiently covered in the reader's initial response. (You

can check off items on your outline, provided you do so un-
obtrusively.) Here are some additional guidelines:

1. In formulating your questions, be sure to retain any
mispronunciations or name changes that the reader used.
At the end of the retelling session, you can ask about such
words: for example, if the reader said "typeical baby" for
typical baby, you can ask "What is a 'typeical baby,' anyhow?"

2. Also in asking questions, be careful not to supply any
information that the reader has not already given you.
And try not to suggest insights that the reader has not
acquired on his or her own.

3. Avoid questions that the reader can answer with a
simple "yes" or "no." Instead, mostly use questions that
begin with the so-called WH-words. Often, you can introduce these questions by referring to information the
reader has already given you, as do the following examples
keyed to the basic elements of a story:

Characters:	What else can you tell me about so-and-so?
	Who else was in the story?
Events:	What else happened in the story?
	What happened after such-and-such?
	Where/when did such-and-such happen?
	How did such-and-such happen?
Plot:	Why do you think such-and-such hap-pened?
	What was so-and-so's main problem?
Theme:	How did you feel when such-and-such happened?
	What do you think the author might have been trying to tell us in this story?

5. At the end of the session, ask about key words that
were mispronounced or miscued—for example, "topical"
or "typeical" for **typical**, "carrot" for **canary**, and so
forth. Indeed, it is wise to ask about *any* key words or
concepts you think the reader might not have understood.

6. Throughout the session, avoid reacting to the con-

tent or accuracy of the reader's responses. Just be generally encouraging and appreciative of whatever the reader says.

ANALYZING AND EVALUATING THE RETELLING

You will need to replay the tape so that you can make thorough notes on the retelling. Using your original outline of what you thought the reader should recall and understand, you can simply check off those items that the reader dealt with adequately, and cross out items that the reader did not deal with at all. When the reader misremembered or misunderstood something, you will need to make specific annotations on your outline. Once you have done this preliminary work, you are ready to evaluate the retelling.

In the *RMI Manual*, Goodman and Burke recommend assigning a certain number of percentage points to various aspects of a story or informational selection. For example, they assign 30 points to character recall and development; 30 points to events; 20 to plot; and 20 to theme (p. 24). You may find it useful to adopt some such scheme. On the other hand, it may be just as satisfactory (and easier) to evaluate the retelling more subjectively, after you have made careful note of what the reader remembered and understood from the story. In fact, you might simply use a scale like the following to rate each aspect of the retelling and for the reader's apparent comprehension of the whole:

1	2	3	4	5	6	7
poor		adequate		good		excellent

If you are using a variety of materials with different individuals, I suspect that a subjective scale of this sort might actually produce more consistent and comparable results than an objective scheme like that suggested in the *RMI Manual*. In any case, you should formulate some consistent method of evaluation that suits you and that is adequate for your purposes.

One or two warnings may be in order. Some readers may do relatively poorly with a reading selection simply because they are not interested in it, or because the concepts are too difficult (despite your best intentions). In that case, a reassessment is in order. Some readers comprehend relatively little when they read aloud, yet comprehend well when reading silently. For such readers, the oral reading session is still important, because it enables you to determine the reader's strategies. But if the subsequent retelling is less successful than the reading led you to expect, you should check the reader's comprehension after silent reading. That is, you should have the person read a different but equally difficult selection silently, and then conduct another retelling session.

PREPARING THE MISCUE WORKSHEET

Before you can anaiyze or evaluate the reader's miscues, you must of course mark them on your copy of the selection(s) read. The following examples indicate the markings most commonly used in miscue analysis:

Substitution   "Blow your nose into the Kleenex."

(The substitution is simply written over the text.)

Omission   "I will make you some hot tea."

Insertion   "You should just suck cough drops."

Reversal   "No, no," said Boris.

Correction   I first saw Claribel when I was working in my office.

(The underlining attached to the © indicates what part of the text was repeated as the reader made the correction.)

If other symbols are needed, you can consult the *RMI Manual* or devise your own symbols. Sometimes it is easiest just to write brief explanations in the margins.

Once you have marked the miscues on your copy of the reading selection, it is time to number those miscues that you intend to analyze. As noted before, if you have collected 35 or more miscues on one selection, it is usually a good idea to discard the first 10 or so (when the reader is just getting acquainted with the selection) and code the next 25 miscues. In most cases, 25 consecutive miscues will provide a representative sample of the reader's strategies.

In numbering the miscues for analysis, it is usually wise to adopt the following principles:

1. If the reader omits most or all of a line of text (or more), do not number the miscue for later analysis. But make note of such omissions, if they occur at all frequently.

2. If a reader more than once makes *the same substitution* for a content word, number and analyze only the first occurrence.

3. If one particular miscue seems to have caused one or more others, it may be best to consider them together as a single miscue. Here is one such example:

much about
Ain't ever heard (anybody)

(call) her (a) beauty.

Instead of three omissions and one insertion, what we seem to have is a longer substitution miscue: "much about her beauty," instead of **anybody call her a beauty.** Regardless of how we first marked these miscues on the worksheet, it is probably best to number and analyze them as a single miscue.

As you become more experienced at analyzing reading miscues, you will probably add some other guidelines for determining how miscues should be selected and numbered for analysis.

ANALYZING THE MISCUES

Before analyzing the miscues, it helps to read the completed worksheet once or twice, reproducing all the miscues made by the reader. This should give you a better "feel" for the reader's strategies. Then you will be ready to transfer the miscue data to the analysis form. This form can be simple or complex, depending on the kinds of information you want to obtain. The form in figure 7.1 is somewhere in between the extremes: simple enough to be used by most teachers, but thorough enough to suggest what kind of instructional help the reader needs.

For each miscue, you will first need to indicate what the text itself said, and what the reader said. This information should be entered in the **Text** and **Reader** columns, respectively. Then, for each miscue, you can ask the following questions (the numbers correspond to those of the questions on the form):

1. *Did the miscue go with the preceding context?* If the answer is a simple "yes," put a check in the *yes* column. If the miscue fit with the preceding grammar but not with the preceding meaning (or vice versa), put a check in the column labeled *partially*. If the miscue was not at all acceptable with the preceding context, put a check in the *no* column.

2. *Did the miscue go with the following context?* Again, if the answer is a simple "yes," put a check in the *yes* column. If the miscue fit with the following grammatical context but not with the following meaning (or vice versa), put a check in the *partially* column. And if the miscue was not at all acceptable with the following context, put a check in the *no* column.

3. *Was the miscue corrected?* If so, put a check in the *yes* column. If not, put a check under *no*.

4. *Was the miscue either acceptable in context, or else corrected?* To answer this question, you will have to look at your responses to questions 1–3. If the miscue was corrected, it automatically gets a *yes* for this last question. If the miscue was not corrected, then look to see if it

Reader's name _____

Date _____

Reading selection _____

TEXT	READER	(1) DID THE MISCUE GO WITH THE PRECEDING CONTEXT?			(2) DID THE MISCUE GO WITH THE FOLLOWING CONTEXT?			(3) WAS THE MISCUE CORRECTED?		(4) WAS THE MISCUE EITHER ACCEPTABLE OR CORRECTED?	
		Yes	Partially	No	Yes	Partially	No	Yes	No	Yes	No
1.											
2.											
3.											
4.											
5.											
6.											
7.											
8.											
9.											
10.											
11.											
12.											
13.											
14.											
15.											
16.											
17.											
18.											
19.											
20.											
21.											
22.											
23.											
24.											
25.											
TOTALS											
PERCENTS											

Figure 7.1 *Miscue analysis form*

received a *yes* check for both of the preceding questions on context. If so, put a check in the *yes* column for question 4. Otherwise, put a check in the *no* column.

In effect, the *yes* column indicates which miscues initially or ultimately resulted in *no significant loss of comprehension.*

EVALUATING AND INTERPRETING THE MISCUE ANALYSIS

Once you have answered these four questions for each miscue, calculate the percentage of responses for each column. If you have coded 25 miscues, then all you need to do is count the number of checks in each column and multiply by 4. I would not want to suggest a rigid or simplistic way of evaluating and interpreting your results, but the following is offered as a general guideline (again, the numbers are keyed to the questions on the analysis form):

1. *Did the miscue go with the preceding context?* If fewer than 60 percent of the reader's miscues rated a *yes* answer to this question, this pattern is probably a matter for concern—at least if the reader did not correct the miscues. If a substantial percentage of miscues were checked as *partially* acceptable with the preceding context, this probably means that the reader was using grammatical cues but not meaning. If necessary, you can look at the miscue worksheet again to confirm or correct this interpretation. At any rate, a reader with fewer than 60 percent *yes* answers probably needs help in learning to use grammar or meaning, or both, to predict what is coming next.

2. *Did the miscue go with the following context?* If fewer than 60 percent of the reader's miscues rated a *yes* answer, this again may be a matter for concern—at least if the miscues were not corrected. Again, if a substantial percentage of miscues were checked as *partially* acceptable with the following context, it probably means that the reader was using grammatical cues but not

meaning. In any case, a reader with fewer than 60 percent *yes* answers probably needs help in learning to use following grammar and/or meaning in order to check the tentative identification of a word.

3. *Was the miscue corrected?* If fewer than 30 percent of the miscues were corrected, this is again a matter for concern, *unless most of these miscues were acceptable in context.* We need to look at question 4 before we can draw any firm conclusions about the reader's use of correction strategies.

4. *Was the miscue either acceptable in context, or else corrected?* This is the most crucial question for assessing the reader's ability to comprehend as he or she reads. If a miscue was not acceptable in context but was corrected, this is a sign of comprehension.[2] On the other hand, if the miscue was not corrected but was acceptable in context, this too is a sign of comprehension. In short, the *yes* column indicates the percentage of miscues which ultimately reflected no significant loss of comprehension. And of course the *no* column indicates the percentage of miscues which ultimately reflected partial or complete loss of comprehension.

Although my method of determining comprehension loss is not entirely the same as that in the *RMI Manual*, Goodman and Burke's generalizations should be applicable. Extensive experience with miscue analysis has led them to suggest the following correlations between reading proficiency and the percentage of miscues which show no loss of comprehension (pp. 116–119):

Effectiveness in using reading strategies	*Miscues showing no loss of comprehension (% of* **yes** *answers for question 4)*
Highly effective	60% to 100%
Moderately effective	40% to 79%
Somewhat effective	15% to 45%
Ineffective	no more than 14%

[2] More technically, this is a sign that the reader was comprehend*ing* during the *process* of reading.

As you may have noted, there is some degree of overlap in the percentages for the different categories. In order to make a more definitive assessment, one also needs to evaluate the reader's retelling. The *RMI Manual* may be helpful in this respect, but it is probably just as well to use your own best judgment.

What can be learned from the retelling and the miscue analysis? The miscue questions help us understand how the reader goes about the task of reading. Specifically, the questions on context and correction tell us whether or not the reader needs help in using preceding and/or following context to identify words and, more importantly, to get meaning. Question 4, on acceptability and correction, provides us with a measure of how well the reader comprehends during the actual process of reading; this is sometimes called the *comprehending score*. The retelling provides us with an estimate of how well the reader can remember and interpret what he or she has read; this is sometimes called a *comprehension score*. The comprehending score reflects the *process* of reading, while the comprehension score reflects the *product*. Together, these various measures give us a fairly accurate picture of how a person reads.

ASSESSING THE MISCUE ANALYSIS FORM

Miscue analysis forms are usually somewhat too complicated, or too simple, or both at the same time! And the form presented here is no exception. It is unnecessarily complicated and time-consuming when a reader's strategies are obvious.[3] At the same time, it is in some ways too simple. Unlike the form in the *RMI Manual*, my form does not give

---

[3] One way of simplifying our miscue analysis form would be to replace the two questions about context with a single question like this: "Did the miscue fit with preceding and following context?" The response columns could be labeled *Both*, *Preceding Only*, and *Neither*. The disadvantage of such a simplification is that we would have no way of differentiating, even indirectly, between syntactic acceptability and semantic acceptability. Thus we might underestimate the strengths of those readers who (like Tony) make good use of syntactic cues but not much use of semantic cues.

the reader credit for at least *attempting* to correct a miscue. Also, although my simpler form requires us to note a miscue's appropriateness with the following context (question 2) and to note whether or not the miscue was corrected (question 3), the form does not require us to relate the two questions. There is no question requiring us to note whether a miscue is corrected *if* following context fails to confirm its appropriateness.

Another shortcoming is that my simplified form does not relate a reader's use of grapho/phonic cues to his or her use of syntactic and semantic cues (context). We know from years of miscue research that the best readers typically make miscues which show less grapho/phonic similarity to the text word than the miscues of poorer readers. Less proficient readers make less effective use of syntactic and especially semantic cues: they read to identify words, and they often deal with these words almost as if the words occurred in isolation. In many cases it would be interesting and potentially useful to compare a reader's use of grapho/phonic cues with his or her use of syntactic and semantic cues. The Goodman-Burke form provides for this (see the *RMI Manual*), but with my simpler form, one would have to settle for informal observations written, say, on the back of the form. For instructional purposes, such observations are probably adequate.

There are at least three uses for a form like the one presented here. First, practice with this form can help teachers better understand the nature of the reading process and the typical differences between good and poor miscues. Indeed, practice with such a form can enable teachers to become experienced enough to analyze and evaluate many miscues upon first hearing them, or after a quick glance at a miscue worksheet. Second, and particularly if the teacher can call upon the services of a reading specialist, such a form could be used as a pretest and posttest for analyzing each student's miscues and strategies at the beginning and end of the school year. Third, the form can be used to analyze the strengths, weaknesses, and needs of those students whose reading strategies are *not* readily apparent to the teacher. In each case, of course, miscue analysis should be supplemented by an evaluation of the reader's ability to remember and explain what has been read.

If the teacher cannot obtain the services of a reading specialist, then for most analysis and record-keeping he or she may have to use a simpler form, like the one presented in the section optimistically entitled "How to Do Miscue Analysis and Survive."

MISCUE ANALYSIS IN ACTION

Miscue analysis is an invaluable way of determining a reader's use of language cues and reading strategies. But we must remember that miscue analysis does not give us a complete or necessarily accurate picture of a reader's ability to comprehend what he or she reads. A miscue analysis must be balanced by a more direct measure of comprehension, an analysis of the reader's ability to remember and explain what has been read. We need both the *comprehending* score (the percentage of miscues which show no loss of comprehension) and the *comprehension* score (as determined from an analysis of the retelling).

This need for balance should be kept in mind, even though here we are examining just the *miscues* of two readers, Jay and Tony. In both cases, we have fewer than 25 miscues in the available sample. As so often in everyday experience, we must make do with what we have.

Let us begin by looking once again at Jay's miscues on a passage from "Jimmy Hayes and Muriel":

After a hearty supper Hayes joined the smokers about

the fire. His appearance did not settle all the questions in

the minds of his brother rangers. They saw simply a loose,

lank youth with tow-colored sunburned hair and a berry-

ingenious ⑤
brown, ingenuous face that wore a quizzical, good-natured

smile.

"Fellows," said the new ranger, "I'm goin' to interduce

much about ⑦

you to a lady friend of mine. Ain't ⟨ever⟩ heard ⟨anybody⟩ ⑥

⑦

⟨call⟩ her ⟨a⟩ beauty, but you'll all admit she's got some fine *a* ⑧

points about her. Come along, Muriel!"

ⓒ ⑨

He held open the front of his blue flannel shirt. ⟨Out ⟨of⟩

⑨ *toad* ⑩

⟨it⟩ crawled a horned frog. A bright red ribbon was tied

the ⑪

jauntily around its spiky neck. It crawled to its owner's

it ⑫

knee and sat there motionless.

's ⑬

"This here Muriel," said Hayes, with an oratorical wave

⑬. *She's* ⑬

of his hand, "has got qualities. She never talks back, she

⑭

always stays ⟨at⟩ home, and she's satisfied with one red

dress for everyday and Sunday, too."

d ⑮

"Look at that blame insect!" said one of the rangers

toads ⑯

with a grin. "I've seen plenty of them horny frogs, but I

ⓒ ⑰

never knew anybody to have one for a ⟨side⟩ partner. Does

the blame thing know you from anybody else?"

her ⑱

"Take it over there and see," said Hayes.

We hardly need to analyze these miscues in order to see that
Jay uses good reading strategies. Jay's miscues are a good

starting point, for this very reason: they are relatively easy to analyze. It would be a good idea to photocopy the blank miscue analysis form (figure 7.1) and try to analyze the miscues yourself, before reading further. Figure 7.2 reflects my own analysis of Jay's miscues. As always with miscue analysis, I have made a few idiosyncratic and perhaps arbitrary decisions. In most cases, however, we should agree on the answers to the miscue questions.

Jay's miscue "ingenious" for **ingenuous** illustrates yet another problem with a simplified form like that presented here. The word fits the preceding context and even the following context reasonably well, syntactically and also semantically. But it does not preserve the meaning of the original. In deciding whether or not a miscue fits with the semantic context, we have to decide what criterion to use. Does the miscue merely have to make a sensible sentence, regardless of whether the meaning of the original sentence is significantly changed? Or does the miscue have to preserve the essential meaning of the original sentence? I have chosen the latter and stricter interpretation.

The following summary of Jay's miscues should hardly be surprising:

100% fit completely with the preceding context
83% fit completely with the following context
17% were corrected
89% were entirely acceptable in context, or were corrected

In short, it appears that Jay is a highly effective reader, one who is well able to predict what is coming next and to correct those miscues that do not fit with the following context. His low percentage of correction is not a matter for concern, since most of his miscues were originally acceptable in context. His 89 percent comprehending score suggests that he understands what he reads, and this was confirmed by his excellent job of retelling the story.

Tony, however, is another matter, as we see in this sample of his miscues from *A Camel in the Sea*:

Reader's name **Jay**

Date **April 1977**

Reading selection **"Jimmy Hayes and Muriel"**

#	TEXT	READER	(1) DID THE MISCUE GO WITH THE PRECEDING CONTEXT? — Yes	Partially	No	(2) DID THE MISCUE GO WITH THE FOLLOWING CONTEXT? — Yes	Partially	No	(3) WAS THE MISCUE CORRECTED? — Yes	No	(4) WAS THE MISCUE EITHER ACCEPTABLE OR CORRECTED? — Yes	No
1.	about	around	✓			✓				✓	✓	
2.	—	at all	✓			✓				✓	✓	
3.	saw simply	simply saw	✓			✓				✓	✓	
4.	youth	young	✓			✓			✓		✓	
5.	ingenuous	ingenious	✓				✓			✓	✓	
6.	ever	—	✓			✓				✓	✓	
7.	anybody call her a much about her beauty	much about her beauty	✓			✓				✓	✓	
8.	some	a	✓					✓		✓		✓
9.	Out of it crawled	Out crawled	✓			✓				✓	✓	
10.	frog	toad	✓			✓				✓	✓	
11.	it's	the	✓			✓				✓	✓	
12.	—	it	✓			✓				✓	✓	
13.	This here Muriel... has got qualities	This here's Muriel she's got qualities	✓			✓				✓	✓	
14.	at	at	✓			✓				✓	✓	
15.	blame	blamed	✓			✓				✓	✓	
16.	frogs	toads	✓			✓			✓		✓	
17.	side	—	✓				✓		✓		✓	
18.	it	her	✓							✓		✓
19.												
20.												
21.												
22.												
23.												
24.												
25.												
TOTALS			18	0	0	15	2	1	3	15	16	2
PERCENTS			100%	0%	0%	83%	11%	6%	17%	83%	89%	11%

Figure 7.2   *Analysis of Jay's miscues*

Mo- ①
Mohamed (mo-hah'med) loved to go swimming in the sea.

2 **Sammon** ②   ③
1 **sam-**
How lucky he was to live in a Somali (so-mah'lee) (village)

ran ④
right on the Indian Ocean! The sandy shore rang with the happy

souts ⑤   ⑥
shouts and cries of the (village) boys and girls. They liked

high ⑦
to race one another into the surf, splashing and spraying
                                              ∧
drase ⑧
the water into a white dancing foam before they dove into the

Mola ⑨   **yūng** ⑩   **Asla** ⑪
waves. Mohamed and his young sister, Asha (ie'shuh),

(spent all the time they could in the cool, clean) sea,

swimming and playing water games. They were good swimmers

because their mother had taught them.

expert ⑫   **Molda** ⑬
⑭ Every day except Friday, Mohamed went to school with the
nother viner ⑮
other village boys. The class was outdoors, and the children

beaches ⑯ **frose** ⑰   **shape** ⑱
sat on little benches in front of the teacher in the shade

of a tall palm tree. They did not have books, so the boys
ramped ⑲
repeated everything the teacher said, over and over, until

other classrooms hurt. ⑳   **vengil** ㉑
they knew their lessons by heart. The girls of the village

did not go to school, for the people thought that school was
imprentice ㉒   **to** ㉓
not as important for girls as it was for boys.

In analyzing Tony's miscues (figure 7.3), I have made
certain assumptions, partly on the basis of his retelling
session. First, I have assumed that his nonword miscues on
the proper names reflect no essential loss of meaning. He

Reader's name __Tony__

Date __April 1974__

Reading selection __excerpt from__

__A Camel in the Sea.__

TEXT	READER	(1) DID THE MISCUE GO WITH THE PRECEDING CONTEXT?			(2) DID THE MISCUE GO WITH THE FOLLOWING CONTEXT?			(3) WAS THE MISCUE CORRECTED?		(4) WAS THE MISCUE EITHER ACCEPTABLE OR CORRECTED?	
		Yes	Partially	No	Yes	Partially	No	Yes	No	Yes	No
1. Mohamed	Mo-	✓					✓		✓		✓
2. Somali	Sammon	✓			✓				✓		✓
3. village	—		✓			✓✓			✓		✓
4. rang	ran			✓			✓		✓		✓
5. Shouts	souts		✓		✓✓				✓	✓	
6. village	—		✓		✓✓				✓		✓
7. —	high	✓✓			✓				✓	✓✓	
8. dancing	drase		✓			✓			✓		✓
9. Mohamed	Mola	✓				✓			✓		✓
10. Young	yung	✓				✓			✓	✓	
11. Asha	Asla	✓				✓			✓	✓	
12. except	expert	✓✓				✓			✓		✓
13. Mohamed	Molda	✓				✓			✓		✓
14. other	nother	✓			✓				✓	✓	
15. village	viner		✓			✓			✓		✓
16. benches	beaches		✓		✓				✓		✓
17. front	frose		✓		✓				✓		✓
18. shade	shape	✓				✓			✓	✓	
19. repeated	ramped	✓				✓			✓		✓
20. their lessons by heart	other classrooms hurt					✓			✓		✓
21. village	Yengil		✓✓			✓✓			✓		✓✓
22. important	imprentice		✓✓			✓✓			✓		✓
23. it	to			✓			✓		✓		✓
24.											
25.											
TOTALS		10	10	2	8	11	4	0	23	8	15
PERCENTS		45%	45%	10%	35%	48%	17%	0%	100%	35%	65%

Figure 7.3   Analysis of Tony's miscues

at least knows that these are names of people and places, and that "Mola/Molda" is a boy and "Asla" is his sister. On the other hand, I have assumed that Tony's other nonwords reflect a loss of meaning and that they should therefore be considered unacceptable with the preceding and following semantic context. Note, however, that most of these miscues *do* seem to be acceptable with the *syntactic* context. In part, syntactic acceptability can be determined from the reader's intonation. In addition, word endings often suggest that the miscue is the same part of speech as the original. The most obvious examples are "souts" for **shouts** and "ramped" for **repeated**; both of these miscues retain the grammatical ending of the original. Lacking evidence to the contrary, I have assumed that all of the nonwords other than proper names should be interpreted and analyzed in this way: as syntactically but not semantically acceptable in context. Hence, they are all marked as being *partially* acceptable with what precedes and what follows.

Tony's miscues show certain strengths. If at first he does not get a word, he does not merely give up: he makes several attempts at the word **village**, for example, after initially omitting it. Some of his miscues clearly show a concern for meaning, as when he inserts "high" in "splashing high and spraying the water." He makes good use of grapho/phonic cues, especially at the beginnings and ends of words. And even his nonword miscues seem to preserve the grammar of the original, resulting in a high percentage of miscues analyzed as partially acceptable with the preceding and following context. Note, however, his other percentages:

45% fit completely with the preceding context
35% fit completely with the following context
0% were corrected
35% were entirely acceptable in context, or were corrected

His miscues suggest that he needs help in predicting something that makes sense with what comes before and in correcting anything that does not make sense with what comes after. His comprehending score (the last percentage listed) suggests that his use of reading strategies is only somewhat effective.

Before drawing such a conclusion, however, we should compare the miscue data with the analysis of his retelling session. Some readers will reproduce the text fairly accurately, yet get little meaning from what they read. Others may get the essential meaning of the text, yet still try (perhaps unsuccessfully) to sound out the exact words. And some readers will correct nonsensical miscues silently rather than overtly. For such reasons as these, it is not wise to evaluate a person's reading ability from miscue analysis alone. We need also to find out how well the reader can retell and explain what has been read. In Tony's case, unfortunately, the retelling was no more encouraging than the miscue analysis: it is clear that he needs to learn to read for meaning, and to use semantic as well as syntactic and grapho/phonic cues.

You may have realized that the miscue form itself did not supply us with all of these conclusions. Rather, the insights came from the *analysis* that was necessary in order to respond to the questions about each miscue. This, of course, will always be true: at best, a form does nothing more than help us get our analysis together.

For analyzing Tony's miscues, a slightly different form might have been more helpful. Instead of the two questions about context, we might better have had two questions like the following (see figure 7.4): Did the miscue create a grammatical sentence? Did the miscue preserve the essential meaning of the sentence? These questions would quickly have pinpointed Tony's basic strength and his basic weakness: he uses syntactic cues, but seems to make little use of semantic cues (see figure 7.5). This conclusion is confirmed by looking at his correction pattern: he has corrected none of the miscues which fail to preserve meaning.

HOW TO DO MISCUE ANALYSIS AND SURVIVE

First, you need to know what you're doing. For most people, there is just one way to learn: you must work your own way through a few detailed miscue analyses. After such a baptism, you should have a firm enough understanding of mis-

Reader's name _____

Date _____

Reading selection _____

TEXT	READER	DID THE MISCUE PRESERVE GRAMMAR? ①			DID THE MISCUE PRESERVE MEANING? ②			WAS THE MISCUE CORRECTED? ③		WAS THE MISCUE EITHER ACCEPTABLE OR CORRECTED? ④	
		Yes	Partially	No	Yes	Partially	No	Yes	No	Yes	No
1.											
2.											
3.											
4.											
5.											
6.											
7.											
8.											
9.											
10.											
11.											
12.											
13.											
14.											
15.											
16.											
17.											
18.											
19.											
20.											
21.											
22.											
23.											
24.											
25.											
TOTALS											
PERCENTS											

Figure 7.4 *Alternative miscue analysis form*

Reader's name _Tony_

Date _April 1974_

Reading selection _excerpt from_

A Camel in the Sea

		(1) DID THE MISCUE PRESERVE GRAMMAR?			(2) DID THE MISCUE PRESERVE MEANING?			(3) WAS THE MISCUE CORRECTED?		(4) WAS THE MISCUE EITHER ACCEPTABLE OR CORRECTED?	
TEXT	READER	Yes	Partially	No	Yes	Partially	No	Yes	No	Yes	No
1. Mohamed.	Mo-	✓			✓				✓	✓	
2. Somali	Sammon		|	✓	✓				✓		✓
3. village	—	✓					✓		✓		✓
4. rang	ran	✓			✓				✓	✓	
5. shouts	souts	✓					✓		✓		✓
6. village	—	✓					✓		✓		✓
7. —	—										
8. dancing	high	✓					✓		✓		✓
9. Mohamed.	drase	✓					✓		✓		✓
10. young	Mola.	✓					✓		✓		✓
11. Asha	yung	✓					✓		✓		✓
12. except	Asla.	✓					✓		✓		✓
13. Mohamed	expert	✓			✓				✓	✓	
14. other	Molda	✓					✓		✓		✓
15. village	nother	✓			✓				✓	✓	
16. benches	viner	✓					✓		✓		✓
17. front	beaches	✓			✓				✓	✓	
18. Shade	frose	✓					✓		✓		✓
19. repeated	shape	✓			✓				✓	✓	
20. their lessons by heart	ramped.			✓	✓				✓	✓	
21. village	other classrooms hurt	✓					✓		✓		✓
22. important	vengil	✓					✓		✓		✓
23. it	imprentice	✓					✓		✓		✓
24.	to										
25.											
TOTALS		20	0	2	8	0	15	0	23	8	15
PERCENTS		90%	0%	10%	35%	0%	65%	0%	100%	35%	65%

Figure 7.5 _Alternative analysis of Tony's miscues_

cues to be able to create and use a variety of shorter forms, depending upon your purpose and the time and assistance available.

For "problem" readers whose miscues cannot readily be interpreted, a fairly thorough miscue analysis would probably be best. You might use the forms and procedure recommended in Goodman and Burke's *Reading Miscue Inventory Manual*, one of the forms presented in the preceding sections of this chapter, or a similar form which you yourself devise. The analysis to help you determine the strengths, weaknesses, and instructional needs of problem readers needs to be supplemented by a retelling analysis, and it is also a good idea to talk with the readers, to find out how *they* perceive their reading difficulties.

Such a thorough analysis may not be necessary for determining the instructional needs of most students. However, a simple form of miscue analysis should be extremely useful for assessing each reader at the beginning and end of the school year. Perhaps a reading specialist can assist the classroom teacher with such analysis and with record-keeping. One might simply ask a single question about each of the miscues analyzed: *was the miscue either acceptable in context or corrected?* This will tell us what percentage of miscues showed no loss of meaning. For record-keeping purposes, this comprehending score may be adequate, but it would be best to supplement and balance this score with notes on each reader's retelling.

If even this degree of careful analysis is not possible, then the knowledgeable teacher can settle for a brief, impressionistic evaluation of each reader's miscues. For example, you might devise a short form with questions something like these:

	seldom	sometimes	usually
1. Does the reader use preceding context to predict what is coming next?	1 2	3	4 5
2. Do the reader's miscues make sense in context?	1 2	3	4 5
3. Does the reader correct those miscues that do not make sense in context?	1 2	3	4 5
4. Are the reader's miscues either sensible in context, or corrected?	1 2	3	4 5
5. Does the reader pay too much attention to grapho/phonic cues and too little attention to syntactic and/or semantic cues?	1 2	3	4 5

Once you have acquired some experience with miscue analysis, you should be able to use such a brief form quickly and reliably.

A brief form could be used not only for twice-yearly assessment and record-keeping, but also for monthly or bimonthly checks upon a reader's progress. I am not recommending basal readers and oral reading groups: quite the contrary. But if you do use a basal reading series and have children organized into such reading groups, the regular reading session would provide a good opportunity for periodic reading assessment. This will require some reeducation on the part of most students, but that is advisable anyway. Instead of being allowed to correct their peers, students should be encouraged (even virtually forced) to keep quiet while someone else is reading. Once you have helped them understand the difference between good and not-so-good miscues, you can ask them to listen attentively for any particularly *good* miscues that a reader makes. Such miscues can be discussed when the reader is through.

This procedure has many advantages. Obviously, it helps students better understand the nature of proficient reading and the strategies they themselves are using or should be using. It encourages each reader to develop and rely on his or her own resources for dealing with problems. It helps everyone emphasize each reader's strengths rather than weaknesses. And it provides the teacher with an opportunity to make at least a quick and tentative assessment of the reader's strengths, weaknesses, and instructional needs.

Miscue analysis is almost infinitely variable. Whatever your purposes and resources and needs, miscue analysis can and should be at the heart of your reading assessment program. The one essential ingredient is not any particular assessment form, but the underlying philosophy and view of reading. Any form devised or chosen should, I think, reflect essentially those characteristics mentioned earlier. It should emphasize the fact that getting meaning is more important than reproducing surface structure; help identify a reader's strengths as well as his or her weaknesses; examine miscues in context; recognize the importance of correcting miscues that do not fit the context; provide insight into a reader's use of language cues and reading strategies; and enable us to determine, in general terms, what kinds of strategy lessons a reader might need.

The next chapter gives considerable attention to such strategy lessons, and the final chapter deals with other aspects of a psycholinguistically based reading program. Before going on, however, let us briefly consider how one can determine a child's readiness for reading and for reading instruction.

ASSESSING READINESS FOR READING

There are several broad factors which are relevant to children's readiness for school in general and for reading in particular: health, mental development, emotional maturity, and so forth. In addition, there are some specific kinds of experiences and abilities that facilitate reading and reading instruction. The following list is suggestive rather than exhaustive:

1. Children need to have attained an appropriate level of cognitive development. In Piagetian terms, it seems

highly desirable for them to understand one-to-one correspondence, if they are to match spoken words and phrases with their written counterparts. An understanding of class inclusion and seriation is also important for reading (see chapter 3, p. 52).

2. Children need to have had experience in listening to literature read aloud to them. It is especially helpful if they are acquainted with literature that has predictable patterns: rhymes, folktales, and so forth.

3. Children need to have had experience not only in listening to literature, but in responding to literature. Such experience should be both specific and general. They need experience in predicting what will happen next as they listen, as well as experience in talking about their reactions to the characters, plot, setting and so forth. In addition, children will profit from the understanding gained by pantomiming some of the actions in the story; using dialogue in acting out certain parts of the story; drawing or making clay figures based on the story; dictating a new story involving one or more of the original characters; and other activities of this nature.

4. Children need to have acquired a basic understanding of how books are read. Through extensive experience in handling books, children need to have learned that in English we read books from front to back, we read pages from top to bottom, and we read each line more or less from left to right.

5. Children need to have had experience following along in a book as a story is read to them (either live, or from a record or tape).

6. Children need to have had experience dictating a story to someone, and having it read back to them or reading it back themselves.

7. Children need to have attained some understanding of the terms "word," "letter," and "sound," as commonly used in reading instruction. These terms and concepts are perhaps easiest to learn when children are encouraged to express themselves in writing. Early writing

is extremely helpful in facilitating beginning reading (see, for example, Clay 1975).

8. Children need to have had experience role-playing themselves as readers. They need to think of themselves as readers, even though they may only be able to "read" along with someone else, to turn the pages at more or less appropriate times as they retell a familiar or memorized story, or to move their finger along the lines of a story they themselves have dictated or written.

In sum, beginning reading instruction is facilitated by an appropriate level of cognitive development in the child; by opportunities for the child to listen to and respond to literature; by opportunities to handle books and more or less follow in a book as a story is read to the child; by opportunities for the child to create his or her own sentences and stories, orally and in writing; and by opportunities to play the role of a reader.

All too often, our reading readiness programs concentrate not upon such experiences that make reading meaningful as well as possible, but upon perceptual skills for dealing with the bits and pieces of language. We concentrate upon such minutiae not only because of the common notion that reading must be taught from the bottom up, beginning with the smallest units, but also because this is what the standardized reading readiness tests are designed to measure: auditory discrimination, visual discrimination, knowledge of letter names, ability to associate a letter with an appropriate sound, and so forth. However, such skills can be learned through early experiences with reading itself. They are not necessarily prerequisites to reading or so-called reading instruction. Indeed, such skills are far less important than an understanding of what reading is all about and a desire to learn to read, both of which are fostered by the more global kinds of experience just listed.

If reading readiness programs are to emphasize global experiences rather than skills in dealing with letters and sounds, we must discard or at least downplay the typical methods of assessing reading readiness. As Pikulski suggests (1978), the best way to assess a child's readiness for reading is to give the child opportunities to "read" (see also Durkin 1976, pp. 79–85). The teacher can then determine the answers to questions as the following:

1. Does the child handle a book appropriately, holding it right side up, turning the pages from front to back, and so forth?
2. Does the child expect to get meaning from books?
3. Does the child predict or construct a story that goes with the pictures in a book?
4. Does the child try to "read" a familiar book by retelling the story and turning the pages at more or less appropriate times?
5. Does the child show curiosity about the printed word by asking, at least occasionally, "What does that say?" or "What's that word?"
6. Can the child recognize and write his or her own name? Can the child recognize at least a few signs and labels in the environment (such as "STOP," "McDonald's," "Chicken Noodle")? Can the child recognize any of the words in a familiar story?

We might also ask whether the child seems to enjoy listening and responding to literature, whether the child shows interest in dictating and writing his or her own stories, and so on.

In sum, there should be no sharp division between getting ready to read and beginning to read. In a classroom where children have frequent opportunities to interact with books, the acquisition of reading will come naturally for most children. We will know they are ready to read when they begin reading.

ACTIVITIES AND PROJECTS FOR FURTHER EXPLORATION

1. To gain practice in analyzing and evaluating miscues, you might begin by analyzing David's (pp. 7–8) or Anne's (p. 97) or Billy's (pp. 120–121). Use one of the more detailed forms suggested

here (p. 177 or p. 190), or else devise a similar form. Then, to gain further practice, analyze Betsey's miscues as illustrated below. You should begin by reading the passage as she read it, complete with all her miscues. As you will see, her miscues improve as she gets further and further into the story. Decide which consecutive stretch of 25 miscues to analyze, and again use one of the more detailed forms. Judging by your examination and analysis of Betsey's miscues, what are her reading strengths? What are her weaknesses? What kind of reading instruction and assistance do you think she needs? Discuss your conclusions and recommendations.

The reading selection is adapted from Lee Garrett Goetz, *A Camel in the Sea* (1966, pp. 11–30). Again, the line divisions reflect the way the material was presented to the reader. To give a more balanced picture of the reader's strategies, this time I have numbered only the first substitution for each of the proper names, even though the subsequent substitutions are not always the same.

Mahoad① s② -minging③
Mohamed loved to go swimming, in the sea. How lucky he was ⑤
island④
to live in a Somali village right on the Indian Ocean! The sandy⑥

shore rang with the happy shouts and cries of the village boys ⑦
⑥ 2 surfy sp.
1 surfing
and girls. They liked to race one another into the surf, splash-
form⑧   the⑨
ing and spraying the water into a white dancing foam before they
Mohema   2 Ala ⑩
1 Aimea
dove into the waves. Mohamed and his young sister, Asha, spent

all the time they could in the cool, clean sea swimming and play-

ing water games. They were good swimmers because their mother

had taught them.
especially⑪ Mohema   ⑫
Every day except Friday, Mohamed went to the school with
another ⑬
the other village boys. The class was outdoors, and the children
a⑭   ⑮   and⑯ 2 shell ⑰
1 sand
sat on little benches in front of the teacher in the shade of

⑱ the

a tall palm tree. They did not have books, so the boys repeated

•⑲   were learned ⑳

everything the teacher said, over and over, until they knew their

it ㉑   ㉒

lessons by heart. The girls of the village did not go to school,

ⓒ taught ㉓   sⓒwere ㉔

for the people thought that school was not as important for girls

as it was for boys.

Sunday ㉕   Madoona

On sunny days, as soon as school was over, Mohamed went with

Ashes ⓒ wa- ㉖   'S ㉗

his mother and Asha to wash the family clothes. His mother stood

the   2 putty   ㉘
       1 pondy

in the water and scrubbed and pounded the clothes until they were

ⓒ had ㉙   2 Madoona   Ash
           1 Madoo

clean. Then she handed them to Mohamed and Asha, who took them

agreed ㉚

and arranged them on the beach to dry.

Madoona   ㉛ ed

Mohamed had helped his mother and Asha wash the clothes ever

since he could remember. He was very much surprised, therefore,

one day not long before his tenth birthday, when his mother told

㉜

him not to come with her and Asha.

ⓒ don't ㉝   2 Madoona
               1 Madoosa

"I do not want you to help us any more, Mohamed," his mother

Ashes

said. "It is time that Asha had more work to do around the

㉞   taught ㉟

house. Besides, in two more years you will be thought of as a

troubles ㊱   ㊲

man by our tribe, and it is not fitting that people see you

will ㊳

always doing women's work. From now on, you help your father in

ship ㊴   we ㊵

the shop and Asha will help me at home."

Madoona   suprized ㊶

That first day, Mohamed felt quite grown-up and superior

Azza

when he saw his mother and Asha carrying a heavy basket to the

beach. But this feeling did not last long. He had no one to

42̂ had Azza

play with! He and Asha had played together for so long that the

other children were used to his not playing with them.
2 Madoona
1 Madoosa
Mohamed stood and watched the other boys play "kick(the) 43̂

the 44̂   45̂
ball" and "hunt for robber" and "water tag" When no one

the 46̂
called him for a game, he turned and walked down the beach, 50̂ thoughtful
47̂   a 48̂   tried 49̂
kick(ing) up the sand with one foot, and trying to look as though

©did 51̂   ed 52̂
he really didn't care or want to play.
                                                        53̂ Hamasam

Finally, he decided to take his problem to his father, Hassan.
                                        's 54̂
"Mother doesn't want me to help wash the family clothes any more,
Madooha   Ashes
Father," Mohamed told his father. "Asha has her work and her

friends, but now I have no one to play with."
Probably 55̂   Madooha
"Perhaps your mother is right, Mohamed," his father said,
                        © help 56̂
and he put down the piece of board that he held in his hand.
                                        ship
"It is time that you should learn to help me in the shop."
                        © when 57̂
Hassan was a builder of fishing boats that went out to sea

every morning and returned to the shore every evening. His
ship
small shop was right on the beach.
                                        Madooha
"When you come home from school each day, Mohamed," said
                                        trouble 58̂
his father, "I will show you the beginning of your trade. You

will be a builder of boats like me."
                                        Madooha
"But father, when will I have time for games?" Mohamed asked.

"You help me a little, and I shall see that you have plenty
            Hansa   slowly 59̂
of time to yourself," Hassan promised. He laughed softly. "I

do remember that boys need to have time to think and play. You

shall have it, my son."

desert ⑥⓪

That summer was the driest one that anyone—even the oldest

Madooha's ㉖①

people in Mohamed's village—could recall. It did not rain at

all. Each day the people would look up at the sky to see if they

could see any rain clouds. But each day the sun shone brightly.

2 hiding ㉖② ㉖③
1 hidden

There was not even one cloud to hide the sun's face for a while.

Soon all the leaves of the trees started to turn brown. The

㉖④ dropped ㉖⑤

flowers drooped lower and lower on their stems. Finally they

became dry as paper. When the wind blew the dry leaves, they

's ㉖⑥

made a noise like a snake slipping through the sand.

Day after day the sun beat down, and there was no shade from

leaves ㉖⑦ Jane ㉖⑧ Julie

the leafless trees. June and July came and went without rain.

August was nearly over and still no rain.

2. After you have practiced analyzing some miscues that have already been
recorded and numbered, it is time to try the whole procedure discussed in this chapter: everything from preparing for the reading session, to analyzing and evaluating the retelling and the
reader's miscues, and finally to interpreting the results and making
recommendations for reading instruction. As a valuable learning
experience, I would recommend that you try one of the following:

   a. Compare a good reader (someone who usually comprehends)
   with a poor reader (someone who usually has trouble comprehending). Pay attention to the differences in their miscues. It should be interesting to have both persons read the
   same material. But in order to do this, you may have to
   select students from different grade levels: for example, a
   good third-grade reader and a relatively poor fourth- or
   fifth-grade reader. After you have collected and analyzed

the data from each reader, compare the results. Do the two readers seem to use the same reading strategies? Discuss this question in detail.

b. If you know of two teachers who have widely differing views of reading and/or methods of reading instruction, choose one of the poorer readers from each class, and compare them. Do they seem to use the same reading strategies? In each case, does there seem to be any relation between the teacher's views or methods, and the student's approach to reading? Discuss in detail.

3. Once you have become fairly comfortable with miscue analysis, try to use the short, impressionistic form on p. 193. At first, it is a good idea to tape record the person's reading, so that you can listen to the miscues two or three times if necessary. Then, record your overall impressions on the short form. If at all possible, compare your analysis with that of someone who is more experienced in miscue analysis.

READINGS FOR FURTHER EXPLORATION

Smith, Laura, and Weaver, Constance. "A Psycholinguistic Look at the Informal Reading Inventory, Part I: Looking at the Quality of Readers' Miscues: A Rationale and an Easy Method." *Reading Horizons* 19 (Fall 1978): 12–22. Presents another form for analyzing miscues and determining instructional needs.

Taylor, Jo Ellyn. "Making Sense: The Basic Skill in Reading." *Language Arts* 54 (September 1977): 668–672. Presents an easy way to assess readers' concern for meaning, with a particularly interesting discussion of self-taught readers.

Watson, Dorothy J. "Helping the Reader: From Miscue Analysis to Strategy Lessions." In *Miscue Analysis: Applications to Reading Instruction*, edited by Kenneth S. Goodman. Urbana, Ill.: ERIC Clearinghouse on Reading and Communication Skills and the National Council of Teachers of English, 1973, pp. 103–115. Shows how to use miscue analysis as a guide in developing appropriate strategy lessons (with one student as an example).

Maring, Gerald H. "Matching Remediation to Miscues." *The Reading Teacher* 31 (May 1978): 887–891. Suggests appropriate reading strategy lessons, working from such traditional miscue categories as "substitution," "omission," and "insertion."

Goodman, Yetta M. "Reading Strategy Lessons: Expanding Reading Effectiveness." In *Help for the Reading Teacher: New Directions in Research*, edited by William D. Page. Urbana, Ill.: National Council of Teachers of English, 1975, pp. 34–41. Suggests useful strategy lessons for various needs.

Goodman, Yetta M. "Strategies for Comprehension." In *Findings of Research in Miscue Analysis: Classroom Implications*, edited by P. David Allen and Dorothy J. Watson. Urbana, Ill.: ERIC Clearinghouse on Reading and Communication Skills and the National Council of Teachers of English, 1976, pp. 94–102. Offers several valuable suggestions for helping readers focus on comprehension.

Allen, P. David, and Watson, Dorothy J., eds. *Findings of Research in Miscue Analysis: Classroom Implications*. Urbana, Ill.: ERIC Clearinghouse on Reading and Communication Skills and the National Council of Teachers of English, 1976. Of particular use to those interested in miscues and the results of miscue research are the sections entitled "The Three Cue Systems" (pp. 75–93) and "Developing Reading Proficiency" (pp. 113–127).

Geissal, Mary Ann, and Knafle, June D. "A Linguistic View of Auditory Discrimination Tests and Exercises." *The Reading Teacher* 31 (November 1977): 134–141. An outstanding article demonstrating some of the reasons why auditory discrimination tests should not be considered valid predictors of a child's ability to read.

Pikulski, John. "Readiness for Reading: A Practical Approach." *Language Arts* 55 (February 1978): 192–197. A language experience approach is recommended for kindergarteners, with language arts for all and reading for those who are ready.

McDonnell, Gloria M., and Osburn, E. Bess. "New Thoughts about Reading Readiness." *Language Arts* 55 (January 1978): 26–29. Presents a rationale and a sensible method for assessing reading readiness.

8

how can we help readers develop good reading strategies?

Reading strategy lessons help the reader focus on meaning. The main strategy which a reader must employ is continuously asking, "Does this make sense to me?" Each strategy lesson must be selected or written with this in mind.—Yetta Goodman

Questions for Study and Discussion

1 How can we help readers learn to predict as they read, to anticipate what is coming next?

2 How can we help readers learn to sample grapho/phonic cues, to confirm or modify their predictions in light of the text itself?

3 How can we help readers learn to confirm/correct as they read, continually to ask themselves "Does that make sense?"

4 How can we help readers learn to use all of these strategies (predicting, sampling, and confirming or correcting) more or less simultaneously?

5 How can we help readers learn to use their own store of knowledge and experience plus information explicit and implicit in the text itself, in order to comprehend?

PRACTICING READING STRATEGIES

We want students to practice good reading strategies in all the reading they do. But many will need help in learning to use one strategy or another, so a sound instructional program should provide for reading strategy lessons tailored to each individual's needs. Such strategy lessons help the reader focus on the use of one or more strategies, but always by dealing with whole sentences and paragraphs rather than with words and pieces of words. Even when attention is fo-

204

cused on grapho/phonic cues, these are always presented in an appropriate context.

This chapter deals with several concerns. First, we will examine some activities for helping readers understand their own reading strengths, particularly their ability to use grammatical knowledge in reading. The next three sections focus on 1) the use of syntactic and semantic context of all kinds to *predict* what is coming next, 2) the *sampling* of grapho/phonic cues to test predictions and arrive at tentative interpretations, and 3) the use of following syntactic and semantic context to *confirm or correct* one's interpretation of the text. The following section discusses lessons that explicitly encourage integration of the language cue systems and the simultaneous use of predicting, sampling, and confirming or correcting strategies. Finally, we will focus on using textually explicit information in order to comprehend.

Though some reading strategy lessons may be appropriate for a variety of readers, students should not be routinely dosed with the lessons. Rather, such activities should be assigned on an individual basis, and only when miscue analysis has revealed the individual's *need* for a certain kind of strategy lesson.

HELPING READERS LEARN THEIR STRENGTHS

It is particularly important to build up the confidence of those who think they cannot read. There are many ways to do this. One way is to have such readers dictate or write some of their own reading materials; another is to use a language immersion component as part of the total reading program. The next chapter discusses these and other ways to help readers become more confident of their own abilities, as well as more convinced that reading is worthwhile. At the moment, however, we want to focus on helping students become aware of their strengths in syntax. They know, unconsciously, a great deal about how sentences are put together, and they should be aware of their own ability to use this knowledge as they read.

Even with prereaders and beginning readers, teachers can use sentence-completion exercises that require children to supply a word or phrase that would fit at the end of a sentence or paragraph. For example:

Mommy fell in the _____.

At the age of five, my own son offered the following possibilities: "well," "pond," "tub," "big ocean," and "whale's tummy." Once you have received and perhaps written such responses on the blackboard, you can help children explain why their suggestions would work, whereas words like "played" and "slowly" would not. As with so many of the better activities, syntactic and semantic cues both play a part in signaling appropriate choices. Hence such an activity actually does double duty.

Teachers might help older students become aware of how much they know about word endings, function words and word order. Students are usually pleased to find that they can complete most of the sentences in something like the "Crashe Helmutt" exercise from Mark Lester's *Words and Sentences* (1973, pp. 31–33). Below are the first few sentences from that exercise. The object is to choose the most suitable of the four nonsense words to fill each blank:

I _____ a movie on television last night.
        (frabs, zinged, flumping, vorpous)
Crashe Helmutt was the _____ of the movie.
        (turgoons, frib, mogged, flonkish)
He played the role of a _____ chifforobe salesman.
        (yaggiest, nunky, mimpier, burfles)
His wife, played by Wednesday Rivet, nagged him _____.
        (ferd, mongous, zizzed, gabbingly)

Such activities are fun not only to do and discuss, but to create. And they help readers realize what vast resources they themselves bring to the task of reading.

A related type of activity would be to have students supply the function words for a passage, as we did with the news story about the Kent State riots, from the *New York Times*

(p. 117). It might be best to have students read and discuss the information in the passage *before* trying to supply appropriate function words. The same can be done with the more common kinds of cloze activities, where every fifth or seventh or tenth word is omitted. Thus in addition to helping students recognize their own strengths in syntax and semantics, such activities can help demonstrate that proficient reading does not necessarily involve the precise identification of every word.

Other activities from earlier in this book would also be suitable for helping older students learn to appreciate their own syntactic resources, their own command of grammar. One example is the "Bloopy and Glit" activity, on p. 93. Many students are surprised and delighted to find that they can read this poem and actually get some "meaning" out of it. Typically, they are also pleasantly surprised that they can read something like the "corandic" paragraph and answer the accompanying comprehension questions (pp. 92–93). Here is another example, an adaptation of an activity from my colleague Jim Burns. See if you can read the following paragraphs and answer the comprehension questions:[1]

The blonke was maily, like all the others. Unlike the other blonkes, however, it had spiss crinet completely

---

[1] The nonsense words are actually "lost words" that have been resurrected. The following definitions are from Susan Kelz Sperling, *Poplollies and Bellibones: A Celebration of Lost Words* (New York: Clarkson N. Potter, 1977). Given the brevity of her definitions, it is possible that some words may have been misused in our story.

Bellytimber—Food, provisions
Blonke—A large, powerful horse
Blore—To cry out or bleat and bray like an animal
Crinet—A hair
Drumly—Cloudy, sluggish
Fairney cloots—Small horny substances above the hoofs of horses, sheep, and goats
Flosh—A swamp or stagnant pool overgrown with weeds
Givel—To heap up
Icchen—To move, stir
Kexy—Dry, juiceless
Lennow—Flappy, limp
Maily—Speckled
Quetch—To moan and twitch in pain, shake
Samded—Half-dead
Shawk—Smell
Sparple—To scatter, spread about

covering its fairney cloots and concealing, just below one of them, a small wam.

This particular blonke was quite drumly—lennow, in fact, and almost samded. When yerden, it did not quetch like the other blonkes, or even blore. The others blored very readily.

It was probably his bellytimber that had made the one blonke so drumly. The bellytimber was quite kexy, had a strong shawk, and was apparently venenated. There was only one thing to do with the venenated bellytimber: givel it in the flosh. This would be much better than to sparple it in the wong, since the blonkes that were not drumly could icchen in the wong, but not in the flosh.

Comprehension questions

1. *Literal*: Where was the small wam?
2. *Translation*: What is "drumly"?
3. *Inference*: Why weren't the other blonkes drumly?
4. *Reorganization*: In what way(s) was the drumly blonke like/unlike the others?
5. *Evaluation*: If bellytimber is venenated, is it wise to givel it in the flosh?
6. *Appreciation*: Are the significant ideas expressed clearly and coherently? Are they expressed in an appropriate style?

Such activities can provide an interesting challenge for the more proficient reader.

All of these activities will be most beneficial if they are discussed in a group. Students need the opportunity to compare their responses with the responses of others, and they also need to learn to justify their answers by giving good reasons. Especially at first, the teacher will need to keep pointing out how much the students actually know about language.

Spiss—Thick, dense
Venenate—To poison
Wam—A scar, cicatrix
Wong—Meadowlands, commons
Yerd—To beat with a rod

A variety of other activities can also be used to help readers become aware of their syntactic resources and how they can use their understanding of grammar as they read. For younger children, one useful activity is to build sentences from word cards. The following is one possible way to proceed: have the child dictate a sentence; then write each word of the sentence on a separate piece of tagboard and put the word cards together to form the sentence that the child dictated; scramble the word cards and have the child reconstruct the sentence; finally, invite the child to add more details to the sentence (a modifying word or phrase, for example). Offer some suggestions, if necessary, and then repeat the procedure.

One advanced four-year-old started with the simple sentence **William went to the zoo**, then wanted to add what he saw at the zoo, who he went with, and so forth. He finally produced the following sentence:

After school, when William and Tony went to the zoo on the bus to see a sick tiger and a nice lion, they had a good surprise as they walked to William's house.

This example suggests, then, that even young children can manipulate words and sentence structures. The *Breakthrough to Literacy* material is particularly useful in the classroom (Bowmar, 1973). This is a language experience program for beginning readers and writers, grades K–3. Children are encouraged to construct their own sentences, using separate word cards.

Older students might be asked to rearrange words into sentences, then organize the sentences into a coherent paragraph. The following example is adapted from an activity by Joyce Teele, an innovative teacher in Norfolk, Virginia:

To Bill Swim Learns

1   showed him the to swimming swim and teacher how breathe
2   to of Bill swim wanted he to learn was the but afraid water
3   the now Bill never be will afraid of again water

4   him during his lessons mother the let take summer
    swimming
5   into and end to finally swam the deep he the of jumped
    end the pool shallow
6   Bill so after not afraid that was quite

One advantage of this activity is that there is sometimes
more than one way to order the words within a sentence. By
comparing their answers, students can discover for themselves that there are alternative ways of writing and reading something.

In addition to *creating, expanding,* and *organizing* sentences, students of various ages can be encouraged to *substitute* one word or construction for another in a sentence;
to *reduce* sentences by eliminating optional modifiers; and
to *rearrange* sentence parts without changing the meaning.
The following are some examples; see also the Teacher's
Edition section in the teacher's edition of any of Martin and
Brogan's *Sounds of Language* readers, published by Holt,
Rinehart and Winston.

Substitution

There   was   an   old   woman

                        ↑   ↑

                     purple   cow
                      nice   bat
                      silly   horse
                      lazy   ghost
                     scary   vampire
                      ugly   computer
                     morose   engine

Reduction

We played ball ~~for hours~~.

The grouchy policeman, ~~who yelled at us yesterday~~,
just slipped on a banana peel.

~~Tired and hungry~~, the old man crawled into bed,
~~pulling the covers up to his chin~~.

Rearrangement

> The grouchy policeman was old and tired.
> The old policeman was tired and grouchy.
> The tired old policeman was grouchy.

Sentence-combining activities can also help students appreciate the possibilities of rearrangement. Take, for example, the following sentences (Weaver 1979, *Grammar for Teachers*, p. 50):

> The man was old.
> The man was tired.
> The man was hungry.
> The man crawled into bed.
> The man pulled the covers up to his chin.

Now, how many ways can you combine these ideas without changing the meaning? Here are just some of the possibilities:

> The old man was tired and hungry. He crawled into bed and pulled the covers up to his chin.
> Tired and hungry, the old man crawled into bed, pulling the covers up to his chin.
> The tired, hungry old man crawled into bed, pulling the covers up to his chin.
> Pulling the covers up to his chin, the old man crawled into bed. He was tired and hungry.
> The hungry old man crawled into bed and pulled the covers up to his chin. He was tired.

Again, the value of such an activity lies mainly in the *discussion*. Is any version clearly not as good as the others? Which version emphasizes what ideas? Is any one version definitely the best? By doing and discussing such an exercise, students will gain not only an understanding of how sentences can be combined and rearranged, but also some understanding of the fact that a given deep structure can be expressed in more than one surface structure. And they will at least begin to gain some appreciation of style.

Another way to gain an appreciation of style is to chunk a stretch of prose into groups of words that have some kind of syntactic and semantic cohesiveness. Take, for example, the following sentence from President Richard Nixon's inaugural address of January, 1969. Nixon was quoting Archibald MacLeish's comments on the Apollo astronauts who spoke from the moon to the people of earth on Christmas eve, 1968:[2]

> In that moment, their view from the moon moved poet Archibald MacLeish to write: "To see the earth as it truly is, small and blue and beautiful in that eternal silence where it floats, is to see ourselves as riders on the Earth together, brothers on that bright loveliness in the eternal cold—brothers who know now they are truly brothers."

Without consciously thinking about grammatical units or rules, how might we divide this short stretch of prose? The following is just one of the various possibilities:

In that moment,
    their view from the moon
    moved poet Archibald MacLeish to write:
        "To see the earth as it truly is,
        small and blue and beautiful
        in that eternal silence where it floats,
            is to see ourselves
        as riders on the earth together,
            brothers
        on that bright loveliness
        in the eternal cold—
            brothers
        who know now
            they are truly brothers."

[2] Lester Thonssen, ed., *Representative American Speeches: 1968–1969*, vol. 41, no. 4 (New York: H. W. Wilson, 1969), p. 120.

Discussing and arguing for *their* way of chunking the selection can help give students a feel for how language works. And it will help them focus upon units larger than the word, units that lead to some understanding of style.

In the following sections, there are many other ideas for helping readers learn to appreciate and use their own syntactic and semantic resources in order to read more effectively and efficiently.

HELPING READERS PREDICT

We learn to predict long before we come to school. The baby learns to "predict" that if he or she cries, somebody will bring a bottle or change the dirty diaper. And if the very young child is immersed in oral literature, he or she will soon learn other patterns that make prediction possible. Take, for example, the nursery rhyme "This little pig went to market." As I remember it, the first line begins "This little piggy went to market." And as you say these words, you tug on the baby's big toe. "This little piggy stayed home" —and you tug on the second toe. "This little piggy had roast beef" (tug on the third toe); "This little piggy had none" (tug on the fourth toe). Last is something like this: "And this little piggy cried 'Wee, wee, wee, wee' all the way home" (tug on the little toe and run your fingers up the baby's leg, like the piggy running home). After a few repetitions of this rhyme and the toe-tugging procedure, the baby *knows* what is going to happen next. The predictable pattern has been established.[3]

Perhaps not all children will have been exposed to nursery rhymes in the home. But most children will have learned to predict patterns in other kinds of language use: if not nursery rhymes, then perhaps church hymns, popular songs, familiar stories, and so forth. In any case, teachers usually find that prereaders and beginning readers can easily learn

[3] I am indebted to my friend and colleague Maryellen Hains for this example.

to recognize some of the patterns of oral and written literature, and to use such patterns to predict what is coming next.
Before discussing such patterns, it would be well to mention one kind of visual literature: the wordless picture book. My all-time favorite is Margaret A. Hartelius's *The Chicken's Child* (1975), which graphically details the adventures of a chicken and her alligator baby. Other favorites are Mercer Mayer's *A Boy, A Dog, and a Frog* (1967), and *Frog Goes to Dinner* (1974). In all of these books, the facial expressions are a major clue to what is going to happen next. All three are available from Scholastic Book Services. For other titles, see Larrick (1976), which is listed at the end of this chapter. Such wordless picture books are a valuable way of helping prereaders and beginning readers learn to predict. Children can also dictate sentences to accompany the pictorial text. In some cases, there is enough room to write such sentences at the bottom of each page, thus creating a personalized book for the child to read. Older children may enjoy helping beginners create such books. In fact, it would be good for an upper elementary class to "adopt" a class of kindergarteners or first graders, and to work with them in various ways.

Indeed, both age groups would benefit not only from working with wordless picture books, but from experiencing and even verbalizing some of the literary patterns that can help them predict. In the teacher's edition of Martin and Brogan's *Sounds of Language* readers, there is a separate Teacher's Edition section that discusses the value of using literary materials with patterns that encourage semantic predicting and, inevitably, syntactic predicting as well. The following patterns of sequencing are discussed:[4] repetitive sequence, cumulative sequence, interlocking sequence, familiar cultural sequence (cardinal and ordinal numbers, days of the week, months of the year, etc.), chronological sequence, problem-centered sequence, rhyme-rhythm sequence. The books in the *Sounds of Language* series (grades K–8) are replete with

---

[4] The following discussion is from my book *Grammar for Teachers: Perspectives and Definitions* (1979).

literary selections illustrating these predictable patterns. One example is "Over in the Meadow," which begins as follows:

> Over in the meadow
> in the sand
> in the sun
> Lived an old mother turtle and her little turtle one.

The selection illustrates four kinds of sequences: repetitive, cultural, and rhythm and rhyme. After the first three verses of the rhyme, Martin and Brogan give children clues to help them figure out how the rest of the rhyme goes (see *Sounds of a Powwow*, pp. 62–73):

1. The first four words of each verse are exactly the same.
2. The next few words tell where the creatures live.
3. The next few words tell who the mother is and how many babies she has.
4. The mother tells the babies to do something and they obey.
5. The verse ends by repeating what the babies did and where they were.

Each successive stanza is written with fewer and fewer words included, until finally with verse 10 there is just a picture of a mother beaver saying "Beave," accompanied by this stanza frame:

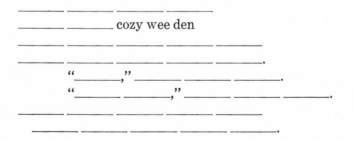

This marvelous example illustrates only a few kinds of predictability. Work with poetry (traditional and otherwise) needs to be balanced by work with prose, where students can gain practice in predicting from character, setting, plot, and so forth (for some specific ideas, see Stauffer and Cramer 1968).

To see how such prediction might work in actual practice, try it with the following story. If possible, read the story with some other people. Each time you come to the octagonal stop sign, stop and reflect. What do you think will happen next? What makes you think so? Share your opinions with others, then read to the next stop sign. Continue through the story this way, predicting and modifying your predictions as necessary. The story is Quentin Reynolds's "A Secret for Two" (1936, p. 44). This particular adaptation was given to me by Carolyn Ewoldt, of Gallaudet College:

A Secret for Two
Quentin Reynolds

Montreal is a very large city, but, like all large cities, it has some very small streets. Streets, for instance, like Prince Edward Street, which is only four blocks long. No one knew Prince Edward Street as well as did Pierre Dupin, for Pierre had delivered milk to the families on that street for thirty years.

During the past fifteen years Pierre's milk wagon had been drawn by a large white horse named Joseph, who knew the route as well as Pierre. Pierre used to boast that he did not need reins—he never touched them. Each morning Pierre reached the stable of the milk company at five o'clock. The wagon would be loaded and Joseph hitched to it; then this splendid combination would stalk proudly down the street.

The wagon, without any direction from Pierre, would roll three blocks down St. Catherine Street, turn right two blocks along Roslyn Avenue; then left, for that was Prince Edward Street. The horse would stop at the first house, allow Pierre perhaps thirty seconds to get down from his seat and put a bottle of milk at the front door, and would then go on, skipping two houses and stopping at the third. So down the length of the street. Then Joseph, still without any direction from Pierre, would turn around and come back along the other side. Yes, Joseph was a smart horse.

Pierre would boast at the stable of Joseph's skill. "I never touch the reins. He knows just where to stop. Even a blind man could handle my route with Joseph pulling the wagon."

So it went on for years. Pierre and Joseph both grew old together, but gradually, not suddenly. Pierre's huge mustache was pure white now, and Joseph didn't lift his knees as high or raise his head quite as much. Jacques, the foreman of the stable, never noticed that they were both getting old until Pierre appeared one morning carrying a heavy walking stick.

"Hey, Pierre," Jacques laughed. "Maybe you got a little rheumatism, eh?"

"Well, Jacques," Pierre said a bit uncertainly. "One grows old. One's legs get tired."

"You should teach that horse to carry the milk to the front door for you," Jacques told him. "He does everything else!"

One morning the owner of the milk company came to inspect the morning deliveries. The foreman pointed Pierre out to him and said, "Watch how he talks to that horse. See how the horse listens and how he turns his head toward Pierre? See the look in that horse's eyes?

You know, I think those two share a secret. Pierre is a good man, but he gets old. Would it be too bold of me to suggest that he be retired and be given a small pension?" he added anxiously.

"But of course," the owner laughed. "I know his record. He has been on this route now for thirty years and never once has there been a complaint. Tell him it is time he rested. His salary will go on just the same."

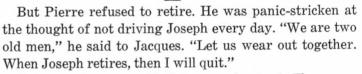

But Pierre refused to retire. He was panic-stricken at the thought of not driving Joseph every day. "We are two old men," he said to Jacques. "Let us wear out together. When Joseph retires, then I will quit."

Jacques, who was a kind man, understood. There was something about Pierre and Joseph that made a man smile tenderly. It was as if each drew some hidden strength from the other. When Pierre was sitting in his seat, and when Joseph was hitched to the wagon, neither seemed old. But when they finished their work, Pierre would limp down the street slowly, seeming very old indeed, and the horse's head would drop and he would walk very wearily to his stall.

Then one morning Jacques had dreadful news for Pierre when he arrived. It was cold and still pitch-dark. The air was like iced wine, and the snow, which had fallen during the night, glistened like a million diamonds piled together.

Jacques said, "Pierre, your horse Joseph did not wake up this morning. He was old, Pierre; he was twenty-five, and that is the same as being seventy-five for a man."

"Yes," Pierre said, slowly, "I am seventy-five. And I cannot see Joseph again!"

"Of course you can," Jacques soothed. "He is over in his stall, looking very peaceful. Go over and see him."

Pierre took a few steps forward then turned. "No—no —you don't understand, Jacques."

Jacques clapped him on the shoulder. "We'll find another horse just as good as Joseph. In a month you'll teach him to know your route as well as Joseph did. We'll—"

The look in Pierre's eyes stopped him. For years Pierre had worn a heavy cap, the peak of which came low over his eyes, keeping the bitter morning wind out of them. Now Jacques looked into Pierre's eyes, and he saw something which startled him. He saw a dead, lifeless look in them. The eyes were mirroring the grief that was in Pierre's heart and soul. It was as though his heart and soul had died.

"Take today off, Pierre," Jacques said, but already Pierre was hobbling down the street, and if one had been near one would have seen tears streaming down his cheeks. Pierre walked to the corner and stepped into the street. There was a warning yell from the driver of a huge truck that was coming fast, and there was the scream of brakes, but Pierre apparently heard neither.

Five minutes later an ambulance driver said, "He's dead. Was killed instantly."

Jacques and some of the milk-wagon drivers had arrived. They looked down at the still figure.

"I couldn't help it," the driver of the truck protested, "he walked right into my truck. He never saw it, I guess. He just walked into it as though he were blind."

The ambulance doctor bent down. "Blind? Of course the old man was blind. See those eyes? This man has been blind for years." He turned to Jacques. "Didn't you say he worked for you? Didn't you know he was blind?"

"No—no—" Jacques said softly, "none of us knew it. Only one knew—a friend of his named Joseph. . . . It was a secret, I think, just between those two."

At what point did you figure out the secret that Pierre and Joseph shared? Think about the kinds of information you used in making and modifying your various predictions. To what extent did you use your understanding of plot, character, setting, and other cues within the story? To what extent did you draw upon your previous store of knowledge and experience?

As this example suggests, stories with an element of suspense or mystery are especially good for predicting. So are folktales, because they often contain several predictable patterns, and because they can be used with students of various ages. Take, for example, the tale of "The Fisherman and His Wife." One might begin by using a modified cloze procedure on the first paragraph, with blanks replacing certain key words. The paragraph is from *Grimms' Fairy Tales* (1945):

There once was a fisherman who lived with his _____ in a miserable little _____ close to the sea. He went to fish every day, and he fished and fished, and at last one day as he was sitting looking deep down into the shining _____, he felt something on his line. When he hauled it up, there was a big _____ on the end of the line.

After the students explain and defend their answers, the teacher can help them compare their choices with the words of the original: **wife, hovel, water,** and **flounder.**

From the very first paragraph, we can begin to speculate about the role that the flounder will play in the story. When we learn that the flounder is an enchanted prince, we naturally expect something mystical and magical to happen—and it does, after the wife sends her husband back to ask a favor of the fish. First he gives her a pretty little cottage, then a big stone castle, and then—we are prepared to predict an even bigger and better dwelling. This is precisely what the woman gets, when the flounder grants her wish to be king.

What more could she possibly want? Perhaps to be God? We are prepared for the wife's eventual downfall by the progressively deteriorating condition of the natural elements. When the fisherman first asks the flounder to give them a pretty little cottage, the sea has already begun to deteriorate: it is no longer bright and shining, but dull and green. By the time the fisherman asks that his wife be made king, the sea is dark, gray, rough, and evil-smelling. And conditions keep getting worse, until finally the woman is sent back to her hovel.

The tale of the fisherman and his wife lends itself to predicting through sentence structure, plot, characterization, setting, sequence, archetypal pattern, and other aspects of meaning. The classroom techniques can be equally various. First, the story can be read *to* students, or *by* them. With either approach, the reading can be stopped at intervals for the students to predict what is coming next and to discuss and justify their predictions. What do they think the wife will ask for next? How do they think the sea will look the next time the fisherman asks a favor? What do they think will happen when the woman asks to be made Lord of the Universe? Students can be invited to respond to such questions through discussion and by drawing, dictating, writing, or dramatizing their predictions.

Students who have learned to *predict*, to use context *first*, are well on their way to becoming proficient readers. As Constance McCullough noted in her 1975 presidential state-of-the-art letter to members of the International Reading Association,

> The reading process appears to include active consideration of the meaning of what has been read and concern for what will be encountered; raising one's own questions, forming expectations of ideas to come, correcting interpretations when the expected does not occur, proceeding to new expectations and new questions, seeing pattern in the author's design of thought and expression, and predicting how the pattern will be extended.

It is becoming increasingly clear that even the beginning reader should establish these habits in order to become a good reader. Because prediction is so important, I include the following brief annotated bibliography of literary works that lend themselves to predicting activities. It was prepared in collaboration with two of my colleagues, Maryellen Hains and Theone Hughes. Rhodes (1977) provides a more extensive bibliography of predictable books to use with beginning or older ineffective readers.

LITERATURE FOR PREDICTING

I. *Early Childhood—up to about Age 8*

Brown, Marcia. *Once a Mouse* . . . New York: Scribners, 1961.
The fable from the Hitopodesa is presented in an award-winning picture book that lends itself to prediction through the extraordinary woodcuts, the placement of type on the page, the progression from little to big, an understanding of natural enemies, and one's knowledge of human nature as mirrored in the arrogant behavior of the tiger and the facial expressions on the quiet hermit.

Brown, Marcia. *The Three Billy Goats Gruff*. New York: Harcourt Brace Jovanovich, 1957. The Scandinavian folktale collected by Asbjorensen and Moe is an excellent introduction to the notion of pattern in folk materials. The motif of the goat crossing the bridge and being threatened by the troll is repeated three times. Each time the events are the same, but the larger goat makes more noise and offers more challenge to the troll. This very basic pattern of repetition and progression is easy for young children to see and imitate. An excellent story for creative dramatics.

Keats, Ezra Jack. *Goggles!* New York: Macmillan, 1969, paperback.
Realistic fiction in a multiethnic setting. Children can predict and act out elements of plot. What's going to happen when the big boys insist that Peter give them the motorcycle goggles he has found?

Milne, A. A. *When We Were Very Young*. New York: Dell, 1924, paperback.
A collection of poems, many suitable for the preoperational child.

For example, in "Disobedience," children will enjoy predicting the outcome when the mother disobeys her three-year-old son and goes to the end of the town alone. In this poem and others, like "The Dormouse and the Doctor," children can also supply the repeated rhyming words. Many are excellent choices for oral dramatization and choral reading.

II. *Middle Childhood—from about Age 8 to about Age 11*

Milne, A. A. *Winnie-the-Pooh.* New York: Dell, 1926, paperback.
A number of chapters in this delightful fantasy lend themselves to predicting from plot and character. One example is *"In Which Piglet Meets a Heffalump."* Pooh predictably goes after the honey that he and Piglet have put in a trap for "Heffalumps." Children might enjoy predicting the ending through creative dramatics.

Myers, Walter Dean. *The Dragon Takes a Wife.* Indianapolis: Bobbs-Merrill, 1972.
Picture-story format is used to present a modern black fantasy in which the hip fairy MayBelle May tries to help Harry, the dragon, win a wife. Her spells are all slightly flawed, however, and the knight pierces Harry's tail in each bout. Children can predict action from characterization and plot structure. How will MayBelle May's spell to make Harry's fire "hotter than hot" work on the battlefield? Will the knight win when Harry becomes the border on the page?

Sobol, Donald. The *Encyclopedia Brown* series. Nashville, Tenn.: Thomas Nelson, 1963.
Although not really literature, these books (many available in paperback) offer an excellent opportunity for predicting. Each chapter is a "case" with all the clues necessary for the young hero-detective and the close reader to solve it. There are ten mysteries in each volume, with solutions at the end.

Other mystery series are also good for predicting. Consider using the Hardy Boys (Frank Dixon) or the Nancy Drew (Carolyn Keene) books. In each case the plot is formulaic, the characters flat, but there is high interest in the action, and the books are fine for predicting clues, false clues, and character through stereotypes and connotative language.

Grimm Brothers. *Household Stories by the Brothers Grimm,* translated by Lucy Crane. New York: Dover reprint, 1886.
Once the pattern of events and types of characters for a specific

story are perceived in these German folktales, children can predict the action themselves—as in "Rumplestiltskin" or "The Fisherman and His Wife."

Larrick, Nancy, ed. *Piping Down the Valleys Wild.* New York: Dell, 1968, paperback.

A wide variety of excellent poems suitable for predicting exercises. "The Little Turtle" by Vachel Lindsay, for example, can be used with young children to predict syntax from repetitive syntactic patterns. Older children will enjoy the same activity with a poem like Patricia Hubbell's "Concrete Mixers." Ciardi's "Mummy Slept Late and Daddy Fixed Breakfast" lends itself to predicting action, description, and rhyme words. What methods might *you* try for cutting the burned waffle?

III. *Later Childhood—from about Age 11 to Young Adult*

L'Engle, Madeleine. *A Wrinkle in Time.* New York: Dell, 1962, paperback.

An award-winning science fantasy novel that transports you through time and space in the search for Meg Murray's father and in the battle of good against evil. From its opening line ("It was a dark and stormy night"), we can begin to predict the tension and adventure to come. From the talk of tramps as the family sips hot chocolate, we can predict who is knocking on the door late at night. But we are only partly right. The book "reads our minds" as Charles Wallace reads Meg's mind. The adventure is not a formula mystery. Mrs. Whatsit is not a tramp in the conventional sense. Once we digest the pattern in this system, we can begin to predict the unpredictable and outwit "IT," a source of evil in the universe.

Lewis, C. S. *The Lion, the Witch and the Wardrobe.* New York: Penguin, 1950, paperback.

The multiple world viewed in this first of the Narnia Chronicles offers a variety of materials suitable for predicting from setting, plot, and character types. For example, what kinds of events do you expect to happen when children wander through the rooms of the old house and find empty rooms opening into other empty rooms? What will happen when one of the children hides in the wardrobe?

Sperry, Armstrong. *Call It Courage.* Englewood Cliffs, N. J.: Scholastic, 1940, paperback.

This award-winning realistic novel in a Polynesian setting can be used to predict character, journey-plot, and rhythmic language. For example, the outcast nature of Mafatu, the hero, can be predicted from his companions: Kivi, the albatross with a twisted foot, who is picked on by other birds; Uri, the yellow mongrel. What will happen when Mafatu again sees the albatross circling in the sky above his canoe? Does Mafatu die at the end? Why is the last paragraph of the novel the same as the first?

Bradbury, Ray. *The Golden Apples of the Sun.* New York: Bantam Books, 1953.

Highly imaginative science fantasy stories that are eminently suitable for predicting with older children. For example, in "The Foghorn," children can be asked to predict from title, setting, character, and elements of plot. What will happen after McDunn first tells Johnny of the monster that came apparently "to worship"? What will happen when they turn off the foghorn? Students might write their own ending from textual clues.

Bierhorst, John. *In the Trail of the Wind.* New York: Noonday, 1971, paperback.

Traditional Native American poetry was oral, relying on strong elements of repetition rather than rhyme for much of its structure and drama. Therefore, many poems in this fine collection lend themselves to predicting from pattern as well as meaning.

HELPING READERS SAMPLE

We have seen, repeatedly, that good readers do not worry overmuch about precise word identification. Because their primary concern is with meaning, they may read "baby" for **child**, "bird" for **canary**, "toad" for **frog**, and so forth— providing these miscues are appropriate in context. In most cases, such readers do not need lessons in how to use grapho/phonic cues.

In contrast, we have readers who say things like "expert" for **except**, "souts" for **shouts**, "ramped" for **repeated**. Such readers are usually making too much use of grapho/phonic cues and too little use of context cues, particularly semantic cues. Beginning and less proficient readers, then, may need help in learning to *sample* grapho/phonic cues in order to identify a word. Of course, we should never insist upon precise identification of all the words as long as the reader gets the essential meaning of the text. Still, readers should at least know how to use grapho/phonic cues effectively and efficiently.

Since the object is to use only as many grapho/phonic cues as necessary, our strategy lessons should always deal with words in context. At first, what is important is simply that children learn to use context to get *meaning*. The teacher might say a sentence like **Rain came in when Sally opened the . . .** , omitting the last word. The children can be encouraged to supply reasonable alternatives, like **door, window, skylight**. In the total context of a story, it may not make much difference what aperture let in the rain. Nevertheless, the teacher can help readers understand that context usually narrows the reasonable alternatives, so that a word can often be identified from a few letters, perhaps even one:

Rain came in when Sally opened the d_____.

Rain came in when Sally opened the w_____.

In context, the initial letter would probably be sufficient to identify the word as **door** or **window**. Children's own dictated experience stories can be used for this kind of activity. The teacher can choose words that are especially predictable from context, and cover all of the word except the initial letter. This should help even young readers understand that when they are predicting and thinking what ought to come next, only a few grapho/phonic cues are ordinarily necessary.

It may also be useful and fun to work with books which systematically omit a certain letter. One example is James Thurber's *Wonderful O* (1957); another is Joseph Moses's *The Great Rain Robbery* (1975). Many children would enjoy creating books of this sort.

For somewhat older and more experienced readers, considerably more variation is possible, as in the following version of part of our story about the wolf and Red Riding Hood (the vowels have been omitted from approximately every fifth word).[5] Don't fill in the blanks, but simply *read* the paragraph as smoothly as possible:

---

[5] Arabic omits the vowels altogether, except in beginners' books (Gibson and Levin 1975, p. 124).

Once upon a t–m– there was a handsome y--ng wolf named Lobo. Lobo l–v–d with his mother and f–th–r at the edge of a d--p, dark woods. Every day L–b– went to hunt at the– north edge of the w--ds, near the little village –f Calais. Sometimes all Lobo c--ld find was a wizened –ld farmer and his wife, w–rk–ng in the fields near th– woods or picking berries –n the thicket. At other t–m–s, Lobo might be lucky –n--gh to find a plump, j--c– child that had disobeyed –ts parents and strayed too f–r from home.

Such a paragraph is a challenge, a kind of puzzle. Provided the content and vocabulary are appropriate, an activity like this can help readers understand that usually they only need to sample grapho/phonic cues if they are using context and reading for meaning.

Older readers may also enjoy and profit from reading something written in code. In the following example Joyce Teele, a teacher in Norfolk, Virginia, has provided only a few of the letter-to-letter correspondences:

H is really S	A is really E
W is really T	M is really D
B is really H	E is really N

The students' task is not to decode the selection one letter at a time, but to read it as efficiently as possible. This excerpt is about skunks:

```
B L X A  / Z U I  / A X A V  / H P A D D A M / L / H T I E T /?/
H   E               E   E      S   E     E D       S   N

O S / Z U I / B L X A / Z U I / T E U J / W B L W / L /
              H   E             N         T H  T

H T I E T / R L E / B L X A / L / X A V Z / K L M / H P A D D /./
S   N       N       H   E        E         D       S   E

W B O H / O H / E U W / K A R L I H A / B A / M U A H E W /
T H  S    S    S   N T   E     S E      H E   D  E S N T

W L T A / L / K L W B /./ L / H T I E T / R L E / F I W / U I W /
T   E       T H          S   N       N       F   T      T

L / K L M / H P A D D / C I H W / J B A E / B A / J L E W H /
    D       S   E       S T      H E N    H E     N T S

W U /./ B A / M U A H / O W / W U / F V U W A R W / B O P H A D S /./
T       H E  D  E S    T T   T T    T E  T    H   S E
```

With such an activity, the teacher can help readers learn to use a maximum of nonvisual information and a minimum of visual information.[6]

Many children who tend to deal with each word as if it stood in isolation will make habitual confusions of one sort of another. They may confuse **then** with **than, the** with **they, and** with **can,** and so forth. The solution is not to drill students on these words in isolation, but to help them learn to use context to disentangle the confusion. The teacher should begin with passages in which both grammar and meaning strongly signal the word intended. For example: if a person commonly reads "can" for **and** and vice versa, one might construct a passage beginning as follows:

> Jim called to ask his friends Bob and Mike, "Can you come to the fort today?" Bob answered, "Yes, we can. But let's go get some pop and cookies to take with us."

The teacher might even initially omit the problem words and ask the reader to supply whichever one is appropriate in context (in this case, **can** or **and**). By learning to use context, most readers can soon eliminate their habitual confusions.

In addition or perhaps prior to these various sampling activities, some readers may need extensive opportunities to internalize the more common spelling–sound relationships. Reading and creating alphabet books can be a valuable activity. This is appropriate for readers of various ages, since many of the commercially available alphabet books are by no means "babyish"; see, for example, some of the books listed in Blatt (1978) and Stewig (1978) (see full references at the end of this chapter). One of my favorite alphabet books is Robert Tallon's *Zoophabets* (1971), which can be used to stimulate reading and writing for virtually all ages.

Language play can help many readers learn basic spelling–

---

[6] The paragraph reads as follows: "Have you ever smelled a skunk? If you have, you know that a skunk can have a very bad smell. This is not because he doesn't take a bath. A skunk can put out a bad smell just when he wants to. He does it to protect himself."

sound relations. In addition, some readers may need the kind of security offered by materials that emphasize *regular* correspondences between letters and sounds. For beginners, an excellent choice would be Al Perkins's *Hand, Hand, Fingers, Thumb* (1969). In addition to emphasizing regular spelling–sound correspondences, this book practically invites the reader to beat out its rhythm on a desk (or whatever), just as the monkeys beat out their rhythms on a drum.[7] Some readers may find the Dr. Seuss books both profitable and enjoyable. And at least some readers may benefit from (if not enjoy) limited practice with the so-called linguistic readers that emphasize the systematic introduction of regular spelling–sound patterns. As usual, I would recommend avoiding any lessons that deal with words in isolation. There are now several linguistic series available, and these usually contain not just word lists, but stories. For ideas on how to coordinate several such series to emphasize particular spelling–sound patterns, see "A Massive Oral Decoding Technique," by Ronald Johnson and others (1972). For those who need to internalize some of the basic spelling–sound patterns, such practice may be appropriate. The problem comes mainly when such practice takes the place of normal reading. Strategy lessons of *any* sort should be only a small part of any individual's reading program.

HELPING READERS CONFIRM OR CORRECT

Do you know what a "scofflaw" is? When I first read the headline "Scofflaw off to a Bad Start," I thought **flaw** must be the base word, so I mentally pronounced the word like this: /sko′ · fla/. I could not even syllabicate or pronounce it correctly until I had read most of the article; it was the third paragraph that finally triggered my understanding:

---

[7] It is interesting to compare this book with others in the Bright and Early series. In some cases, they seem to reflect quite different approaches to reading instruction. For example: you might compare *Hand, Hand, Fingers, Thumb* with Theo. LeSieg's *In a People House* (1972) and with Stan and Jan Berenstain's *Bears in the Night* (1971).

Cooper had ignored 780 parking tickets between 1973 and 1977. He was identified by a computer in 1977 as the city's worst traffic scofflaw. It took nearly a year for police to find him.[8]

In this case, I used following context to correct my tentative stab at the word. Once I realized that a "scofflaw" is someone who scoffs at the law, I was able to syllabicate and pronounce the word correctly.

When proficient readers come to words that they cannot identify or understand just from preceding context and grapho/phonic cues, they usually use following context as an aid. Less experienced and less proficient readers may need help in learning to use following context, especially in learning to correct those miscues that do not make sense with the following context.

One strategy, of course, is simply to ask "Does that make sense?" The teacher should wait at least until the end of the sentence before asking such a question, in order to give the reader ample opportunity to correct his or her own miscue. Since self-correction is the ultimate goal, it may be even better to postpone such a question until the entire selection has been read. At that time, the teacher can ask about some of the miscues that did not make sense in context. The "teacher" does not have to be the classroom instructor: he or she can be an aide, a parent or other adult in the community, an older child, or even one of the reader's peers. It often helps to have the reader tape record his or her own reading, then listen for anything that does not make sense. When the reader encounters something nonsensical, he or she can stop the tape momentarily and supply something that seems to make better sense. Then, the reader should listen to check whether the following context supports this change. Finally, the reader can try reading the text again. Such an activity helps readers get in the habit of using preceding context to predict, and following context to confirm or correct.

[8] *Kalamazoo Gazette*, August 1, 1978, p. A-1. The article was a UPI tidbit originating in Chicago.

There are many other activities that can be used for this purpose. In both fiction and nonfiction, it is often possible to find terms that are clarified by the surrounding context. The term **krait** in Roald Dahl's "Poison" is one such example: to those who know something about snakes, it is usually obvious by the end of the story that a krait is a snake (see p. 77). Here is another example: see if you can determine what word should go in the blanks. The excerpt is from Ray Bradbury's *The Golden Apples of the Sun* (1953, p. 18):

He had some theories about the _____ itself.

"One day many years ago a man walked along and stood in the sound of the ocean on a cold sunless shore and said, 'We need a voice to call across the water, to warn ships; I'll make one. I'll make a voice like all of time and all of the fog that ever was; I'll make a voice that is like an empty bed beside you all night long, and like an empty house when you open the door, and like trees in autumn with no leaves. A sound like the birds flying south, crying, and a sound like November wind and the sea on the hard, cold shore. I'll make a sound that's so alone that no one can miss it, that whoever hears it will weep in their souls, and hearths will seem warmer, and being inside will seem better to all who hear it in the distant towns. I'll make me a sound and an apparatus and they'll call it a _____ and whoever hears it will know the sadness of eternity and the briefness of life.' "

Obviously the first sentence suggests little more than that the missing word is a noun. But by the time you have reached the second blank, it should be clear that the missing word is something like **foghorn**.

With this particular paragraph, the response **foghorn** is probably most appropriate (in Bradbury's story, the word is written **Fog Horn**). Generally, however, it is better to choose some paragraphs which allow for several different but appropriate responses. Another example from Bradbury allows for different dialectal variants. What word or words would *you* put in the blanks below? Essentially the same

thing belongs in each blank. The paragraph is from Bradbury's *Dandelion Wine* (1957, p. 34):

> Somehow the people who made _____ knew what
> boys needed and wanted. They put marshmallows and
> coiled springs in the soles and they wove the rest out of
> grasses bleached and fired in the wilderness. Somewhere
> deep in the soft loam of the _____ the thin hard
> sinews of the buck deer were hidden. The people that
> made the _____ must have watched a lot of winds
> blow the trees and a lot of rivers going down to the lakes.
> Whatever it was, it was in the _____, and it was
> summer.

I would probably choose **tennis shoes** or **gym shoes**, but there
are other possibilities that would be equally "correct." In
fact, I think the word **sneakers** is very appropriate, given
the context. Such an activity can help readers understand
that a given deep structure can be expressed in more than
one surface structure. And it can also help readers see that
in a given context, one surface structure may be more appropriate or effective than others.

Once students have had experience with context activities
such as the foregoing, they may enjoy creating and sharing
their own missing word puzzles. Indeed, they may be able to
help *you* think of other ways to emphasize the use of strategies for confirming or correcting.

HELPING READERS INTEGRATE THE CUE SYSTEMS

The most important way of helping readers "get it all together" is to give them plenty of opportunities to read. It is
also helpful, though, for a teacher to give direct guidance
after an individual has read a selection aloud. For example:
when the reader has made a nonsensical miscue and left it
uncorrected, the teacher can later reread the sentence to that
point and ask "What would make sense here?" Then the
teacher can help the reader use following context to confirm
the appropriateness of the word supplied or to supply an-

other word that is more appropriate. If desired, the teacher can then direct the reader's attention to the word on the page, to the grapho/phonic cues. Context, however, comes first.

The cloze procedure is particularly valuable in helping readers learn to use syntactic and semantic cues, to predict and to confirm or correct. First developed by Wilson Taylor in 1953, the cloze procedure is based upon the observation that language is redundant, that about one out of every five words in a stretch of text can be predicted from context. Hence the basic cloze procedure involves filling in every fifth word that has been omitted from a text. The "Beaver" activity (p. 69) is an example of this kind of cloze. And as you may remember, we needed to use various kinds of context in order to fill the blanks with reasonable responses. At one time or another, we needed to use preceding and/ or following context within the sentence; context within the preceding and/or following sentences; and our own personal context, our knowledge of beavers. Little wonder, then, that this kind of activity is so valuable in helping readers use all kinds of nonvisual cues.

Various modifications of the cloze procedure can be used to help readers get it *all* together, to learn to use *all three* cue systems simultaneously in order to get to meaning. We can encourage such integration simply by using cloze activities that omit not entire words, but selected parts of words. The various paragraphs and versions of our wolf and Red Riding Hood story provide an example.

Whatever the variation(s) used, it is important for students to read through the entire cloze activity before filling in any of the missing parts. This should help them see the value of using following context to identify and/or get the meaning of difficult words. It is crucial for students to discuss their answers to a cloze exercise. They need the opportunity to share and compare their responses with those of other students, and the challenge of defending their choices or rejecting them in favor of something better.

Some additional suggestions and recommendations for using the cloze procedure follow:

1. Vary the technique, beginning with relatively easy exercises. With beginning readers, you might start by eliminating the last word of sentences they themselves have dictated (or by eliminating all but the initial letter of the last word.) With somewhat older students, you can use such variations as these: a) omit parts of words, to help them learn to *sample* the grapho/phonic cues; b) omit inflectional endings, to help them realize their own syntactic strengths; c) omit function words, to help them realize their ability to predict these words from the content words, word order, and context; d) omit key concept-carrying words, to help them see how words can be understood from context; e) omit every fifth word (or whatever) and have them read just for meaning, not to fill in the words, in order to help them see that comprehension is ordinarily possible without identifying all the words; and so forth. There are many possibilities.

2. Use a variety of materials: songs, stories, and poems; content-area textbooks; newspapers and magazines; and anything else that might be suitable.

Many of the ideas just listed are culled from one or another of the articles cited at the end of this chapter.

Besides being a valuable instructional strategy, the cloze procedure is also useful for assessing a reader's use of context in reading, assessing a reader's ability to comprehend a given reading selection or book, and determining the suitability of specific reading materials for a given group of children. If you are interested in these other uses you might first consult Culhane (1970). To my knowledge, Bormuth (1975) presents the most comprehensive discussion of how to use the cloze procedure to match reading materials with children.

HELPING READERS COMPREHEND

The reason for integrating the language cue systems is, of course, to comprehend. It is common to divide comprehension into categories, depending on the degree of involvement supposedly required of the reader. A popular "taxonomy" of reading comprehension deals with literal recognition or *recall, inference, evaluation,* and *appreciation* (Barrett, in R. Smith and T. Barrett 1974, pp. 53–57). Each of these is important: readers need to recall at least selected information from what they have read; to draw appropriate inferences; to evaluate evidence and arguments; and to appreciate the structure and style of literary works. All of these are the *products* of comprehension, the results of having comprehended. Even the most basic category, recall, depends upon comprehension. Perhaps you have found, as I have, that students have very poor recall when they do not understand the material read or discussed in class.

I would argue that recall, inference, evaluation, and appreciation are not *kinds* of comprehension but possible *results* of comprehension. They are products of the comprehension *process*. We may need to focus instructional attention on the process itself if we want students to comprehend.

One way to "teach" comprehension is by asking questions and helping students learn how to go about determining appropriate answers. Pearson and Johnson's comprehension taxonomy (1978) helps teachers understand what kinds of information readers can draw upon in answering questions about a text. The answers to recall and inference questions are either *textually explicit, textually implicit,* or "*scriptally implicit.*" To discover what these terms mean, read the paragraph below and answer the following comprehension questions (Pearson and Johnson 1978, p. 157):

Will Wends His Way

Right after the Civil War, many distraught soldiers made their way West to find fame and fortune. Some could not go home because there were no homes to go to. The war had devastated them. One young man, Will Goodlad, made his fortune in the hills of Colorado. He found gold in a little river near Grand Junction. His fortune was short-lived, however. In 1875, he declared bankruptcy and returned to the land of his birth—the Piedmont of South Carolina.

1. When did Will Goodlad declare bankruptcy?
2. Where did Will Goodlad discover gold?
3. When did Will Goodlad discover gold?

The answer to the first question is textually explicit: it says right in the text that Will Goodlad declared bankruptcy in 1875. The answer to the second question is also textually explicit: the text tells us that Goodlad discovered gold in a little river near Grand Junction. But suppose you answered that Goodlad discovered gold in Colorado. That information is not directly stated in the text, but is textually implicit: it is a logical inference, given the sentence about Goodlad's making his fortune in the hills of Colorado and the subsequent sentence about his finding gold. Finally, when did Will Goodlad discover gold? The answer to that question is textually implicit: though the text does not explicitly say when Goodlad discovered gold, we can infer from the paragraph as a whole that this discovery took place sometime between the end of the Civil War and 1875. But suppose you answered that Goodlad discovered gold between 1865 and 1875. In that case, you were using information that was only scriptally implicit, part of your knowledge or internalized "script" about the Civil War.

Thus we see that it is not so much questions as *answers* that draw upon information which is textually explicit, textually implicit, or scriptally implicit. Although a question may be explicitly answered in the text, readers may draw instead upon information which is textually only implicit, or upon information which is drawn from their prior knowledge or mental "script" for the topic. If one is familiar with Grand Junction, Colorado, one might have used such prior knowledge in saying that Goodlad discovered gold in Colorado.

Perhaps it is obvious that many students will need help in learning to bring their own store of knowledge and experience to the interpretation of what they read. It is also true that many will need guided practice in dealing with the meanings explicit and implicit in the text itself. One reason is that written language uses sentence patterns and even grammatical signal words (like **as though, consequently**) that occur only infrequently in speech. Thus the text itself may cause problems that would not be typical of the spoken language. Then, too, readers cannot use intonation as a guide to meaning: one must understand at least the grammar of a text in order to read it with appropriate intonation. Also, readers will have difficulty with comprehension if they read word by word, simply trying to identify each word in succession. Many readers seem unaware that written language is supposed to make sense, just like spoken language.

The following are just some of the problems readers may have in dealing with information that is explicit or implicit in the text itself. For related discussions, see Hittleman (1978, pp. 225–274), and Pearson and Johnson (1978, pp. 108–125). The discussion here will be followed by brief illustrations of how teachers can help students deal with such problems in processing a text.

1. Even when the information is presented fairly straightforwardly, some readers may have trouble determining such things as *who* or *what* was involved as doer or "recipient" of an action; *what happened*; and *when, where,* or *how* the action took place.

   a. *Who* or *what* was involved as doer or recipient

   Happiness at their concern was so strong in her that **her panic** fled . . .
   —Madeleine L'Engle, *A Wrinkle in Time*
   (What happened here? We do not usually expect something inanimate to be the "doer" of an action.)

   Men scanned the skies anxiously, watching for the dreaded signs which might spell the destruction of their world.
   —Armstrong Sperry, *Call It Courage*
   (Who or what was watching?)

b. *What happened*

Sharon **opened a book** and **pretended to read.**

> Judy Blume, *Freckle Juice*
> (What did Sharon do? There are two answers, and
> the second is syntactically complicated: she did not
> actually read, she just **pretended** to read.)

c. *When, where,* or *how* the action took place

Later, Kapugen's Aunt Martha told her that he had lost
his mind **the day her mother died.**

> —Jean Craighead George, *Julie of the Wolves*
> (When had Kapugen lost his mind? The answer
> might be easier to determine if the relevant phrase
> were introduced by a preposition: **ON the day her
> mother died.** Pronoun reference is a problem here
> too.)

She slept at times **in** the warmth of **his big sealskin
parka.**

> —Jean Craighead George, *Julie of the Wolves*
> (Where did she sleep? The answer is partially ob-
> scured by **the warmth of,** which suggests *how* she
> slept—warmly.)

She saw them **through a scarf of tiny crystals that was
her breath on the cold night air inside the house.**

> —Jean Craighead George, *Julie of the Wolves*
> (How did she see them? Readers may have difficulty
> figuring out that the "scarf" was her breath.)

2. Readers may also have difficulty determining the refer-
ent of pronouns and other words which take the place
of a more specific word or phrase (see also Pearson and
Johnson 1978, pp. 124–125).

a. *Pronouns,* taking the place of a more specific noun
or noun phrase

There was plenty of food for breakfast, and lunch and
dinner, too, for that matter; but still the sight de-
pressed her, for **it** was the same tiresome fare they had

been eating every day, every meal, for the last month.
—Robert C. O'Brien, *Mrs. Frisby*
and the Rats of NIMH
(What does **it** refer to? At first, the word **it** seems to
refer to **the sight.**)

b. *Pro-adverbs*, taking the place of a more specific
adverb or adverb phrase

I early learned that the harem was the women's quar-
ters, and that the *hareem* was the group of women who
lived **therein**, whether many or few or only one.
—Dorothy Van Ess, *Fatima and Her Sisters*
(What place is indicated by the word **therein**?)

c. *Pro-verbs*, taking the place of a more specific verb
or verb phrase

"You wouldn't do anything to hurt her."
"No, but she thinks I **might.**"
—Ray Bradbury, *I Sing the Body Electric*
(She thinks I might do what? The answer is in the
preceding sentence.)

3. Readers may also have difficulty processing the information in subordinate clauses, perhaps because they
fail to understand the import of the signal word intro-
ducing the clause, or because the signal word is not
present in the surface structure.

a. *Adjective* or so-called *relative clauses*

As he stood there surveying his world, the wind **that**
swept up from the wide Pacific beat hard against him,
whistling in his ears.
—Armstrong Sperry, *Call It Courage*
(What does **that** refer to? What swept up from the
wide Pacific?)

The haunted house was half in the shadows of the
clump of elms **in which** it stood.
—Madeleine L'Engle, *A Wrinkle in Time*
(What does **in which** refer to?)

Sometimes still I feel the smile **I learned from her,**
printed on my cheek at three in the deep morn . . .
                              —Ray Bradbury, *I Sing the Body Electric!*
(What did I learn from her? The adjective clause
may be hard to process precisely because it is *not*
introduced by a word like **that** or **which.**)

b. *Adverb clauses*

There was plenty of food for breakfast, and lunch and
dinner, too, for that matter; but still the sight de-
pressed her, **for** it was the same tiresome fare they had
been eating every day, every meal, for the last month.
                              —Robert C. O'Brien, *Mrs. Frisby*
                              and the Rats of NIMH
(What does the signal word **for** mean? In the first
instance, **for** means "because." This use of **for** is
seldom encountered in speech.)

Kapugen's back would grow taut **as** he lifted his arms
and fired his gun.
                              —Jean Craighead George, *Julie of the Wolves*
(What does the signal word **as** mean in this sen-
tence?)

I figured something drastic must have happened in his
life, **as** it is very unusual for a hound to be traveling all
alone.
                              —Wilson Rawls, *Where the Red Fern Grows*
(What does the word **as** mean here?)

As the valleys of a main stream and its many tribu-
taries change in size and shape, the landscape as a
whole must change.
                              —Robert L. Heller et al., *Earth Science*
(In this sentence, the first **as** has still another shade
of meaning: it suggests necessary correlation, or
perhaps even cause.)

Half an hour passed, **the sun sinking lower in the west**
all the time, before she heard a slight scratching noise
up above . . . .
                              —Robert C. O'Brien, *Mrs. Frisby*
                              and the Rats of NIMH

(Here, we have not an adverb clause but a constructtion which can be paraphrased as an adverb clause: **while the sun sank lower in the west all the time.** Without the overt signal word **while,** the original construction may be difficult to interpret.)

c. *Noun clauses*

Meg had realized **that** some of the "games" her parents played with her were tests of some kind, and **that** there had been more for her and Charles Wallace than for the twins.
    —Madeleine L'Engle, *A Wrinkle in Time*
(The word **that** introduces the noun clauses, the parts of the sentence which tell what Meg had realized.)

"I can't explain **where** it comes from or **how** I get it, and it doesn't happen very often."
    —Madeleine L'Engle, *A Wrinkle in Time*
(The words **where** and **how** introduce the parts of the sentence telling what the speaker can't explain.)

She thought at first **it was a hen,** strayed from the chickenyard—caught by a fox?
    —Robert C. O'Brien, *Mrs. Frisby*
    and the Rats of NIMH
(The noun clause may be hard to process precisely because it is *not* introduced by **that.**)

4. Readers may have problems understanding various other kinds of constructions that are difficult to process in one way or another. The following examples only begin to illustrate the many possibilities:

"But we really didn't mean **you to know about the sheets.**"
    —Madeleine L'Engle, *A Wrinkle in Time*
(This construction may be difficult because the signal word **for** has been omitted. More typically, the sentence might read "But we really didn't mean **for you to know about the sheets.**")
Dark gold and soft brown were the old men who sat

around Kapugen's camp stove and talked to him by day
and night.

—Jean Craighead George, *Julie of the Wolves*
(What were the old men like? To Julie/Miyax, they
were **dark gold and soft brown**. The inversion of
normal word order may make the sentence difficult
to process.)

As soon as the details of how much they would charge
at the door and how much of that Stub would get were
settled, the job of moving began.

—Carl Carmer, *Listen for a Lonesome Drum*
(This sentence is difficult to process because the
main clause occurs at the end of the sentence, after
a lengthy adverbial clause that contains an interrupted passive construction: **As soon as the details
. . . were settled.**)

The space above the streets and between the build-
ings becomes an oasis in the cement jungle, a people-
oriented environment with grassy playgrounds, flower-
ing shrubs and chattering squirrels.

—James W. Hudson, "We Can Build Space Age
Cities Now," in *National Wildlife Magazine*
(The potential problem here is the appositive: **a
people-oriented environment.** Will readers realize
that this phrase is supposed to clarify the nature of
the oasis in the cement jungle?)

Many of these potential problems involve specific kinds of
syntactic constructions and/or function words that signal
relations between other words. If readers have trouble with
such constructions and signal words, should we teach them
grammar in the hope of improving their reading? I say
definitely not. A considerable body of research suggests that
the formal study of grammar has little positive effect on
students' reading, writing, speaking, and listening (see my
Grammar for Teachers, 1979). Also, we have seen that
even beginning readers have considerable intuitive understanding of the structure of their language. What we need

to do is encourage readers to *use* that knowledge to predict what is coming next and to confirm or correct their tentative interpretations.

More specifically, students may need guided practice in dealing with difficult syntax. Consider the following sentence:

> Men scanned the skies anxiously, watching for the dreaded signs.

To proficient readers, this sentence may not appear syntactically difficult. However, less proficient readers may have difficulty figuring out who did the watching. One way to help such readers may be through sentence-combining activities (see, for example, Hughes 1975). Teachers can help students learn how to create various kinds of sentences, step by step. Given the underlying sentences **Men scanned the skies anxiously** and **Men watched for the dreaded signs**, teachers can show students how to combine the sentences in various ways:

> Men scanned the skies anxiously and watched for the dreaded signs.
>
> Men, who watched for the dreaded signs, scanned the skies anxiously.
>
> Men, who were watching for the dreaded signs, scanned the skies anxiously.
>
> Men, watching for the dreaded signs, scanned the skies anxiously.
>
> Watching for the dreaded signs, men scanned the skies anxiously.
>
> Men scanned the skies anxiously, watching for the dreaded signs.

Additionally, one can reverse the order and emphasis of the two underlying sentences to produce such results as these:

> Men watched for the dreaded signs and scanned the skies anxiously.

Scanning the skies anxiously, men watched for the dreaded signs.

Men watched for the dreaded signs, scanning the skies anxiously.

Activities of this sort can be used with older students, while simpler sentence-combining activities can be used in the early elementary grades. Such direct attention to sentence *creation* aids in sentence *comprehension*, particularly when the teacher explicitly links the two. For a summary discussion of sentence-combining, see my *Grammar for Teachers* (1979).

Besides needing help with complicated syntax, readers may need help with particular function words. However, we saw with the newspaper passage about the Kent State riots (p. 117) that readers can often supply many of the function words in a text, given the content words, word order, and a comprehensible topic. This fact suggests that we can use *context* to teach the function words that students are not familiar with (see Goodman and Greene 1977, pp. 27–29). In the following sentences what function word would you supply, using meaning and grammar as your guide?

Their boots squeaked in the cold and their voices sounded far away, _____ the temperature was far below zero.

The fox's brown fur of summer was splotched with white patches, reminding Miyax again that winter was coming, _____ the fur of the fox changes each season to match the color of the land.

Provided our experiential background is adequate, most of us would probably put **because** or **since** in both blanks. Having shown students that they *can* comprehend such sentences, the teacher may then introduce the signal word that occurred in the original sentences from *Julie of the Wolves*: the word **for**. In speech we do not often use **for** to mean "because," so teachers may have to help students learn to recognize this use of the word in the literature they read. We can use information *implicit* in the text to help students understand and recognize an *explicit* syntactic signal! Note, too, that there is no need to teach a grammatical label for this use of **for**. What matters is not that it is a subordinating conjunction, but that it is roughly equivalent to **because.**

Students may need help, then, in learning to deal with function words that are fairly common in certain kinds of written language, but relatively rare in speech. They may also need guided practice in comprehending relations that are implicit rather than explicit. One particular study found that fourth graders did not seem to understand the cause-effect relations implicit in the following pairs of sentences (Bormuth et al. 1970, p. 354) :

> The gear slipped off. The machine stopped.
> (The first sentence gives the cause, while the second sentence gives the effect.)
> The machine stopped. The gear had slipped off.
> (The first sentence gives the effect, while the second sentence gives the cause.)

The need for help in learning to understand textually implicit relations is not confined to elementary school students. If they have not learned to read for meaning, many junior high and high school students need such assistance too (see also Palermo and Molfese 1972, pp. 415–423).

Whatever their individual needs, students benefit most from *guided practice* in understanding textually explicit and implicit information. By themselves, workbooks and worksheets do little to *teach* students. Rather, students learn from the teacher and from their peers as they work through a lesson together, discussing the text and how it can be comprehended. The key to success is verbal *interaction.*

Students also need help in learning to use scriptally implicit information in order to comprehend what they read. That is, many students need guided practice in using their prior knowledge and experience as an aid to comprehension. This is especially important in the content areas, where teachers may need to help students build concepts through experience *before* trying to read and understand the textbook. But before discussing such matters in the next chapter, I want to emphasize that reading strategy lessons (of whatever kind) should never take the place of actual reading and that reading strategy lessons should constitute only a small part of the total reading curriculum.

ACTIVITIES AND PROJECTS FOR FURTHER EXPLORATION

1. In connection with the foregoing chapter, you presumably analyzed the miscues of one or more readers. Choose one of these readers, and prepare a set of reading strategy lessons appropriate to the reader's needs, interests, and abilities.
2. Begin collecting or adapting or creating reading strategy lessons for a specific group of students, real or hypothetical. Specify the age(s) and needs of the group.

READINGS FOR FURTHER EXPLORATION

Watson, Dorothy J. "Helping the Reader: From Miscue Analysis to Strategy Lessons." In *Miscue Analysis: Applications to Reading Instruction*, edited by Kenneth S. Goodman. Urbana, Ill.: ERIC Clearinghouse on Reading and Communication Skills and the National Council of Teachers of English, 1973, pp. 103–115. Shows how to use miscue analysis as a guide in developing appropriate strategy lessons (using one student as an example).

Cooper, Charles R., and Petrosky, Anthony R. "A Psycholinguistic View of the Fluent Reading Process." *Journal of Reading* 20 (December 1976): 184–207. An outstanding article that outlines a reading program for secondary students and includes an especially valuable bibliography.

McCay, David, et al. *Breakthrough to Literacy*. Glendale, Calif.: Bowmar, 1973. A language experience program for beginning readers and writers, grades K–3, in which children are encouraged to construct their own sentences, using separate word cards.

Larrick, Nancy. "Wordless Picture Books and the Teaching of Reading." *The Reading Teacher* 29 (May 1976): 743–746. Offers some good suggestions, plus a useful bibliography of wordless picture books.

Tovey, Duane R. "The Psycholinguistic Guessing Game." *Language Arts*

53 (March 1976): 319–322. Provides some useful suggestions for helping readers predict.

Stauffer, Russell G. "Productive Reading-Thinking at the First Grade Level." *The Reading Teacher* 13 (February 1960): 183–187. Provides an extended example of how readers can predict, then read to confirm or modify their predictions—a method suitable for all ages.

Blatt, Gloria T. "Playing with Language." *The Reading Teacher* 31 (February 1978): 487–493. Offers a wealth of practical suggestions and an extensive bibliography with a section on alphabet books.

Stewig, John Warren. "Alphabet Books: A Neglected Genre." *Language Arts* 55 (January 1978): 6–11. Suggests using alphabet books as an introduction to visual literacy, with an extensive bibliography of alphabet books useful for various purposes.

Johnson, Ronald J.; Johnson, Karen Lamb; and Kerfoot, James F. "A Massive Oral Decoding Technique." *The Reading Teacher* 25 (February 1972): 421–423. Suggests using a variety of linguistic readers to help students master various spelling–sound patterns.

Bortnick, Robert, and Lopardo, Genevieve S. "An Instructional Application of the Cloze Procedure." *Journal of Reading* 16 (January 1973): 296–300. Offers practical suggestions for teachers at all levels; an excellent introduction to the cloze procedure.

Blachowicz, Camille L. Z. "Cloze Activities for Primary Readers." *The Reading Teacher* 31 (December 1977): 300–302. Has some interesting and useful suggestions.

Pikulski, John J. "Using the Cloze Technique." *Language Arts* 53 (March 1976): 317–318, 328. More interesting and useful suggestions.

Farnes, N. C. *Reading Purposes, Comprehension and the Use of Context.* Bletchley, Buckinghamshire, England: The Open University Press, 1973. Illustrates various activities that could help readers understand how to use context as an aid to comprehension.

Pearson, P. David. "A Psycholinguistic Model of Reading." *Language Arts* 53 (March 1976): 309–314. Illustrates activities that focus on one, two, or all three of the language cue systems.

Hittleman, Daniel R. *Developmental Reading: A Psycholinguistic Perspective.* Chicago: Rand McNally College Publishing, 1978. Two sections are particularly relevant: "Strategies for Reconstructing Meaning" (pp. 225–274) and "Using Context to Determine Unknown Words" (pp. 286–292). There are also useful discussions of DRTA, the so-called Directed Reading-Thinking Activity: pp. 200–206, 227–235, and 328–330.

Pearson, P. David, and Johnson, Dale D. *Teaching Reading Comprehension.* New York: Holt, Rinehart and Winston, 1978. Two sections are particularly relevant to our discussion of comprehension: "Proposition Level Tasks (Continued)," pp. 108–125, and "A Simple Taxonomy of Questions," pp. 157–168.

Weaver, Constance. *Grammar for Teachers: Perspectives and Definitions.* Urbana, Ill.: National Council of Teachers of English, 1979. Provides a useful summary of sentence-combining research and activities, with a bibliography of resources for the teacher.

Goodman, Yetta, and Greene, Jennifer. "Grammar and Reading in the Classroom." In *Linguistic Theory: What Can It Say about Reading?* edited by Roger W. Shuy. Newark, Del.: International Reading Association, 1977, pp. 18–30. Illustrates reading strategy lessons for helping readers overcome problems with syntactic markers like **as though, even though,** and **although.**

9

how can we design a psycholinguistically based reading program?

Students learn to read most successfully within the context of a total language arts experience, *which includes speaking and listening activities, writing, leisure reading, and reading within a variety of content areas, such as the sciences, vocational education, social studies, mathematics, and so on.*—Michigan Department of Education

Question for Study and Discussion

1   How might we design a multifaceted reading program appropriate for a wide range of instructional levels?

A READING PROGRAM FOR ALL SEASONS

The general public tends to have not only an inaccurate view of proficient reading, but also an inadequate view of reading "instruction," unfortunately. People often think that reading means merely identifying words, with meaning taking care of itself, and that reading instruction involves merely teaching children how to succeed at word identification.

We have seen, however, that reading is not a simple matter of translating written words into their spoken counterparts. Rather, it is a complex process of determining meaningful relations among words. Because it entails an interaction between mind and print, reading requires the active involvement of the reader. Thus even if helping children learn *how* to read were our only goal, their motivation and involvement would be crucial. To be most successful in our task, we must engage the enthusiastic cooperation of the learner, and so a primary part of our job is to create in the child an interest in reading, a desire to gain information and pleasure from the printed word. Such motivation is both an end in itself and a means to an end: it facilitates the process of learning to read.

The reading program outlined in this chapter is broad and multifaceted. Reading strategy lessons are only one of the six suggested components. Depending somewhat upon their reading experience and proficiency, readers need to have frequent and meaningful opportunities for:

Creating reading materials
Being immersed in reading
Practicing reading strategies
Sustaining silent reading
Sharing and experiencing reading
Reading for a specific purpose

We have already discussed the third component, lessons for practicing reading strategies. The nature of each of the other components will be clarified in the sections that follow. The first two components are especially important for the beginning or less proficient reader. The last component is especially important for the more experienced and more proficient reader, particularly beyond the early elementary years. But *all* readers should have not only whatever kinds of reading strategy lessons they might need, but also frequent opportunities to read for and by themselves, and to share and experience what they read. It is also important for teachers at all levels to read to students, in order to expose them to more sophisticated writing styles than they could handle by themselves, to model fluent oral reading, and to demonstrate that reading can indeed be pleasurable.

Such a multifaceted program obviously makes no sharp distinction between beginning reading, developmental reading, and remedial reading. Rather, it emphasizes the needs which are basic to all readers, regardless of their reading experience and proficiency: we all need opportunities to read and to make reading a significant part of our lives.

Doubtless the reading program suggested here is not quite

a reading program for all seasons. Actually it is not really a program but an *outline* for a comprehensive program that might span most of the years from kindergarten through high school. Armed with such an outline and guided by your own understanding of the reading process, you should be able to structure and implement a multifaceted reading program that is suited to your particular students and circumstances. Instead of using commercially prepared textbooks as if they were the beginning and end of reading instruction, you can design a reading program that permeates and reflects every aspect of the curriculum. More than anyone or anything else, you, the teacher, hold the key to your students' reading enjoyment and success.

CREATING READING MATERIALS

A "language experience" approach is particularly important for beginning and nonproficient readers. They need to know that what can be said can be written, and vice versa, and they need the motivation inherent in dictating and writing their own stories, poems, and so forth. Such experience ought not be confined to the very young or the very nonproficient, however, for virtually every reader can profit from the opportunity to create some of his or her own reading materials.

At first, young children will need to dictate their ideas and sentences for others to write. This is not the kind of dictation taken by a secretary. Rather, there is constant interplay between the child or children and the person doing the writing, constant shuttling back and forth between the discussion of ideas and the actual composition of sentences to be written.

Perhaps the class will discuss their trip to a farm, with each child offering a sentence about something the children saw or did. Or perhaps the class will discuss the space exhibit they have seen at a museum, with various children contributing sentences to a written description of a moon rover or a command module. In any case, the teacher can not only guide the discussion, but ensure that the written product has some sort of logical structure. Instead of asking for *any* sentence about the farm trip, for example, the teacher might ask only for sentences that describe how one of the animals looked or walked or sounded or smelled. Often the teacher can encourage the use of descriptive or figurative language. If someone suggests "The giraffe had a long neck," the teacher might say something like "He sure did, didn't he? Can you think of anything else that is long like a giraffe's neck? Anything that his neck looked like?" With responses such as "like a tree," "like a big building," "like a telephone pole," the class might create a whole poem about the giraffe's neck!

Class compositions can be aesthetically satisfying as well as useful for reading instruction. Together, the class can compose and "write":

1. Descriptions of things they have seen, places they have been, animals or other things in the classroom, a castle they would like to live in, a robot they would like to have, and so forth.
2. Stories about a real or imaginary person, animal, plant, or whatever.
3. Directions for making clay, baking cookies, concocting a witches' brew, and so forth.
4. Poems of various sorts, such as those in which each child contributes a line that begins in the same way (for example: "I wish . . ." or "I dreamed . . ." or "I remember . . .").

Often it helps for the teacher to read a model of the kind of composition that the children are going to do. For example, if the class is going to write a collaborative wish poem, it would help to read first a few lines or poems that other children have composed (see Kenneth Koch's *Wishes, Lies, and Dreams,* 1970).

After writing the children's composition on the blackboard or on a large chart, the teacher can conduct a variety of reading activities. The teacher should read the finished composition at least once or twice, moving a finger under each line of print in the process. Then the teacher can invite the children to read along as best they can. In addition, the teacher can: 1) ask each child in turn to read the line he or she has contributed; 2) invite children to try reading the entire composition individually; 3) ask children if they can locate certain words; 4) ask children if they can locate words beginning with a certain letter or sound, and so forth. As usual, these are only some of the many possibilities.

Of course, children need opportunities to compose their own individual stories and poems, too. Even those who can write for themselves can often benefit from having someone available to discuss their ideas with them and to act as their scribe. Here, for example, is a story my son composed at the age of seven. The immediate stimulus was four transparent "suncatchers": a boat, a bird, a flower, and a butterfly. The resulting story is far superior to anything he had written on paper himself:

There Once Was a Lost Ship

There once was a bird that had red in the middle, shaped like a heart. It had blue all around it, and red on the top, like a chef's hat. The bird flew down onto a ship with a red flag at the top, and a crystal sail. The boat had a blue, glowing bottom when you looked into it. Then once the ship stopped at a land nearby, and no one could ever find the ship again. There they saw a nice tulip, with kind of orange in the middle, shaped like a diamond. This diamond shape had dark purple around it, like a ship with a green trigger at the bottom, and when you pulled the trigger it would shoot all different colored buds out, into flowers.

Then a bright yellow butterfly with silver antennas flew down, like the gentle wind. And then the bird flew over to the butterfly, and they swooped down next to the tulip into the light green grass. They had their picnic in the cool shade of a green tree. When you touched it, you would find ten, twenty, or even fifty dollar bills.

In this place, nothing lives except animals, and beauty, and food the animals can eat. And the bird never wanted to leave that land again, for now that was his home. The bird and butterfly and tulip were happy and safe together.

For a long time afterwards, my son enjoyed reading and rereading this story to anyone who would listen. It gave him the opportunity to practice good reading strategies, too, because he did not "know" all the words at sight and repeatedly had to predict, sample, and confirm or correct as he read.

If they are especially poor readers, even high school students and adults can benefit from the opportunity to dictate and later read their own compositions. The possible topics are virtually endless. They can dictate poems, personal reminiscences, stories involving their favorite heroes (real or imaginary), myths and fables, answers for the advice columns of a newspaper, advertisements for something they would like to sell, explanations of how to do something, and so forth. The teacher can use this reading material in a variety of productive ways.

The following item of folklore is from a middle-grade student in a remedial reading class. It was first related informally, rather than dictated. The teacher, Mary Sue Piper, later transcribed the story this way, using the boy's own language patterns:

Burying Turnips

My teacher reads a lot. She says she learns a bunch of stuff that way . . . But I don't know about that! I don't read a lot, but I know a bunch of stuff—like she had to ask me something she read about that she didn't know nothing about, and I didn't read it nowhere but I already knowed about it. My teacher read about burying turnips, but she didn't know what it meant. She asked me and I knowed. I knowed all about it! I didn't read it, I just knowed it.

You bury turnips when your kinfolks die. You bury the turnips in the land they owned or lived on. You always do. You do it so they can rest easy. If you don't bury them you could be sorry. Like my Daddy—now *he really* was sorry!

Well, my Grandaddy died and we buried him, but my Daddy didn't bury no turnips. He just thought it was old-fashioned and we didn't need to bury no turnips. But that wasn't the right thing to do, so Grandaddy was disturbed.

He came back and talked to my Daddy one night in a dream. He said, "Son, you knowed better than to lie to your Mama. You promised her that you wouldn't take that crescent wrench I gave you to work with you at your job." That really disturbed my Daddy. The next morning he couldn't find that crescent wrench nowhere. He really looked for it, too.

My Grandaddy come to me in a dream and told me I knowed better than to plan to take my firecrackers to the county fair. When I looked for my firecrackers the next day, I couldn't find them nowhere. But I didn't tell nobody what happened to *me*. Nobody in *my* house!

My Daddy decided we better bury some turnips! Quick! I didn't tell them so, but I was shorely happy about his deciding that. I was scared!

We went to my Granddaddy's land and buried about four turnips. That put my Daddy's mind at ease, too. But best of all, it put my dead Granddaddy at rest and he never came and bothered us no more after that.

That's how I knowed about it. I didn't read it nowhere. But I really knowed about it.

By using such material for reading practice and instruction, the teacher built upon the reader's strengths: he already knew the essence of what the story said, and he was able to use this prior knowledge to help him read. Furthermore, the task was inherently motivating: he wanted to read the story he had told. Since many of his classmates have similar folk traditions from the Ozarks, they too were interested in reading his story and in creating similar stories of their own.

If the teacher could give students such individualized writing and reading help just once a semester or once a year, it would still be well worth the effort. But the wise teacher will find ways of enlisting others to help, perhaps even on a regular basis. Parents are often quite willing, if only they are asked. Grandparents and elderly persons in the community may be glad to feel needed. And older students (even nonproficient and reluctant readers) can often benefit from reading to younger children and helping them compose and write their own stories.

So far, we have talked only about having someone else act as a scribe for the student. But it is equally important that children try their own hand at writing, even before they learn to read. In fact, there seems to be a natural transition from drawing to writing to reading. Teachers can encourage this transition by labeling some of the objects in the pictures children draw. Soon, the children themselves will try to write "me," "my dog," "sun," "sky," and so forth. And from single words, it is but a short step to sentences that the children can write and read. The important thing to remember, for both younger and older students, is that deep structure is more important than surface structure: conveying meaning is more important than spelling and punctuating everything "correctly."

Younger children, especially, want and need to write about themselves: their families, their pets, their friends, their feelings, their wants and needs, their adventures, and so forth. But even older students and adults benefit from the opportunity to think and write about themselves. The mere injunction to "write about yourself" usually produces deadly results, so try instead to think of some imaginative way to foster introspection and self-expression. One such idea is a "collage" poem about oneself. To get their thoughts going, writers might ask themselves such questions as these, taken mainly from Mimi Brodsky Chenfeld's *Teaching Language Arts Creatively* (1978):

What color(s) am I?	What place(s) am I?
What sound(s) am I?	What kind(s) of food am I?
What time(s) of day am I?	What kind(s) of sports am I?
	What kind(s) of clothes am I?
What season(s) am I?	What kind(s) of tree or flower
What holiday(s) am I?	am I?
What book(s) am I?	

As usual, a few examples may help to stimulate the imagination. Here are some collage poems from students in Victoria Pachulski's reading improvement classes:

> I am a skateboard rolling away in a boring class.
> I am a bowl of jello on a cold night.
> I am a slippery snake with a piece of soap on a Halloween
>   night.
> I am a *Teen* magazine.
> I am a bird flying high on a cold, dark night.
> —Gary Sleeman, Grade 7

> I am a hard cement floor.
> Sometimes I'm pizza.
> I am an ice cube in a hot oven.
> I am the sun, bright and warm in the morning.
> I am a bolt of lightning when I get mad.
> Sometimes I'm a hat.
> I'm a robot at home.
> I'm green, gold, blue and black.
> —Robert Lewman, Grade 7

> I am 7:00 in the morning.
> I am a skirt and a shirt, jeans, and socks.
> I am Spring, blooming with something new every day.
> I am the Fourth of July, with all the colors.
> I am pudding, pizza, grapes, and candy bars.
> Sometimes I am a turtle, and sometimes I am a bird.
> I am a forest.
> I'm really a blank piece of paper, a plant, and a sports car.
> —Sheri Lipes, Grade 7

> I am a stamp with George Washington on it.
> I am Sunday.
> I am a shirt with a hole in it.
> I am a summer with flowers, trees, lakes, rivers, and
>   oceans.
> I am a steak that cooks and sizzles.
> I am wind.
> I am a sponge that is slushy and soggy.
> I am a road that people drive on.

I am a house where people can sleep and keep warm.
I am a chair.
                              —Norman Marble, Grade 8

I am a single engine plane all alone in the wild.
I am mellow music when I'm by myself, and rock music
    when I am with other people.
I am a good fight, with lots of hard hitting.
I am fancy clothes and a Corvette.
I am a front-loader, tearing things up.
I am a strange, colorful picture, full of animals.
I am bleachers after a good game.
I am a ship on the ocean, late at night, crushing the waves.
                              —Mark Mitchell, Grade 9

The next two collage poems are from prospective teachers
in a college class, while the last poem is one of my own:

I am basic blue jeans with bare feet
I am country with mountains and meandering streams
I am 10:00 a.m.—active and always on the go—
        Iran, Russia, Germany, Scotland
                U S of A
            I am American
I am Christmas—joyous and giving
I am 2 a.m.—quiet and serene.
I am like a cactus—
        I can be very sticky and prickly
I am the Philadelphia Phillies
        and the Detroit Lions
                              —Cathy McCabe

I am ten o'clock, steadily ticking
        toward noon
A calculator, tracking my progress,
        planning my future
I am concrete, a foundation for the
        architecture of my life.

Yet I am also a string instrument,
        vibrating with living melodies

A prism, absorbing the spectrum of life
and tossing out multicolored glints
Hungry, determined, I am my own canvas
never complete.

—Pat Reeves

I'm a sugary, sprinkly donut,
but sometimes just the hole;
A lemony cool drink,
but sometimes just the rind;
A super supreme pizza,
but sometimes just the anchovies;
A ten-speed Free Spirit,
but sometimes just low gear,
A tumbling, rainbow waterfall,
but sometimes just dry stones
in a neglected riverbed.

—Connie Weaver

Of course not all of these writers needed to use their poems as the basis for reading practice and instruction. But they all enjoyed reading and sharing their collages with others. We all need opportunities to find language and reading personally meaningful.

Remember that there are at least three benefits from having students dictate or write some of their own reading materials. First, such composition helps students understand that written language is parallel to oral language, and that the purpose of both is to convey feelings, experiences, information, ideas. Second, it gives students confidence that they can read something, and it provides motivation to read. Third, it provides materials for the teacher to use in helping students develop good reading strategies.

The following references should be helpful in conceptualizing and implementing this aspect of a comprehensive reading program.

READINGS FOR FURTHER EXPLORATION

Hall, MaryAnne. *Teaching Reading as a Language Experience.* 2nd ed. Columbus, Ohio: Charles E. Merrill, 1976. For the elementary teacher, an excellent introduction to the language experience approach to reading.

Lee, Dorris M. and Rubin, Joseph B. *Children and Language: Reading and Writing, Talking and Listening.* Belmont, Calif.: Wadsworth, 1979. An outstanding introduction to the language experience approach.

McCracken, Robert A., and McCracken, Marlene J. *Reading Is Only the Tiger's Tail.* San Rafael, Calif.: Leswing Press, 1972. Presenting a language experience approach, this book is especially useful to early elementary teachers.

Platt, Penny. "Grapho-linguistics: Children's Drawings in Relation to Reading and Writing Skills." *The Reading Teacher* 31 (December 1977) : 262–268. Offers practical ideas for helping children move from drawing into writing and reading.

Hildreth, Gertrude. "Early Writing as an Aid to Reading." *Elementary English* 40 (1964) : 15–20. Discusses several reasons why early writing facilitates beginning reading.

Blatt, Gloria T. "Playing with Language." *The Reading Teacher* 31 (February 1978) : 487–493. Discusses a wealth of books that can be used to stimulate language play and language development, many of which can stimulate children's own writing and reading.

Lipson, Greta B., and Morrison, Baxter. *Fact, Fantasy, and Folklore: Expanding Language Arts and Critical Thinking Skills.* Carthage, Ill.: Good Apple, 1977. Suggests using folktales as a starting point for a variety of oral language activities, many of which could easily lead to writing and reading. The basic ideas can be modified for use with almost any age.

BEING IMMERSED IN READING

Some children learn to read much as they learned to speak: by being immersed in language. Through interaction with the environment, they learn to recognize the word **STOP** on the octagonal red sign, the word **McDonald's** attached to the golden arches, and the words **Chicken Noodle** on the soup can. Surrounded by television and the world of advertising, most preschool children can recognize at least a few such words in their specialized contexts. These children have begun to learn an essential reading strategy: use the total context in order to identify words and get meaning.

Other children are even more advanced in their reading

by the time they enter school, having followed along in books as people read to them or as they listened to a record or tape recording. They may have memorized a favorite book and begun to investigate the relation between the spoken language and the written language, usually with the help of someone to answer questions like "What's that word?" or "What sound does this letter make?"

In short, the "natural" readers have usually been immersed in the written language, and they have usually had someone to assist them in their individual exploration of the relation between spoken language and written language. However, they have learned to read without really being "taught."

Research suggests that such language immersion and assistance can be highly effective in the classroom, particularly with beginning readers and with so-called disabled or remedial readers (see the references at the end of this section). Different researchers have given different names to their particular approaches, but they all have one thing in common: the child works with whole stories, rather than with bits and pieces of language. If any attention is given to words and parts of words, it is only after the entire selection has been read.

A language immersion technique can be used not only with an individual child, but with a group of children. If the teacher can obtain several copies of various trade books, then he or she can read aloud while the children each follow along in their own copy of the book. As a starter, the teacher might get the school to purchase about four to six copies of one of Scholastic's "libraries" of books. These are sets of books assembled for a particular grade level and/or according to a particular topic; each library usually contains from thirty to forty different books.[1] Another excellent resource is the *Sounds of Language* reading series, by Bill Martin, Jr., and Peggy Brogan.[2]

It helps if the teacher can obtain or make a *large* copy of

---

[1] For a catalog of their paperbacks and related materials, write to Scholastic Book Services, 904 Sylvan Avenue, Englewood Cliffs, N.J. 07632.

[2] This series is published by Holt, Rinehart and Winston. For a

the book: then the teacher can hold this book up for the children to see, and run a finger under each line of print while reading to the children. After the children have followed along with the teacher's reading two or three times, the teacher can invite the children to read aloud with the teacher, as best they can. At first the children's efforts may be halting and timid, but the teacher should continue to read at a steady, fluent rate. As the children become more competent and more confident about their own reading of the story, the teacher can try such additional steps as these:

1. Invite just one or two of the children to read aloud with the teacher, at least for a page or two.
2. Invite two children to read a page or more aloud without the teacher. (But if *both* readers stumble, the teacher can supply words to keep the flow of reading going.)
3. Invite the children to ask questions about words and parts of words, and perhaps invite them to choose one or more words they would like to add to a personal word collection.
4. Ask the children questions about words and parts of words. For example, the teacher might ask if they can find a certain word on a certain page, or if they can find two words that begin with a certain letter or sound. Such activities should obviously be geared to the abilities and needs of the readers.

As usual, these suggestions do not exhaust the possibilities. There are many ways to vary and build upon this basic technique of reading *to* and then *in unison with* children.

One advantage of this reading immersion technique is that it can be carried out not only by the classroom teacher, but by teacher's aides, parents and grandparents, other children —by anyone who can read the necessary materials fluently and with expression. In fact, much of the work can be done

---

catalog of their reading and language arts and English materials, write to Holt, Rinehart and Winston, Inc., 383 Madison Avenue, New York, N.Y. 10017.

by a record or a tape recording. The child can first listen to a record or tape while following the story silently in a book. Then the child can gradually begin to read along until he or she can "read" the entire book independently.

Sometimes it helps if the selected story or stories can be tape recorded specifically for a given child or group of children who are similar in their reading habits. In particular, it helps if someone can record the selected story at a speed approximating the child's or children's own reading rate.[3] Commercially recorded materials also work quite well; Scholastic Book Services is again a valuable resource, offering a wide variety of record-and-book and cassette-and-book combinations. For the early elementary grades, there are not only individual titles, but a set of about sixty record-and-book combinations and a set of over thirty cassette-and-book combinations. There are a few combinations offered for the upper elementary grades and for junior high and high school students.

For some children, the first book will take weeks of daily practice; for others, less time will be necessary. But the second and subsequent books will usually take much less time to master—perhaps about a week. Instead of being bored by such extended practice, children usually find it challenging and exciting, particularly if they have never before experienced success at reading. Of course, reading an extremely familiar text is not the same as reading a totally new book, but it often gives beginning and nonproficient readers enough confidence to tackle something new. And it helps them learn to use context for dealing with problem words and for getting meaning.

Even high school and college students will enjoy and benefit from being read to, if the selection is interesting and the reading is fluent and expressive. We can read aloud ourselves, invite guest readers, or use records and tapes. In addition to such oral interpretation of literature, though,

---

[3] Of course there would have to be some signal telling the child when to proceed to the next page. It is best to use short tapes (about 15 minutes to a side) and record just one story on each side.

we should provide a systematic reading immersion program for prereaders and beginning readers, and for most nonproficient or reluctant readers. Such assistance seems to be particularly valuable for the "phonics-bound" student (Heckelman 1969, p. 281). In describing the eight-year-old readers with whom she worked, Carol Chomsky has in effect described many such readers (1976, p. 288):

> These children were not non-readers. They had received a great deal of phonics training and had acquired many phonetic skills. They met regularly with the remedial reading teacher with whom they had worked intensively since first grade. After much effort, they could "decode," albeit slowly and painfully. What was so frustrating was their inability to put any of this training to use, their failure to progress to even the beginnings of fluent reading. . . . In spite of their hard-won "decoding skills," they couldn't so much as read a page of simple material to me. The attempt to do so was almost painful, a word-by-word struggle, long silences, eyes eventually drifting around the room in an attempt to escape the humiliation and frustration of the all too familiar, hated situation.

Such children need the opportunity to read in a nonthreatening situation, where they can gradually begin to chime in with another reader (a live reader or a record or tape). And they need the satisfaction of learning to read an entire story fluently and confidently, by themselves.

To be successful, a reading immersion program takes time and effort. Most of the experimental programs seem to have involved the child for about fifteen minutes each day, over a period of at least three or four months. Teaching time will of course vary according to the particular methods and materials used. But one thing is certain: in most cases, the results should be ample justification for the time and effort spent. Children become not only better able to read, but more willing to read. Indeed, many children have become downright eager to read as a result of such reading immersion.

This discussion provides only the broad outlines for a reading immersion program. Before initiating a program of their own, teachers would be well advised to consult such references as the following, each of which has some particular aspects or suggestions that might prove helpful.

READINGS FOR FURTHER EXPLORATION

Hoskisson, Kenneth, and Krohm, Bernadette. "Reading by Immersion: Assisted Reading." *Elementary English* 51 (September 1974): 832–836. Describes a reading immersion program used with a second grade class.

Chomsky, Carol. "After Decoding: What?" *Language Arts* 53 (March 1976): 288–296, 314. Describes a reading immersion program used with a group of eight-year-olds.

Heckleman, R. G. "A Neurological-Impress Method of Remedial-Reading Instruction." *Academic Therapy* 4 (Summer 1969): 277–282. Describes a program used with a group of children about to enter the seventh grade.

Hollingsworth, Paul M. "An Experimental Approach to the Impress Method of Teaching Reading." *The Reading Teacher* 31 (March 1978): 624–626. Instead of having a person read with the child as in Heckleman's method (see the preceding reference), Hollingsworth used a machine that would enable the child to hear, simultaneously, a tape recording and the child's own voice as he or she read along with the tape. The children in this study were upper elementary students.

Martin, Bill, Jr., and Brogan, Peggy. *Sounds of Language.* New York: Holt, Rinehart and Winston, 1972ff. Among these supplementary readers for K–8, the early readers are especially useful in a reading immersion program.

SUSTAINING SILENT READING

Once when I asked my young son what books he read in school, he replied "Oh, we just 'do' reading. You know, workbooks and stuff. We don't read books in school." Alas, the situation is not much better for older readers, at least not for those who are relatively nonproficient. They are kept so busy with exercises and the learning of rules that they are seldom given the opportunity to engage themselves with an entire story or other reading selection. Often they deal with nothing longer than a paragraph. This limits their reading in at least two significant ways: it provides little motivation for reading, and it provides little opportunity for building up enough context to use as a means of identifying words and getting meaning.

Students need not only numerous opportunities to read extensively *in the classroom*, but also the experience of practicing sustained silent reading. Parodoxically, some students will never come to see reading as anything but a chore, unless they are virtually forced to learn to read for their own purposes and their own pleasure.

Therefore, I would recommend that "sustained silent reading" (SSR) be one component of any reading program, from kindergarten through high school and beyond. Doubtless there must be many ways to provide for sustained silent reading. At the outset, however, it seems wise to learn from the experience of others. On the basis of his own experience and that of thousands of other teachers, Robert McCracken recommends that the following six rules be followed rigidly, until the habit of sustained silent reading is fully established (1971):

1. *Each student must read silently.* Prereaders and beginning readers may in fact read the pictures more than the words, but no one is allowed to get away with the claim "I can't."

2. *The teacher reads,* and permits no one to interrupt his or her reading. If there are any other adults in the classroom (teacher's aides, parents, or whoever), they too must read. The teacher and other adults set an example by becoming engrossed in something of interest. McCracken and McCracken (1978) have concluded that such modeling may be *the* most crucial element in a sustained silent reading program. If the adult(s) in the classroom do not read, the program is likely to fail.

3. *Each student selects a single book, magazine, or newspaper* and stays with that choice for an entire reading session. No changing of materials is permitted, because some students would spend more time switching materials than reading. In order for the program to be successful, however, there must be a wide range of mate-

rial from which to choose. McCracken warns that no student should be chided for reading an easy book. If a student is reluctant to choose, the teacher can select the book, require what is to be read, and perhaps even give the student questions to answer for homework. After that experience, most students will be glad to choose their own reading material.

4. *A timer is used* to signal the end of the sustained silent reading period. A wall clock will not work, because some students become clock watchers; and the teacher's watch will not work, because students will interrupt to ask if time is up. McCracken recommends that the teacher start by setting the timer for five to ten minutes, but encourage students to read longer if they wish. In his experience, almost all classes will sustain silent reading for twenty-five minutes or more within a week's time, if there are daily sessions.

5. *There are absolutely no reports or records of any kind.* Nothing should be required of the students except read-in itself, so that the nonproficient or reluctant readers will participate more readily. But by the second week of daily practice, the teacher can begin to encourage responses. Again, the teacher serves as a model: by commenting on something particularly interesting in his or her own reading, by reading aloud a passage that is especially well written, by commenting on an unusual word, and so forth. Through such indirect means, the teacher can encourage students to share what they have been reading.

6. *Begin with whole classes or even larger groups of students, heterogenously grouped.* McCracken warns that if the group is too small (say, ten or fewer), the students tend to interrupt each other with comments or requests for help. Also, it is wise to have a wide range of reading abilities in the group. If the reading group consists of just poorer readers, it may take three or four months to establish the habit of sustained silent reading.

A sustained silent reading program can be established not only in an elementary classroom or a secondary English or reading class, but in an entire elementary, junior high, or high school. In the case of an entire school, the program works best if the sustained silent reading is carried out at a different time of day throughout the week: first period on Monday, second period on Tuesday, and so forth. According to McCracken, many teachers have found success in requiring reading that is related to their content area. For example, the social studies teacher might require students to choose from among a number of relevant news magazines, biographies and autobiographies, historical novels, and so forth. Whether or not the reading is limited to a certain content area, a schoolwide program of sustained silent reading is certain to have many benefits.

McCracken suggests that the six rules not be relaxed or modified until all students have acquired the habit of sustaining their reading for at least thirty minutes. It takes about a month to get the habit well established.

The teacher does not need to wait that long, however, to begin encouraging students to share what they have read. Indeed, as suggested earlier, the teacher can begin to model such behavior by about the second week of the program. Even when the program is well established, it would be wise to accept McCracken and McCracken's advice: "we suggest that teachers require nothing of children after sustained silent reading that they do not do themselves willingly and naturally. Usually this eliminates writing book reports, making lists of unknown words, filling in worksheets of any type, or taking tests" (1978, p. 407). Such activities make reading a burden rather than a joy.

The following bibliography includes not only articles on sustained silent reading itself, but bibliographies that may help teachers and librarians or students themselves locate reading materials of interest.

READINGS FOR FURTHER EXPLORATION

McCracken, Robert A. "Initiating Sustained Silent Reading." *Journal of Reading* 14 (May 1971) : 521–524, 582–583. Includes McCracken's six basic rules for initiating a sustained silent reading program.
McCracken, Robert A., and McCracken, Marlene J. "Modeling Is the Key

to Sustained Silent Reading." *The Reading Teacher* 31 (January 1978): 406–408. Emphasizes the importance of modeling sustained silent reading.

McCracken, Robert A., and McCracken, Marlene J. *Reading Is Only the Tiger's Tail.* San Rafael, Calif.: Leswing Press, 1972. Provides some valuable suggestions for starting a SSR program in kindergarten classes (pp. 21–23).

Mason, George E., and Mize, John M. "Twenty-two Sets of Methods and Materials for Stimulating Teenage Reading." *Journal of Reading* 21 (May 1978): 735–741. Contains some good suggestions, as well as a useful list of sources, with addresses, where materials can be obtained.

Fader, Daniel N., and McNeil, Elton B. *Hooked on Books: Program and Proof.* New York: Berkley, 1968. For everyone who teaches at the secondary level (or otherwise), a program suggesting the importance of the total learning environment in encouraging young people to read.

Cianciolo, Patricia, et al. *Adventuring with Books: A Booklist for Pre-K–Grade 8.* New ed. Urbana, Ill.: National Council of Teachers of English, 1977. An excellent resource for students, teachers, and librarians. Organized partly by genre (folktales, fantasy, mystery, etc.) and partly by subject matter (conservation and ecology, aeronautics and space, etc.), with most entries annotated.

Walker, Jerry L., et al. *Your Reading: A Booklist for Junior High Students.* New ed. Urbana, Ill.: National Council of Teachers of English, 1975. Another excellent resource, with all entries annotated and grouped into more than forty headings that appeal to students.

Donelson, Kenneth, et al. *Books for You: A Booklist for Senior High Students.* New ed. Urbana, Ill.: National Council of Teachers of English, 1976. Excellent annotated bibliography grouping books into more than fifty categories of interest to students.

White, Marian E. *High Interest—Easy Reading: For Junior and Senior High School Students.* 2nd ed. New York: Citation Press, for the National Council of Teachers of English, 1972. Another annotated bibliography that can easily be used by students; includes mainly books popular with students who do not usually enjoy reading.

SHARING AND EXPERIENCING READING

How can we share and experience books? Let us count the ways . . . .

Happily, no one could possibly enumerate all the ways for making books meaningful and memorable. Even the media are varied and various. We can watch a film or a filmstrip version of a book; we can listen to a book on record or tape; or we can watch a live dramatization of all or part of a book. We can write alternative endings to stories, write letters to a favorite character, or write our own piece, using a literary selection (like a myth or a fable) as a model. We can pantomime some of the action in a story, move in accompaniment to a poem and background music, or put on a puppet show recreating all or part of a story. We can draw pictures of a favorite character in a story, sculpt characters or scenery out of clay, or paint a mural depicting the sequence of events from a story. We can make a film or slide show based upon a particular literary selection. We can draw maps, charts, and graphs to express and clarify our understanding of certain kinds of informational material. We can draw pictures or bake a cake to demonstrate the steps in a recipe. And so forth.

We need not and probably should not resort to the traditional book report. If records *must* be kept, the teacher can always ask students to make out an index card (using a specified format) for every book read. Another possibility is to have students describe the most interesting parts or characters of a book in a journal, or to discuss the most interesting ideas, if they have been reading nonfiction. But there are often more stimulating ways for individuals and groups of children to share books and to extend their appreciation for what they have read.

For convenience, I have talked about sharing "books." But of course students' reading can and should include a variety of materials: books, stories, articles, poems, and so forth. As mentioned earlier, some of the reading material may well stem from the students' own dictation or writing. This reading material too can be shared, perhaps through individually authored and class-authored "books."

Instead of trying to list all the myriad possibilities for making books and other reading materials meaningful, I have chosen to present two specific illustrations of how reading can be integrated with other aspects of the curriculum. It is often such integration that makes reading most meaningful and memorable.

Both illustrations indicate the kind of brainstorming that might occur before specific lesson plans are made. In these two cases the brainstorming was done by teachers, but it would ordinarily be best if students participated in both the initial listing of possible activities and the final selection of activities to be undertaken.

"Chicken Soup with Rice"

The first list of activities is designed to accompany Maurice Sendak's *Chicken Soup with Rice* (1962). As many elementary children and teachers know, this is a narrative poem in praise of chicken rice soup. For each month of the year, the child narrator of the poem has a unique way to enjoy his favorite dish.

With any given class, of course, the teacher would want to choose only a few activities. The following were enumerated in collaboration with three elementary teachers: Katy Hill, Mary Singleton, and Priscilla Weaver. The activities are grouped into various areas of focus: oral activities and dramatization, music and art, drawing and writing, math and science, and listening and reading strategies. The book and most of these activities are especially suitable for children at the early elementary level.

Focus on Oral Activities and Dramatization

Read the poem several times until children are able to join in the refrain.

Have different children read the "new" part for each month, while all join in the refrain.

Have children pantomime the actions as someone reads the stanza for one or more of the months (January, March, May, July, or September might work well). Or have a child pantomime whatever stanza he or she chooses, and let the class guess which stanza is being pantomimed.

Have children do an oral interpretation of the stanza for one or more of the months (January, March, or November might work well).

Focus on Music and Art

Play the record of *Chicken Soup with Rice* (if you can locate a copy; it is no longer available from Scholastic). Alternatively, you might let the children themselves set the poem to music. They can then sing the poem or play it on bells, water glasses, or whatever.

Have children clap the rhythm of the poem or accompany it with rhythm instruments (maracas, castanets, tambourines, or whatever).

Have children make a pictorial calendar or time line showing them enjoying *their* favorite food during each month of the year.

Have children make mosaics out of rice. (Food coloring can be used to color the rice.)

Focus on Drawing and Writing

Have children draw a picture of their favorite food and dictate or write a caption under it (for younger children) or write a story or poem about it (for older or more capable writers).

Write a class poem beginning "I like . . . ." Children could be asked to supply the names of two or three foods that they particularly like. After the initial list is made, perhaps teacher and children can rearrange the items so that at least some lines are alliterative (*"h*ot dogs and *h*amburgers"). The children then might add adjectives, perhaps adjectives that also alliterate. It might even be fun to personify some of the foods (*"h*appy *h*ot dogs and *h*ungry *h*amburgers").

Have children write a poem imitating one of the stanzas of *Chicken Soup with Rice* (for example, the stanza for the month of December).

Have children write a poem about their favorite season. Younger or less experienced writers could be presented with a frame, such as "I like spring because . . . ."

Give the children a list of the ingredients for chicken soup with rice, and have the children write out the steps in the process of making the soup. Alternatively, one might give the children a scrambled list of the steps involved, and have the children put the steps in logical sequence. They could also make a list of the utensils, equipment, and supplies needed. If possible, allow the children to make and serve chicken rice soup in the classroom. (See the section on math and science.)

Focus on Math and Science

Have children study length, using rice. How many grains of rice does it take to measure out one centimeter? One decimeter? One meter?

Have children study area, using rice. How many grains of rice does it take to cover a postage stamp? A postcard?

Have children explore conservation of quantity, using rice instead of liquids. For example, have children measure a cup of rice into two identical containers, then empty the rice from one of the containers into a taller and thinner (or shorter and fatter) container. Do the children realize that the amount of rice is still equal in the two containers?

Have children investigate the principles of a balance scale by measuring rice.

Have children find and compare recipes for chicken rice soup. Which recipe will make the thickest soup, the one with the higher concentration of solids? Which will make the thinnest soup? (One possibility is one-half cup rice for every four cups of chicken broth.)

Have young children count out cups, spoons, napkins, and crackers for serving chicken rice soup, in order to help them attain or solidify the concept of one-to-one correspondence (one cup or whatever for each person).

Have young children measure the water or bouillon for the soup. Have them measure the rice, too, noting how the rice expands and becomes soft after cooking.

Give older children a list of the ingredients for making a relatively small amount of chicken rice soup, and have them determine how much of each ingredient they will need in order to make a serving of a given size for everyone in their class.

Have older children determine which is more economical for making chicken rice soup: canned chicken broth or instant chicken bouillon.

Have children study rice growing, poultry raising, nutrition.

Focus on Social Studies

Have children investigate the foods associated with a certain ethnic group or nationality; you might even focus on soups that are popular with a certain group. If possible, have these foods prepared or at least served in the classroom. (See the section on writing and the section on math and science.)

Have children study how the American Indians prepared wild rice. If possible, have various rice dishes, representing different cultures, prepared or at least served in the classroom.

Have children use a map or atlas to locate the places named in *Chicken Soup with Rice* (Spain, Bombay, the Nile). Children could then study the cultures of these places, perhaps their food specialties in particular.

Focus on Listening/Reading Strategies

Read the selection aloud and have children supply rhyme words (the January, March, and December stanzas would work well for this).

Have children do a cloze exercise, possibly with the first letter of the word supplied. (The May, June, and July stanzas might be good choices for omitting every fifth word, beginning with **best** in line two of the May stanza.)

Have children do syntactic substitution, expansion, reduction, or rearrangement activities (noting, in the process, how the poetry of the original is usually mangled).

Have children predict what the narrator will do with chicken rice soup in the month of October and in the month of December.

"Ethan Frome"

The following activities were designed by Victoria Pachulski, who teaches both remedial reading and literature at the high school level. In order to help certain readers develop good reading strategies and at the same time learn to enjoy good literature, she devised a variety of activities to use with Edith Wharton's *Ethan Frome* (1911). Pachulski explains her reasons for selecting this particular novel:

I personally enjoyed it as a high school junior; the plot of the story lends itself, very well, to the predicting process; the theme of *Ethan Frome* is one that is easily understood by the average sixteen year old; it relies on contemporary, fairly standard, language usage; and the setting of the story is one of a stark, New England farm community, not unlike the community in which the students selected for this project live.[4]

In addition to analyzing the readers' miscues and preparing appropriate strategy lessons, Pachulski outlined the following set of possible activities for helping these readers experience and appreciate *Ethan Frome*.

Language

Discuss how the language in *Ethan Frome* differs from "our" language. Specific examples should be presented by both teacher and students. The sentences should be read aloud by several students, and analyzed as to their effectiveness. The group should discuss *why* the language of *Ethan Frome* is somewhat different from our language.

Students should keep individual journals, recording any "odd" language structure they come across. With the teacher's help if necessary, these phrases should then be rewritten so that they make sense to the individual student.

Students could write the continuing "saga" of *Ethan Frome* in comic book form, using language typical of the original.

Using actual passages from the novel, the teacher could prepare sentence-combining activities.

Students could read aloud various poems written by New Englanders of the period. The language as well as the typical themes could be discussed.

Isolate one bulletin board in the room as the "Write-On" board. When students encounter words that are characteristic of the writer, the novel, the characters, or the setting, let them go to the board and write the word on an appropriate sheet of paper. "Ethan graffiti" may soon begin to appear.

---

[4] "Teaching a Novel by Strengthening Student Predicting Abilities" (unpublished paper, Western Michigan University, 1978).

Culture, Setting

Take time to examine maps of Massachusetts. Compare the geographical area to that of the students.

Explore farming techniques of the period represented in *Ethan Frome*. Students could compare their findings with modern methods of farming.

Have students who are interested in history or antiques prepare a presentation dealing with the average farm home of a century ago.

Display and discuss a series of reproductions of Andrew Wyeth paintings of New England. Assign a paper titled "Does Wyeth Know Starkfield?"

Discuss the differences in morals and family life, then and now.

Character, Plot

Ask a student who is interested in art to attempt portraits of the various characters. Does the rest of the class agree with the physical characteristics represented?

Have students keep a journal of their personal reactions to the emotional problems that Ethan, Mattie, and Zeena face.

Assign a "How would *you* feel" paper, with Ethan's desperation as the starting point.

Have students write a "collage" poem [like those earlier in this chapter], for one of the characters in the novel.

Have students conduct "character interviews" in which one student acts as a reporter, while another acts as a character from the book. The interviewer should ask some questions dealing with the character's feelings about the setting, other characters, the character's own past (students can invent these "pasts"), and the character's expectations for the future.

Designate several places in the book where students are to stop reading and predict what is coming next. Once the actual events have been discovered, compare the predictions with the way the author preferred things to happen.

Do a daily news broadcast, near the end of the hour, reporting on the latest events in the book. One student can present the news update, while another reviews the particular chapter, much as a critic would review an entire book or film.

Emphasis on Reading

Read aloud to the students, demonstrating that you enjoy reading. Make reading a treat for them too.

Have students conduct an experiment to see whether words are easier to identify in isolation or in context. Students can work in pairs.

Employ the cloze procedure, using paragraphs from the beginning of each chapter. As students progress through the book, this activity should become easier.

Have students practice reading, orally, a favorite section from the novel, then record their readings. Play the tape at the beginning and end of each class period, as students are getting situated or preparing to leave.

Have students read sections of the book to music and slides of New England. This works well with *Ethan Frome* because there are so many descriptive passages.

Produce a permanent tape of the novel being read by various students and present it to the school's media center.

READINGS FOR FURTHER EXPLORATION

Heinig, Ruth Beall. "Creative Drama and the Language Arts." In *The Language Arts Teacher in Action*, edited by Constance Weaver and Rollin Douma, pp. 26–36. Originally published at Western Michigan University in 1977, the monograph is available from the National Council of Teachers of English. In her comprehensive and excellent article, Heinig suggests various ways of integrating literature and creative drama.

Blatt, Gloria T., and Cunningham, Jean. "Movement: A Creative Approach to Poetry." *Elementary School Journal* 75 (May 1975) : 490–500. Suggests a variety of activities to help students experience poetry.

Platt, Penny. "Grapho-linguistics: Children's Drawings in Relation to Reading and Writing Skills." *The Reading Teacher* 31 (December 1977) : 262–268. Suggests how to help young children move from drawing into writing and reading.

Coody, Betty. *Using Literature with Young Children*. Dubuque, Iowa: Wm. C. Brown, 1973. A book filled with ideas for integrating literature into the total curriculum. Focuses on the early elementary child (and younger).

Cullinan, Bernice E., and Carmichael, Carolyn W., eds. *Literature and Young Children.* Urbana, Ill.: National Council of Teachers of English, 1977. Provides excellent suggestions for integrating literature with the total elementary curriculum.

Sebesta, Sam Leaton, and Iverson, William J. *Literature for Thursday's Child.* Chicago: Science Research Associates, 1975. Contains many valuable suggestions for exploring and experiencing literature in the elementary classroom.

Somers, Albert B., and Worthington, Janet Evans. *Response Guides for Teaching Children's Books.* Urbana, Ill.: National Council of Teachers of English, 1979. Provides specific suggestions for teaching twenty-seven well-known children's books, from the picture book to the junior novel.

READING FOR A SPECIFIC PURPOSE

It is commonplace to say that we should vary our reading rate and approach, depending on what kind of material we are reading. We should not read poetry the same way we read novels and short stories, nor should we read nonfiction the same way we read fiction. We should not read textbooks the same way we read newspapers, magazines, and such. Students, then, need to learn to vary their reading rate and approach in accordance with what they are reading. But it is perhaps even more important for students to learn to vary their overall reading strategy in accordance with their specific purposes for reading. The following activities should help you understand this statement.

Activity 1. The following is an excerpt from an article discussing the Supreme Court's decision in the case of Allan Bakke versus the University of California. Read this excerpt specifically to find out whether or not the Court ordered the university to admit Bakke to its medical school. Then read the excerpt again, this time specifically to see whether or not racial quotas are a permissible means of trying to provide equal opportunities for minority group Americans.

But Affirmative Action Stands

**Supreme Court
rules for Bakke**

WASHINGTON (AP) — The Supreme Court today ordered a California medical school to admit Allan Bakke, ruling that he had suffered illegal discrimination because he is white, but said that race can be taken into account in future college admissions programs.

In a 5–4 decision, the court held that the University of California's medical school at Davis had gone too far in considering race when it refused to admit Bakke. But it held that affirmative-action programs intended to benefit minority applicants can properly be a factor in decisions on admitting students.

Bakke successfully sued the university after his application to the university's medical school at Davis was rejected in 1973 and 1974.

He charged that the medical school's special admissions program which reserved 16 of the 100 openings in each entering class for "disadvantaged" students was really only an impermissible racial quota.

Under it, Bakke charged, less academically qualified blacks, Hispanics and Asian-Americans were admitted ahead of him.

The Supreme Court interpreted the Civil Rights Act of 1964 to say that while some race-conscious programs are valid, the program that kept Bakke out of medical school crossed the line into illegal racial discrimination.

Bakke, a 38-year-old civil engineer who lives in Sunnyvale, Calif., and works for the nation's space agency at the Ames Research Center in nearby Palo Alto, never had to prove that he would have been admitted if the school had not had a special admissions program.

The university conceded that it could not prove Bakke would have been excluded if the program had not existed.[5]

---

[5] This excerpt is from the *Kalamazoo Gazette*, June 28, 1978, p. A-1.

How far did you have to read to find out if the Supreme Court ordered that Bakke be admitted to the university's medical school? How did you go about determining whether or not racial quotas are permissible in trying to provide for racial equality?

Activity 2. The next excerpt is from some of my "escape" reading: Anya Seton's *Devil Water* (1962, pp. 515–516). Read specifically to see whether Rob got to his wife Jenny in time to be with her when her father, Charles, was executed. Then read the excerpt again, so that you could explain to someone else how persons of nobility were executed in the middle of the eighteenth century in England.

Again Rob pushed and shoved, heedless of the curses and angry looks he produced. Still he did not quite reach Jenny.

Charles paid the executioner ten guineas, saying that he was a poor man, regretted there wasn't more, and trusted that the axe was sharp. The coffin, covered with black velvet, stood open and ready on the scaffold. The sheriffs stood beside it.

Charles held up his hand almost as though in blessing, and he called out in ringing tones, "I'll not weary you all by a harangue. I've but one thing to say—I die a true, obedient, and humble son of the Catholic Apostolic Church, in perfect charity with all mankind, and a true well wisher to my dear country that can never be happy without doing justice to the best and most injured of kings —James the Third. I die with sentiments of gratitude, respect, and love also for the King of France—Louis the well-beloved . . . I recommend to His Majesty my dear family. I heartily repent of all my sins, and have a firm confidence to obtain pardon from Almighty God, through the merits of His blessed Son, Christ Jesus our Lord, to whom I recommend my soul."

Charles kneeled down beside the block in prayer; all those on the scaffold, including the executioner, kneeled too. It was while Charles rose and the two warders started to divest him of his hat, wig, coat, and waistcoat that Rob finally reached Jenny.

She did not see him. Her face was a silver mask. Her breathing was like the tearing of silk. Her two hands were clamped tight around her throat, her unwinking eyes stared at the scaffold while the executioner rolled down the collar of Charles's shirt.

Rob jumped to the step beside her. He grasped her head in his arm, his hand on her cheek, he forced her face against his shoulder.

"You shall *not* look!" he cried fiercely, and held her face pressed downward on his shoulder.

She made no sound. She went limp against him, nor tried to move.

It was Rob who watched the execution of Charles Radcliffe. He saw Charles cross himself and kneel down with composure, stretching his bare neck across the block. He saw Charles's hand move in the signal. He saw the flashing of the axe under the sunlight as it descended. He saw the fountain spurt of crimson blood, the undertakers running with a red baize cloth to catch the head. He saw the still-quivering trunk stowed in the waiting coffin, the head also carried to the coffin. He saw the hearse draw up beside the scaffold and receive the coffin. The Horse Guards parted to let the hearse through, and it drove away towards Great Tower Street.

How did you go about learning what happened to Rob and Jenny? How did you go about learning and remembering enough details so that you could describe a typical execution?

Activity 3. The following passage is from Yetta Goodman's "Developing Reading Proficiency" (1976, p. 117). Read to see who omits more function words, good readers or poor readers. Next, read to see how omission miscues typically change as a reader becomes more proficient. Then, more generally, read to learn as much as you can from the passage.

As a reader gets older but has not developed very much proficiency, the percentage of omission miscues will decrease as she plods along, reading each word, producing substitution miscues rather than omissions. As a reader develops proficiency, she tends to omit known words which are not significant to the meaning. These may be omissions of function words like *the* or *and* between two independent clauses. Or these may be omissions of redundant features. For example, in some early reading materials, it is not uncommon for a phrase like *old apple tree* to be repeated five or six times. After the initial reading of the phrase, the reader knows the description of the tree and retains this information even if at subsequent readings she omits *old* or *apple* or both. Phrases like *he said* or *John said* are often omitted by proficient readers once the reader knows who is carrying on the dialogue in the story. The story retellings often give added evidence that the readers who are developing proficiency retain meaning even when they omit such words or phrases.

How did you go about reading the passage each time? What did you learn?

In the foregoing activities, strategies will have differed from one individual to another. But the effective *and efficient* reader will in some cases have adopted strategies for scanning and skimming. When looking for particular information, one such strategy is to look initially just at the first sentence of each paragraph. Another strategy is to look for key words and phrases: in the preceding activities, words and phrases like **medical school, quota, Rob, Jenny, function word**, and **omission**(s). Such strategies help a reader determine which part(s) of a text need to be read more carefully in order to find the desired information.

Our overall approach also depends, to some extent, on what we intend to *do* with information and ideas once they have been located. Do we merely want to know the Supreme Court's decision about admitting Bakke to the University of California's medical school, or do we want to understand the Court's position and be able to explain its reasoning? Do we merely want to experience what it might have been like to be executed in mid-eighteenth-century England? Or do we want to master the details well enough to explain the rites to someone else? Do we merely want to comprehend how omission miscues change with increased reading proficiency, or do we want to be able to apply this understanding in some way? And if the latter, then which details do we need to extract from the passage? And how will we store these details: in our heads, on note cards, or what?

Even with fiction, then, there is no single way to read. If we are reading to appreciate an author's style and skill, we may read every word, savoring every detail. But if we are reading mainly to follow the plot or to understand the character development or the theme, we may read more superficially, skipping over some of the details. Furthermore, our approach will depend to some extent on our external reasons for reading: reading for sheer personal enjoyment is one thing, whereas reading to take a test is something else indeed.

With nonfiction, our approaches may be even more varied. Again, however, our general reading strategy should vary according to the particular type of material read, the particular kinds of information or understanding we want to gain from the material, and how we want to use the knowledge gained. Sometimes we merely want to satisfy our curiosity about something—like the Bakke case. Sometimes we want to gain information for practical ends: buying a car, solving our personal problems, shopping for the best bargains at the supermarket. And at other times, we might even want to become an expert on a subject.

Another factor influencing our reading strategy is the relevant knowledge and experience we bring to the reading task. In contrast to the information explicit and implicit in the text itself, this is information which comes from within the reader. Such prior knowledge is what Pearson and Johnson (1978) call scriptally implicit information. That is, our information about various topics is organized into what might be called mental "scripts."

Various kinds of predicting activities are one way to help students learn to use their scriptally implicit knowledge as they read. If they have heard or read a number of folktales, for example, students will often be able to predict many of the events in patterned stories like "The Fisherman and His Wife," where the wife repeatedly demands more and more power, accompanied by bigger and better dwellings. But what of nonfiction, perhaps the kinds of informational selections found in social studies or science textbooks? How can students learn to "predict" with such materials?

One of the best approaches is to help students begin by taking stock of what they already know. This approach is illustrated by the following hypothetical discussion, intended to prepare students to read a selection about the construction of the first continental railroad (Pearson and Johnson, 1978, pp. 189–191): [6]

Instructor: Tell me what you know about the Union Pacific Railroad. (No response.) Well, when was it built? (No response.) Before the Civil War? After? During?

Student 1: Before!

Student 2: After!

Instructor: Now, why do you say before?

Student 1: Just seems right to me. Maybe it had something to do with the Gold Rush?

Student 2: No, it was after!

Instructor: You're sure about that?

Student 2: Pretty sure. There's something about a Golden Spike out West in Utah, or Nevada, or Wyoming, and that country wasn't even settled by the time of the Civil War.

Instructor: Didn't they have railroads before the Civil War?

---

[6] Pearson and Johnson are in turn indebted to W. Dorsey Hammond of Oakland University, who is indebted to Russell Stauffer for the example.

Student 3: Sure the railroads came as early as 1820 or 1830. Right after the steam engine.

Student 4: But they were mostly in the Eastern United States.

Instructor: So no one is sure when it was built. Anyone want to guess about a date (several are offered ranging from 1840 to 1910)? Okay, where did it start and where did it end? (No responses.) Let me draw a map (draws sketchy map of the U.S.). Did it start over here on the East Coast, say Pittsburgh? Did it start up here, say Minneapolis? Did it start here, say St. Louis? Where?

Student 4: I think it was St. Joseph. Something started there.

Student 5: Omaha sounds right to me.

Student 3: St. Louis rings a bell for me.

Instructor: (Who has been jotting down guesses all along.) Well, we have three candidates. I'm not sure either. But we'll find out. Where did it end? Here, in Los Angeles? Here, in San Francisco? Here, in Seattle? Here, in Utah? Where?

Student 6: San Francisco, because Los Angeles was just a small town then.

Student 7: I seem to remember that it was not one railroad but two that built the first transcontinental railroad.

Student 8: That's right. It was a contest.

Instructor: So, when the railroad across the country was built it wasn't built from East to West?

Student 8: No, it wasn't! One company started from the East and the other started from the West.

Instructor: I think you're right. The first transcontinental railroad was built from both ends toward the middle. What do you need to build a railroad?

Student 5: Rails.

Student 4: Railroad ties.

Student 1: Workers.

Instructor: Okay. For the company that went from East to West, I can see how they got their materials.

Student 3: Yeah, they just loaded them onto railroad cars and hauled them to the end of the line.

Instructor: But how did they get their materials on the West Coast?

Student 5: Same way.

Student 7: Not then. No iron ore out there. But they could get ties.

Instructor: I think you're right. I think Pittsburgh was the center of steel production then. It still is, I guess. Well, let's assume they had to transport the rails. How could they do it? Overland Stage?

Student 6: No! Rails would have been too heavy for the wagons. And if they only took one or two it would have taken forever to haul the rails.

Instructor: Pony Express?

Student 6: No! By boat.

Instructor: (Pointing to map.) You mean they went from Pittsburgh to New York then around through the Panama Canal and up to San Francisco? (lots of nos.) Why not, that's about the shortest way.

Student 3: The Panama Canal wasn't built yet. They had to go around South America.

Instructor: How do you know that? We haven't even established when the railroad was built. Maybe the Panama Canal was already finished.

Student 4: No!

Instructor: Did they have to go from Pittsburgh to New York to get a ship? Could they have gone another way?

Student 5: Maybe they went by barge down the Ohio River to the Mississippi, then to New Orleans.

Instructor: Could they? Does the Ohio River go through Pittsburgh?

Student 6: I'm not sure but I bet some river did that eventually went into the Mississippi.

Instructor: What about the ties? Do you think they just got those out in California and Nevada as they went along? Or do you think they hauled those from the Midwest or the East?

Student 7: There's lots of timber in California, in the mountains.

Instructor: But is it the right kind? Can you make ties out of redwood or pine or fir?

Student 4: You could probably use fir, but not redwood or pine. They're too soft.

Instructor: I'm not sure myself. As a matter of fact, I'm not sure about much of this at all. Let's just review what we're not sure about at this point. (Instructor jots down the following points.) When was it built? Where did it start? Where did it end? Where and how did they get the rails and ties? Oh, one other thing—who were the workers?

Student 9: Coolies. Chinese coolies.

Student 7: On the West Coast. But from the East it was the Irish.

Instructor: Why the Irish and the Chinese?

Student 9: They brought in the Chinese just to work on the railroad because they were cheap.

Student 7: The Irish were new immigrants. They were cheap, too. It was the only kind of job they could get. They were discriminated against then.

Instructor: That's one more thing to look for—who built the railroad? And there's one other thing that's always puzzled me. Why did they build it from both ends toward the middle? It would seem to me to make more sense just

to go from the East to the West. Then they wouldn't have
had to worry about transporting materials by boat or
whatever. Well, that's enough to look for. Here's an article
about the railroad. Let's read it to see whether or not we
were right about any of this.

A discussion like the one just quoted serves several valuable
functions. It demonstrates to students that they already
know something about the topic they are going to read about.
Even with relatively unfamiliar material, the teacher can
usually find some way of relating the unknown to something
already known. Moreover, such a discussion enables students
to pool their prior knowledge, their mental "scripts" for a
topic. In addition, such discussion arouses students' curiosity and encourages them to set *their own purposes* for
reading.

Such previewing is part of the Directed Reading-Thinking
Activity (DRTA) advocated by Russell Stauffer; see, for
example, Stauffer (1960) and Stauffer and Cramer (1968).
Basically this approach involves predicting what will come
next and citing evidence to justify one's predictions; reading
to confirm, reject, or modify predictions; making and justi-
fying new predictions; and so forth. The approach is applicable at all grade levels and can be adapted for either fiction
or nonfiction.

For dealing with the kinds of informational material
typically found in textbooks, the so-called SQ3R approach is
valuable. The abbreviation stands for the steps in the procedure: *survey, question, read, recite, review.* The method
was originated by Francis Robinson, who describes the steps
as follows (Robinson 1962, pp. 31–32):

SURVEY   1. Glance over the headings in the chapter to
see the main points which will be developed.
Also read the final summary paragraph if
the chapter has one. This survey should not
take more than a minute and will show the
three to six core ideas around which the discussion will cluster. This orientation will
help you organize the ideas as you read
them later.

QUESTION 2. Now begin to work. Turn the first heading into a question. This will arouse your curiosity and so increase comprehension. It will bring to mind information already known, thus helping you to understand that section more quickly. And the question will make important points stand out while explanatory detail is recognized as such. Turning a heading into a question can be done instantly upon reading the heading, but it demands a conscious effort on the part of the reader to make this a query for which he must read to find the answer.

READ 3. Read to answer that question, i.e., to the end of the first headed section. This is not a passive plodding along each line, but an active search for the answer.

RECITE 4. Having read the first section, look away from the book and try briefly to recite the answer to your question. Use your own words and include an example. If you can do this you know what is in the book; if you can't, glance over the section again. An excellent way to do this reciting from memory is to jot down cue phrases in outline form on a sheet of paper. Make these notes very brief!

Now repeat steps 2, 3, and 4 on each subsequent headed section. That is, turn the next heading into a question, read to answer that question, and recite the answer by jotting down cue phrases in your outline. Read in this way until the entire lesson is completed.

REVIEW 5. When the lesson has thus been completely read, look over your notes to get a bird's-eye view of the points and their relationship and check your memory as to the content by reciting on the major subpoints under each heading. This checking of memory can

be done by covering up the notes and trying
to recall the main points. Then expose each
major point and try to recall the subpoints
listed under it.

In discussing further this approach to dealing with textbooks, Robinson warns (pp. 34–35):

Habits from reading fiction often make textbook reading
difficult, for it has been found that most people read fiction
in order to forget their troubles and not to remember
what is in the book. Such an attitude of comprehending
for the moment, when carried over into textbook reading,
gives rise to a delusion that since the ideas are comprehended as they are read they will, of course, be remembered and unconsciously organized as answers to questions. This is far from the truth. Reading textbooks is
work; the reader must know what he is looking for, look
for it, and then organize his thoughts on the topic he has
been reading.

The SQ3R approach, then, is a method for going beyond surface structure to deep structure, a method for *studying*
informational material. The method is applicable at all grade
levels and can be modified for use in virtually any content
area.

A comprehensive reading program should help students
learn to adjust their approach to the materials read and to
their immediate and ultimate purposes for reading. They
need to learn to skim a novel just to follow the plot, if they
should so choose. They need to learn to gain vital information from the day-to-day materials in their environment:
newspapers, driver's manuals, cookbooks, instruction leaf-
lets, and so forth. And they need to learn how to search for
information in textbooks, encyclopedias, and other resources: how to use a table of contents and an index, how
to select relevant parts of a reference by using chapter titles
and section headings, how to skim sections and paragraphs
to find needed information, and so forth.

Obviously not all of these techniques can be taught at
once, nor should they be. The emphasis depends upon such

factors as the age of the students, their reading ability, and their particular interests and concerns. Ideally, there would be a systematic, schoolwide plan for helping students learn a variety of approaches for dealing with literature, newspapers and magazines, content area textbooks, and so forth. In the absence of such a plan, the individual teacher can at least help students learn to adjust their approach in dealing with some of the kinds of materials they might be expected to read at that particular time in their life.

Most important is the setting of purposes and goals. Every time the student gets ready to read something, he or she should mentally ask such questions as "Why am I reading this?" "What do I already know about this topic and/or this kind of reading selection?" "What kinds of experience/information/ideas do I expect to gain?" "What am I going to do with the knowledge gained?" Such introspection will help students learn to read *for a purpose*, and this in turn will make their reading more effective and efficient.

READINGS FOR FURTHER EXPLORATION

Farnes, N. C. *Reading Purposes, Comprehension and the Use of Context.* Bletchley, Buckinghamshire, England: The Open University Press, 1973. The unit on reading purposes and comprehension demonstrates in detail how a reader's purpose(s) can be used first to judge the relevance of material, then as a guide to handling relevant material. It emphasizes gathering information for a multifaceted school project.

Stauffer, Russell G., and Cramer, Ronald. *Teaching Critical Reading at the Primary Level.* Newark, Del.: International Reading Association, 1968. This little booklet emphasizes the development of purposes for reading, as well as the development of critical thinking and reading habits. The approach advocated is the DRTA, Stauffer's "Directed Reading-Thinking Activity."

Robinson, Francis P. *Effective Reading.* New York: Harper and Brothers, 1962. Presents the author's well-known SQ3R study method.

READING AND THE TOTAL CURRICULUM

We have all known students who did well in one curricular area, but not so well in others. Nevertheless, there seems to be a strong correlation between reading ability and achievement in other areas, particularly in other aspects of the language arts. Time and time again, research has uncovered such parallels. Perhaps most impressive is Walter Loban's thirteen-year study of 211 children from a variety of socioeconomic backgrounds. Loban investigated the students' progress each year, from kindergarten through twelfth grade. Each year, the teachers were asked to rate every student on a number of language factors. In the primary grades, teachers assessed just the children's oral language skills (listening and speaking). Beginning in grade four, the teachers also rated the quality of the students' writing, and their skill and proficiency in reading. The ratings were averaged in order to select the thirty-five most proficient and the thirty-five least proficient language users (Loban 1976, p. 5).

Over the thirteen years of the study, Loban found an amazingly consistent correlation between the teachers' subjective ratings and various objective measures of language facility. The group rated high over these thirteen years exhibited more language complexity and greater use of the resources of language. In measure after measure, the students whose language power impressed numerous teachers are the ones who showed the following characteristics (pp. 88–89):[7]

1. Longer communication units (that is, longer grammatical sentences)
2. Greater elaboration of subject and predicate
3. More embedding in transformational grammar, especially multibase deletion transformations
4. Greater use of adjectival dependent clauses
5. More use of dependent clauses of all kinds
6. Greater variety and depth of vocabulary
7. Better control of mazes (that is, proportionately fewer

[7] Unfortunately, the students' language was not analyzed according to the norms for their own dialect, whatever it might have been. Thus some students' "language power" was doubtless underrated.

hesitations, language tangles, and unnecessary, unintended repetitions in speech)

8. Higher scores on tests of reading ability
9. Higher scores on tests of listening
10. Increasing skill with connectors (**unless, although,** etc.)
11. Greater use of tentativeness: supposition, hypotheses, conjecture, conditional statements

Even though some of the terminology may not be clear, the list is impressive. Again and again, those who excel in one aspect of language have been found to excel in others. Indeed, "those superior in oral language in kindergarten and grade one *before they learned to read and write* are the very ones who excel in reading and writing by the time they are in grade six" (p. 71).

Of course correlation is not the same as cause, and we cannot merely assume, for example, that an extensive reading program will improve students' writing, or vice versa. However, Loban's study does strongly suggest that learning is an integrated whole. Hence it seems wise not to teach reading in isolation from the rest of the curriculum. Learning to read is inseparable from reading to learn. To make reading meaningful, we must make it an integral part of the total curriculum, a vital part of students' lives. Thus are we most likely to see the "miracle" of reading happen.

ACTIVITIES AND PROJECTS FOR FURTHER EXPLORATION

1. Make a list of at least ten creative ways for a student to "report" on something he or she has read.
2. As a prelude to establishing your own comprehensive reading program, do one or more of the following. In each case, plan for a specific grade or range of grade levels.
   a. Investigate the many ways for helping students make their own books. Try some yourself.
   b. Prepare an annotated bibliography of record-and-book and cassette-and-book combinations. If the resources for your

specific grade level(s) seem rather slim, choose materials that you yourself might tape.

c. Brainstorm on the many activities that might evolve from a particular reading selection. Consider a variety of curricular areas in your plans.

d. Prepare an annotated bibliography of the fifty paperbacks you would most like to have in your classroom.

e. Prepare a set of materials and activities for helping students learn to read for specific purposes.

3. Outline a comprehensive reading program for your own classroom. Ideally, you should at least begin to think about the management of time and resources. Who can you get to help with various parts of the reading program: a reading specialist, an aide, parents or other adults in the community, older students, your own students? When and how will you assess each individual's reading strengths, weaknesses, and instructional needs? When and how can you provide for reading strategy lessons and the other kinds of experiences that some or all readers may need? When and how can you integrate reading with other areas of the curriculum?

READINGS FOR FURTHER EXPLORATION

Tiedt, Iris M. *Reading Strategies: Activities to Stimulate Slow and Reluctant Readers.* San Jose, Calif.: Contemporary Press, 1976. An interesting variety of activities for elementary students in particular, though many are suitable for readers at all levels of proficiency.

Lee, Dorris M., and Rubin, Joseph B. *Children and Language: Reading and Writing, Talking and Listening.* Belmont, Calif.: Wadsworth, 1979. Suggests how to build a language arts curriculum based on an understanding of children's cognitive and linguistic development and upon an understanding of the language processes (reading, writing, talking, and listening).

Aaron, I. E. et al. *Reading Unlimited: Scott, Foresman Systems, Revised.* Glenview, Ill.: Scott, Foresman, 1976. A basal reading series for grades K–8 reflecting, more than most others, a psycholinguistic orientation.

Allinson, Alec; Allinson, Beverley; and McInnes, John. *Bowmar Language Stimulus Program.* Glendale, Calif.: Bowmar, 1974. An interesting and integrative language arts program for approximately grades 3 through 6.

Martin, Bill, Jr., and Brogan, Peggy. *The Sounds of Language.* 2nd ed. New York: Holt, Rinehart and Winston, 1972 ff. A supplemental reading series for grades K–8, stressing the integration of various aspects of language.

Moffett, James, et al. *Interaction: A Student-Centered Language Arts and Reading Program.* Boston: Houghton Mifflin, 1973. An integrative program for grades K–12.

appendix
a brief introduction to english grammar

The grammar of a language is like a network or web, with everything related to something else. It is nearly impossible to define one grammatical term without reference to others. For this reason, I have chosen to provide not just a glossary of grammatical terms, but an appendix showing the inter-relations among the terms.

Most of these terms are used in describing surface structure rather than deep structure. Hence this appendix deals mainly with the terms and definitions of traditional school-book grammarians, made more precise through the insights of structural linguists. The discussion deals much less with the insights of the transformationalists, simply because their terms and insights have already been discussed more thoroughly, in chapter 2.

The topics covered here are: 1) the clause and the sentence; 2) content words and function words; 3) grammatical endings; 4) nouns, pronouns, and noun determiners; 5) verbs and their auxiliaries; 6) adjectives; 7) adverbs; 8) clauses and their related function words; and 9) word order and basic sentence patterns. Much of the material is taken nearly verbatim from my book *Grammar for Teachers: Perspectives and Definitions* (1979), which discusses the transformationalists' ideas and insights in much more detail.

THE CLAUSE AND THE SENTENCE

The clause and the sentence are our basic units of expression, the primary vehicles for communicating ideas. We will discuss first the clause, and then the sentence.

In its simplest form, a *clause* consists of a *noun-part* fol-

296

lowed by a *verb-part*. Some nouns are proper names, like **Bob, Joe,** or **Mr. Evans.** Others are pronouns, like **I, you, they, someone, nothing.** Most other kinds of nouns can occur after **the: the boy, the street, the dog, the idea.** Usually the most basic form of a verb can occur after **can: can sleep, can stay, can dance, can work.** Putting such noun-parts and verb-parts together, we can create simple clauses like the following:

> the boy can sleep
> the street can stay
> the dog can dance
> the idea can work

Of course the noun-part and the verb-part may be much more complicated, but these are the two basic parts of a clause. The noun-part is known as the *subject*. The verb-part is known as the *predicate*.

No matter how complicated, the subject part usually has a single "head" noun, also known as the *simple subject*. The predicate part will have a single "head" verb, also known as the *main verb* or the *simple predicate*. In the clauses below, the simple subject and the simple predicate (main verb) are boldfaced:

Subject Part	*Predicate Part*
the **boy**	can **sleep**
the **street**	can **stay**
the **dog**	can **dance**
the **idea**	can **work**

The most basic parts of any clause are the simple subject and the simple predicate.

There are two major kinds of clauses. The first is the *independent clause*, also known as the *main clause*. The independent clause is a subject-plus-predicate construction which can stand alone as a sentence. The clauses in the preceding examples are independent clauses. Following are some more examples:

The elephant sneezes.

The elephant became king.

The elephant eats peanuts.

The girl will bring him peanuts.

Each sentence contains only one clause, an independent clause.

The second major kind of clause is the *dependent clause*, also known as the *subordinate clause*. A dependent clause is only part of a grammatical sentence. It functions like a *noun*; or like an *adjective*, to describe a noun; or like an *adverb* does, usually to describe an action. These three kinds of clauses can be briefly illustrated as follows:

Noun

Everybody knows **that the elephant eats peanuts.**

Adjective

We brought presents to the elephant **who became king.**

Adverb

When the elephant sneezes, everybody runs.

In the first sentence, **that the elephant eats peanuts** is a noun clause specifying what everybody knows. In the second sentence, **who became king** is an adjective clause describing the noun **elephant.** In the third sentence, **when the elephant sneezes** is an adverb clause telling when everybody runs. The noun clause, the adjective clause, and the adverb clause are all *dependent* clauses; they are attached to or embedded within an independent clause.

Grammatically speaking, then, a *sentence* consists of an independent clause, plus any dependent clause(s) that may be attached to it or embedded within it. The following are examples:

The elephant sneezes.

independent clause

Everybody knows that the elephant eats peanuts.

dependent clause

independent clause

We brought presents to the elephant who became king.

independent clause   *dependent clause*

When the elephant sneezes, everybody runs.

dependent clause   *independent clause*

The girl likes the elephant;   therefore, she will bring him some peanuts.

independent clause   *independent clause*

As the last example indicates, a grammatical sentence may be only part of a punctuated sentence. Conversely, a grammatical sentence is sometimes divided into more than one punctuated sentence. The following is an example:

The girl will bring the elephant some peanuts.   Because she likes him.

independent clause   *dependent clause*

This is only one grammatical sentence, but two punctuated sentences. A dependent clause punctuated as an entire sentence is typically called a *sentence fragment*. Upon occasion, the sentence fragment can be stylistically effective. However, it has traditionally been condemned by teachers. So, too, has the *run-on sentence*, in which two independent clauses are unconventionally joined. Again, here is an example:

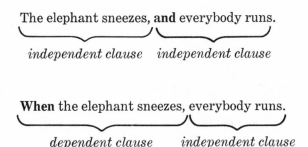

In this case, convention calls for the addition of a word like
and or **when**:

Note that in the first case, we have two independent clauses
and hence *two* grammatical sentences. In the second case,
we have *one* independent clause and hence only one grammatical sentence.

To recapitulate, then, a *clause* consists of a noun-part (a
subject) followed by a verb-part (a *predicate*). A grammatical sentence consists of an independent clause, plus any
dependent *noun, adjective,* or *adverb* clause(s) that might
be attached to or embedded within it. To put it somewhat
differently, a clause consists of at least one noun plus one
verb, and a grammatical sentence consists of at least an
independent clause. Clauses will be discussed more thoroughly later, in the section titled "Clauses and Their Related
Function Words."

CONTENT WORDS AND FUNCTION WORDS

There are two basic kinds of words in a language: *content
words* and *function words*. The content words are the ones
primarily responsible for suggesting the specific meaning of
a sentence. The function words glue these content words

together into a surface structure. In English, the major kinds of content words and function words are as follows:

Content Words	*Function Words*
nouns (and pronouns)	noun determiners
verbs	prepositions
adjectives	verb auxiliaries
adverbs	subordinating conjunctions
	coordinating conjunctions
	conjunctive adverbs

These are the grammatical categories, or *parts of speech*, as they have traditionally been called. Let us focus primarily on the content words. Noun determiners and prepositions will be discussed under the heading "Nouns, Pronouns, and Noun Determiners." Verb auxiliaries will be discussed under "Verbs and Their Auxiliaries." The other three types of function words will be discussed under "Clauses and Their Related Function Words."

GRAMMATICAL ENDINGS

The content words of our language can usually be identified by their *form* and/or their *function*. Their various functions will be discussed in the following sections. Here, however, we will be briefly concerned with *form*, with the grammatical endings by which the content words may tentatively be identified.

There are two major kinds of grammatical endings: *inflectional* and *derivational*. Roughly speaking, an *inflectional* ending is one added to a word as it joins with other words in a sentence. Since there are just a few inflectional endings, these will all be given. The class of *derivational* endings is much larger, consisting of all those that are not inflectional. Many of these endings "derive" one part of speech from another. Following are some of the most common derivational endings for each major part of speech. A much more complete set of examples will be given in subsequent sections.

Regular Inflectional Endings

Nouns

> *Plural,* -s or -**es**
> Johnny saw two bobcats, three lions and four hippopota-muses at the zoo.

> *Possessive*
> -'s for singular possessive
> That bobcat's tail is skinny.

> plural -s or -**es** plus apostrophe for plural possessive
> Those lions' manes are scraggly.
> The hippopotamuses' mouths are big.

Verbs

> *Third Singular,* -s or -**es**
> The lion crouch**es** down and waits for his dinner.

> *Past tense,* -**ed** (for regular verbs)
> Yesterday he look**ed** around, roar**ed**, then wait**ed** patiently for his dinner.

> *Present Participle,* -**ing**
> He is watch**ing** and wait**ing**.

> *Past Participle,* -**ed** (for regular verbs)
> He has wait**ed** for a long time now.

Adjectives

> *Comparative,* -**er**
> This hippopotamus is bigg**er** than that one.

> *Superlative,* -**est**
> The one over there is the bigg**est** of all.

Some Derivational Endings

Noun Endings

-ness	darkness, happiness	-ce	absence, violence
-ty or -ity	royalty, purity	-th	depth, width

Verb Endings

-ize	apologize, idolize
-ify	terrify, dignify
-en	threaten, darken

Adjective Endings

-y	funny, grouchy
-ful	healthful, cheerful
-less	penniless, heartless

Adverb Endings

-ly	slowly, carefully

Note: -ly is also found on a few adjectives, like **lovely** and **friendly**.

As the foregoing examples suggest, a noun designates an entity; a verb commonly expresses action; an adjective describes a noun; and an adverb commonly describes the action expressed by the verb. These partial definitions will be expanded and clarified in the sections that follow.

NOUNS, PRONOUNS, AND NOUN DETERMINERS

NOUNS

A *noun* is traditionally defined as a word that names a person, place, thing, or idea. Structurally, a noun may be defined as any word that takes a noun ending. There are two kinds of inflectional endings by which many nouns may be identified: *plural* (as in **bobcats**) and/or *possessive* (as in **bobcat's** and **bobcats'**; the latter example indicates both plural and possessive). In addition, there are several derivational endings by which some nouns may be identified. The following words illustrate some common derivational endings for nouns: **conveyance, claimant, absence, consistency, employee, baker, communism, physicist, community, agreement, happiness.** Note that -**er** is also an adjective ending (e.g. **hotter**) and sometimes an adjective or adverb ending (e.g. **faster**).

Nouns have five basic functions: they serve as *subject of a clause, direct object of a verb, predicate nominative, object of a preposition,* or *indirect object of a verb.*

1. *Subject of a clause.* A *clause* is traditionally said to consist of a *noun-part* plus a *verb-part*, an entity about which something is predicated. These two basic parts of the clause are the *subject* and the *predicate*, respectively. Thus the most basic function of a noun is to serve as the subject of a clause: **EBENEZER snores, EBENEZER is king, EBENEZER eats peanuts.**

2. *Direct object of a verb.* A direct object is a noun that occurs after the verb and that is traditionally said to "receive the action of the verb." A direct object ordinarily refers to a *different* real world entity than the subject does: **Ebenezer eats PEANUTS, Ebenezer knows ARITHMETIC.**

3. *Predicate nominative.* A predicate nominative is a noun that occurs after the verb (i.e., in the predicate part of the sentence) and that refers to the *same* real world entity as the subject: **Ebenezer is KING, Ebenezer became KING.**

4. *Object of a preposition.* Another way a noun can function is as the object of a preposition; together, the preposition and the following noun constitute a *prepositional phrase*. The following words are those which most commonly function as prepositions: **at, by, for, from, in, of, on, to,** and **with.** Prepositional phrases can be illustrated as follows: **John stared AT EBENEZER, John stood BY EBENEZER, John played WITH EBENEZER.** In each case the noun **EBENEZER** is the object of the preposition.

The following is a more complete list of words which *can* function as prepositions, though some of them have other functions as well:

about	below	in	throughout
above	beneath	into	till
across	beside	like	to
after	besides	near	toward
against	between	of	under
along	beyond	off	underneath
amid	by	on	until
among	concerning	onto	unto
around	down	out	up
as	during	over	upon
at	except	past	with
before	for	since	within
behind	from	through	without

5. *Indirect object of a verb.* Another way a noun can function is as the indirect object of a verb. The indirect object always comes before a direct object and indicates the one to whom or for whom something is given, said, or done: **John gave EBENEZER peanuts, John bought EBENEZER peanuts.** An indirect object can always be paraphrased by a prepositional phrase introduced by **to** or **for**, as in **John gave peanuts TO EBENEZER** and **John bought peanuts FOR EBENEZER.**

In summary, then, we can define a *noun* as any word which takes a noun ending. Any word or construction that functions like a noun can be called a *nominal*. Such a construction can be a phrase, a clause, or a near-clause. A *phrase* ordinarily has a *head word* which is described or "modified" by everything else[1] (as in **Ebenezer eats THE OLD WRINKLY PEANUTS**, where the word **peanuts** is modified by **the, old**, and **wrinkly**). A *clause* has no head word, but rather a subject-plus-predicate structure (as in **Ebenezer thinks THAT JOHN WILL BRING HIM PEANUTS**, where **John**

---

[1] The *prepositional phrase* is an exception to this definition, since the preposition is not usually considered a head word, modified by its following nominal.

is the subject of the noun clause and **will bring him peanuts** is the predicate). A *near-clause* shows evidence of an underlying subject-plus-predicate unit, even though it does not have the normal structure of a clause (as in **Ebenezer likes FOR JOHN TO BRING HIM PEANUTS**, where **John** is the underlying subject of the near-clause and **will bring him peanuts** is the underlying predicate.

PRONOUNS

We turn now to pronouns. Traditionally, a *pronoun* is defined as a word used in place of a noun. There are several kinds of pronouns, and these have varying functions. Here, just three kinds will be illustrated: *indefinite pronouns, demonstrative pronouns,* and *personal pronouns.*

1. *Indefinite pronouns*

 Ebenezer doesn't need **anything**.
 Everyone can go.
 Nothing happened.
 Ebenezer saw **somebody**.

2. *Demonstrative pronouns*

 John likes **this**.
 Ebenezer likes **these**.
 John doesn't like **that**.
 Ebenezer doesn't like **those**.

3. *Personal pronouns*

 I'm telling **you, you**'ve got to watch out for **him**.
 He doesn't like Margaret's story or **mine**.
 We gave **her** the treatment.
 The peanuts are **his**.

Some of these so-called pronouns can also function as noun determiners.

NOUN DETERMINERS

A *noun determiner* has one function: to signal that a noun is coming up. However, a determiner may be separated from its noun by intervening adjectives:

That wrinkled old elephant is Ebenezer.

(noun   (adjectives)   (noun)
determiner)

At first glance, noun determiners look very much like adjectives, for both describe a noun. Unlike adjectives, however, noun determiners cannot be preceded by **very**. We can say **Myrna is very PRETTY** (adjective) but not **Myrna is very THE** (noun determiner).

There are various kinds of determiners, predeterminers, and postdeterminers. Here are just five categories:

1. *Articles*: definite, **the**; indefinite, **a** or **an**. The articles are an infallible signal that a noun is coming up in a sentence.

2. *Demonstratives*: **this, these**; **that, those**. As indicated under "Pronouns," these words can function as nouns: **Ebenezer likes THESE, Ebenezer doesn't like THOSE.** However, these demonstratives can also function as noun determiners: **Ebenezer likes THESE peanuts, Ebenezer doesn't like THOSE peanuts.**

3. *Possessives*: **my, our, your, his, her, its**, and **their**. Examples are **He doesn't like MY story, Here are HIS peanuts.** Note that **his** and **its** can function either as a noun or as a noun determiner: **The peanuts are HIS** (noun) versus **Here are HIS peanuts** (noun determiner).

4. *Cardinal numbers*: **one, two, three**, and so forth. The cardinal numbers can also function as nouns. For example: **Helen bought TWO** (noun) versus **Helen bought TWO jackets** (noun determiner).[2]

---

[2] The ordinal numbers (**first, second, third,** etc.) form a different

5. *Miscellaneous:*

all	every	much
another	either	no
any	few	neither
both	many	other
each	more	several
	most	some

Again, most of these words can function either as a noun or as a noun determiner:

Noun	*Noun Determiner*
Ebenezer doesn't want **any**.	Ebenezer doesn't want **any** peanuts.
Most are good.	**Most** elephants are good.
John doesn't want **much**.	John doesn't want **much** applesauce.
Mike wants **some**.	Mike wants **some** peanuts.

VERBS AND THEIR AUXILIARIES

VERBS

A *verb* is traditionally defined as a word that expresses action or a state of being or becoming. Structurally, a verb may be defined as any word which takes a verb ending or a distinctive verb form. There are four kinds of inflectional endings by which many verbs can be identified: *Third singular present tense, past tense, present participle,* and *past participle.* These are illustrated below:

Third singular present tense, -s or -es[3]

He **plays** the piano.

He **wishes** he could play the piano.

---

kind of category. Unlike the cardinal determiners, the ordinal determiners must be preceded by an article, a demonstrative, or a possessive: **You don't get a SECOND chance,** versus **You get TWO chances.**

[3] The term "third singular" comes from the fact that this is the

Past tense, **-ed**

He **played** well.

Present participle, **-ing**

He is **playing** the piano.

Past participle, **-ed**

He has **played** the piano for years.

The so-called third singular ending is used when the verb is present tense and the subject is a singular noun or nominal other than **I** or **you**: **He PLAYS the piano, That bully PLAYS the piano.** Otherwise the present tense verb has no ending: **I PLAY the piano, Those bullies PLAY the piano.** Note that in all these cases, the action is habitual rather than presently occurring. To indicate a present action we would say, for example, **He IS PLAYING the piano.** For regular verbs, the past participle form is the same as the past tense form, both ending in **-ed.** For irregular verbs, there are usually different past tense and past participle forms: **went** versus **gone, sang** versus **sung, ate** versus **eaten,** and so forth. In any case, the past participle may be defined as the form used after a **HAVE** auxiliary (a form of the verb "to have") : **He has PLAYED the piano for years, They have GONE already, Marvin had SUNG that song many times before.**

There are only a few derivational endings that can be used to identify verbs. The following words illustrate almost all of the possibilities: **complicate, amplify, finish, idolize.** Note that **-ate** can also be an adjective ending (**That's a DUPLI-CATE key**) or a noun ending (**Get me a DUPLICATE**). The **-ish** ending can signal adjective (as in **childish** and **foolish**).

A verb functions as the head word of a predicate: **Ebenezer SNORES, Ebenezer BECAME king, Ebenezer EATS peanuts.** As the first example suggests, a verb is the one absolutely essential part of a predicate.

In summary, then, a *verb* may be defined as any word which takes a verb ending or a distinctive verb form. This

---

verb form used with the so-called third person singular pronouns, **he, she,** and **it**: **He plays the piano, She dances, It works.**

definition includes three kinds of auxiliary verbs, discussed below. Thus we may have a *verbal phrase*, consisting of a *main verb* preceded by one or more *auxiliary verbs*: **He SHOULD LEAVE, He SHOULD HAVE LEFT, He SHOULD BE LEAVING,** and so forth.

VERB AUXILIARIES

There are three major kinds of *auxiliary verbs* that may precede a main verb. These three kinds are as follows:

Modal		*Form of* **HAVE** (the verb "to have")	*Form of* **BE** (the verb "to be")
can	could	have	be
shall	should	has	am
will	would	had	is
may	might	having	are
must			was
			were
			been
			being

Two and even three auxiliaries may precede a main verb, but they must always occur in this order: *modal*, form of HAVE, form of BE. Here are some of the many ways auxiliaries can be used with a verb: **She SHOULD HAVE BEEN driving the jeep, She SHOULD BE driving the jeep, She HAD BEEN driving the jeep, She WAS driving the jeep, She SHOULD HAVE driven the jeep, She HAD driven the jeep, She SHOULD drive the jeep.** Note that if a form of HAVE occurs as an auxiliary, the next word will always be a past participle (by definition). If a form of BE occurs as an auxiliary, the next word will be a present participle (unless the sentence is passive). The first auxiliary is in either the present or the past tense form.[4] If there is no auxiliary, then the main verb is in either the present or the past tense form.

---

[4] The modals **can, shall, will, may,** and **must** are considered to be present tense forms. For historical reasons, the other modals are considered to be past tense forms.

ADJECTIVES

An *adjective* is traditionally defined as a word that modifies a noun. Structurally, an adjective may be defined as any word that takes an adjective ending or that may be preceded by **more** and **most**. (We will see that some words which may be preceded by **more** and **most** can function either as adjectives or as adverbs.)

Many adjectives can add the inflectional endings -**er** and -**est**, while others express the same meaning by taking **more** and **most**:

Myrna is **pretty**.	Myrna is **beautiful**.
Myrna is **prettier** than Myrtle.	Myrna is **more beautiful** than Myrtle.
Myrna is the **prettiest** turtle I know.	Myrna is the **most beautiful** turtle I know.

Forms like **prettier** and **more beautiful** are called the *comparative degree*: they are used when comparing one entity with another (e.g., Myrna with Myrtle). Forms like **prettiest** and **most beautiful** are called the *superlative degree*: they are used when comparing one entity with two or more others (Myrna with all other turtles).

There are also several derivational endings by which some adjectives may be identified. The following words illustrate some common derivational endings for adjectives: **adorable, fatal, important, molecular, arbitrary, confident, helpful, fantastic, childish, active, friendless, friendly, gracious, crazy.** Note that the -**ly** ending appears much less often on adjectives than on adverbs (**quickly, slowly, carefully,** and so forth). The -**ant** ending can also be found on nouns (**claimant, coolant**).

As indicated, an adjective functions to modify (describe) a noun. Thus the base form of a true adjective will fit into both of the two major adjective positions: 1) before a noun, and 2) in predicate adjective position, preceded by the word **very**:

That **pretty** turtle is Myrtle.

Myrtle is very **pretty**.

As the example indicates, a *predicate adjective* is an adjective that occurs in the predicate part of the sentence but that modifies the subject.

In summary, then, we can define an *adjective* as any word that takes an adjective ending or that can be preceded by **more** and **most**. Any word or construction that functions like an adjective can be called an *adjectival*. An adjectival can consist of a word, a phrase, a near-clause, or a clause. The following are just a few kinds of examples:

Word

Myrna and Myrtle are **pretty**.

Jack shut the **barn** door.

The man **inside** stole the money.

We'll never recover the **stolen** money.

Phrase

Myrna is **unusually pretty**.

Here is Ms. Anderson, **our president**.

That bird **in the tree** is a bluejay.

We'll never recover the money **stolen in yesterday's robbery**.

Near-clause

Albert glared at her angrily, **his eyes black with hate**.

Clause

The man **that was inside** stole the money.

We'll never recover the money **that was stolen**.

That bird **that's in the tree** is a bluejay.

Albert, **whose eyes were black with hate**, stared at her angrily.

ADVERBS

An *adverb* is traditionally defined as a word that modifies a verb, an adjective, or another adverb. However, adverbs can also modify an entire clause. Structurally, an adverb may be defined as any word that takes an adverb ending or that can function adverbially and be modified by **more** and **most**. Since this structural definition does not encompass many of the words traditionally considered to be adverbs, we will eventually "define" the class of adverbs through examples.

Like adjectives, a few adverbs can add the inflectional endings **-er** and **-est**, while others express the same comparative and superlative meanings by taking **more** and **most**:

Walk **fast**.	Speak **pleasantly**.
Walk **faster**.	Speak **more pleasantly**.
Walk the **fastest** you can.	Speak the **most pleasantly** you can.[5]

Adverbs which have comparative and superlative forms illustrate one of the major types of adverb, the *manner adverb*. These generally answer the question HOW?

There are only four derivational suffixes by which some adverbs may be identified. These may be illustrated as follows: **quickly, slowly; backward(s), forward(s); lengthways, sideways;** and **lengthwise, sidewise**. The **-ly** ending is by far the most common (there is an adjectival **-ly** also, as in **lovely** and **friendly**). Adverbs that take derivational endings are also manner adverbs.

The term *adverb* is often used to describe not only words that take an adverb ending, but other words that tell WHEN, WHERE, or HOW an action is done.[6] Here are some typical adverbs:

Time Adverbs (WHEN)	Place Adverbs (WHERE)	Manner Adverbs (HOW)
today	here	quickly
tomorrow	there	slowly
yesterday	everywhere	backwards
		lengthways
		sidewise

[5] As this awkward sentence suggests, the superlative of adverbs is rarely used.

[6] The category *adverb* also includes intensifiers like **especially, extraordinarily, really, too,** and **very**.

An *adverbial* is any word or construction that functions like an adverb. Most adverbs tell something about an action and hence modify a verb or, more often, an entire independent clause. The following are just a few examples of adverbials that tell something about an action:

Word

We cleaned the garage **yesterday.**

Phrase

He leaves **this Friday.**

Near-clause

The storm being on its way, we didn't dare go sailing.

Clause

He soaked his toupee **while he was shaving.**

For a list of the subordinating conjunctions that most commonly introduce adverbial clauses, see the next section, on "Clauses and Their Related Function Words."

CLAUSES AND THEIR RELATED FUNCTION WORDS

Earlier, we defined a grammatical *sentence* as an independent clause, plus any dependent clause(s) that might be attached to it or embedded within it. A *clause* was defined as a subject-plus-predicate construction, a noun-part plus a verb-part. An *independent* or *main clause*, then, is a subject-plus-predicate construction that can stand alone as a sentence. Below are some examples:

Ebenezer snores.

Ebenezer is king.

Ebenezer eats peanuts.

John will bring him peanuts.

There are two kinds of words used to join independent clauses: *conjunctive adverbs*, and *coordinating conjunctions*. The words that most commonly function as conjunctive adverbs are as follows: **accordingly, also, anyhow, anyway,** besides, consequently, furthermore, hence, however, indeed, likewise, moreover, namely, nevertheless, otherwise, still, then, and therefore.[7] The coordinating conjunctions are as follows: and, but, or, yet, for, nor, so.[8] Following are examples of how these two kinds of words are used to join independent clauses:

> George couldn't see anything; nevertheless, he plunged ahead recklessly.
>
> George couldn't see anything. He plunged ahead recklessly, nevertheless.
>
> George couldn't see anything, but he plunged ahead recklessly.
>
> George couldn't see anything. But he plunged ahead recklessly.

As these examples indicate, the coordinating conjunctions and the conjunctive adverbs may be punctuated and positioned differently. Another difference is that the coordinating conjunctions can join not just independent clauses, but also words, phrases, near-clauses, and dependent clauses: Those are my books AND magazines (words), We ran in one door BUT out the other (phrases), We asked John to go to the grocery AND Mike to go to the drugstore (near-clauses), and We won't leave if it's snowing OR if it's raining (dependent clauses).

Having defined an independent clause as a subject-plus-predicate construction that can stand alone as a sentence, we logically define a *dependent* or *subordinate* clause as a subject-plus-predicate construction that *cannot* stand alone as a grammatical sentence. There are three types of dependent clauses: a *noun clause*, an *adjective clause*, and an *adverb clause*.

---

[7] Conjunctive adverbs are sometimes called *transitional adverbs, adverbial connectors, sentence adverbials,* or simply *sentence connectors.*

[8] For brevity, I have omitted the pairs of coordinators that are called *correlative conjunctions.* The major pairs are **either . . . or,** and **neither . . . nor.**

A *noun clause* functions like a noun: as subject of a clause, direct object of a verb, predicate nominative, object of a preposition, or (occasionally) indirect object. It is introduced by a *complementizer* (**that**; **if, whether**) or by a *WH-word* (mainly **who, what, which, when, where, why, how**). Note that a complementizer is simply placed in front of a subject-plus-predicate construction, whereas a WH-word is an integral part of that construction:

Ebenezer thinks **that** John will bring him peanuts.

Ebenezer wonders **if** John will bring him peanuts.

Ebenezer wonders **who** will bring him peanuts.

Ebenezer wonders **what** John will bring him.

An *adjective clause* functions like an adjective: to modify a noun. An adjective clause is introduced by a *relative pronoun* (mainly **that**; **who** for humans and pets; **what** for other animates and for inanimates; and **whose** for possessives). Note that the relative pronoun is an integral part of an adjectival clause:

The man **that was inside** stole the money.

We'll never recover the money **that was stolen.**

That bird **that's in the tree** is a bluejay.

Albert, **whose eyes were black with hate,** glared at her angrily.

An *adverb clause* functions like an adverb. Usually an adverb clause modifies an independent clause. An adverb clause is introduced by a *subordinating conjunction*. Note that a subordinating conjunction is simply placed in front of a subject-plus-predicate unit to make an adverb clause:

Wash your hands **before we eat dinner.**

He soaked his toupee **while he was shaving.**

I'd like to go **where Robin went.**

He cried **as if his heart would break.**

He didn't stay, **because dinner was almost over.**

We don't know them, (al) though they've lived here three years.

We won't leave if it's snowing.

Among the most common subordinating conjunctions are the following: **after, although, as, as if, because, before, even though, if, like, since, so(that), though, till, unless, until, when, where, wherever, whether(or not)**, and **while**.

WORD ORDER AND BASIC SENTENCE PATTERNS

Word order is often crucial in determining a word's function in a sentence. In English, the subject usually comes first, then the verb, followed perhaps by an adverb, an object, or a complement of some sort. Thus there are three basic sentence patterns underlying all others:

1. *Subject + Intransitive verb + (Adverb)*

   Ebenezer snores.

   Ebenezer snores loudly.

The parentheses indicate that the adverb is an optional element in this basic sentence pattern. An *intransitive verb* is simply a verb which is followed by nothing or by an adverb, as above.

2. *Subject + Transitive verb + Direct object*

   Ebenezer eats peanuts.

A *transitive verb* is simply a verb which is followed by a direct object, a nominal that "receives the action" of the verb or shows the result of the action. One way of expanding this pattern is by adding an indirect object between the verb and the direct object:

   John gave Ebenezer peanuts.

   John bought Ebenezer peanuts.

Another way is by adding an *objective complement* after the direct object:

   John crowned Ebenezer king.

The word **king** is the objective complement. The objective complement refers to the same real world entity as the direct object.

3. *Subject + Linking verb + Subjective complement*

A *linking verb* is one which is followed by a subjective complement. And a *subjective complement* is simply a predicate nominative or predicate adjective identifying or describing the subject. Hence the following sentences illustrate this basic pattern:

Ebenezer is king. (predicate nominative)

Ebenezer is kingly. (predicate adjective)

bibliography

The following bibliography is divided, somewhat arbitrarily, into two major sections: "References," and "Suggested Readings." Of necessity, many items are listed in both sections. The brief bibliographies at the end of each chapter are designed primarily for those just beginning a study of psycholinguistics and reading. In contrast, the following bibliographies are designed more for those who want to pursue such study in greater depth and detail.

When there is more than one entry for a given author, those entries are listed chronologically.

REFERENCES

The following section includes not all of the references I consulted, but at least most of the ones that helped shape my own views on the nature of the reading process. Most of these references are cited in the text. Almost all of the others were cited in an earlier draft, and are retained here because they may be relevant to those with a scholarly interest in the reading process and related matters. Particularly useful articles and chapters are often listed separately, even when they are printed in one of the books cited. Many such articles and chapters are appropriate for a wide audience, as their titles will suggest.

Abrams, Kenneth, and Bever, Thomas G. "Syntactic Structure Modifies Attention during Speech Perception and Recognition." *Quarterly Journal of Experimental Psychology* 21 (August 1969) : 280–290.

Aitchison, Jean. *The Articulate Mammal: An Introduction to Psycholinguistics.* New York: Universe Books, 1976.

Allen, P. David. "Implications for Reading Instruction." In *Findings of Research in Miscue Analysis: Classroom Implications,* edited by P. David Allen and Dorothy J. Watson, Urbana, Ill.: ERIC Clearinghouse on Reading and Communication Skills and the National Council of Teachers of English, 1976, pp. 107–112.

Allen, P. David, and Watson, Dorothy J., eds. *Findings of Research in Miscue Analysis: Classroom Implications.* Urbana, Ill.: ERIC Clearinghouse on Reading and Communication Skills and the National Council of Teachers of English, 1976.

Anderson, Irving H., and Dearborn, Walter F. *The Psychology of Teaching Reading.* New York: Ronald Press, 1952.

Anisfeld, Moshe. "Language and Cognition in the Young Child." In *The Psycholinguistic Nature of the Reading Process,* edited by Kenneth S. Goodman. Detroit: Wayne State University Press, 1968, pp. 169–183.

Artley, A. Sterl. "Phonics Revisited." *Language Arts* 54 (February 1977): 121–126.

Bailey, Mildred H. "The Utility of Phonic Generalizations in Grades One through Six." *The Reading Teacher* 20 (1967): 413–418.

Ball, Zachary. *Bristle Face.* New York: Holiday House, 1962.

Baratz, Joan C. "Teaching Reading in an Urban Negro School System." In *Teaching Black Children to Read,* edited by Joan C. Baratz and Roger W. Shuy. Washington, D.C.: Center for Applied Linguistics, 1969, pp. 102–116.

Baratz, Joan, and Stewart, William. *Friends.* Washington, D.C.: Education Study Center, 1970.

Barr, Jene. *Little Circus Dog.* Chicago: Albert Whitman, 1949.

Berdiansky, Betty; Cronnell, B.; and Koehler, J. *Spelling–Sound Relations and Primary Form-Class Descriptions for Speech-Comprehension Vocabularies of 6–9 Year-Olds.* Inglewood, Calif.: Southwest Regional Laboratory for Educational Research and Development, Technical Report No. 15, 1969.

Bever, T.G., and Bower, T.G. "How to Read without Listening." In *Project Literacy Reports No. 6,* Educational Resources Information Center, ED 010 312, January 1966, pp. 13–25.

Bever, T.G.; Lackner, J.R.; and Kirk, R. "The Underlying Structures of Sentences are the Primary Units of Immediate Speech Processing." *Perception & Psychophysics* 5 (1969): 225–234.

Biemiller, Andrew. "The Development of the Use of Graphic and Contextual Information as Children Learn to Read." *Reading Research Quarterly* 1 (Fall 1970): 77–96.

Blachowicz, Camille L.Z. "Semantic Constructivity in Children's Comprehension." *Reading Research Quarterly* 13, ii (1977–1978): 188–199.

Blatt, Gloria T. "Playing with Language." *The Reading Teacher* 31 (February 1978) : 487–493.

Bloomfield, Leonard. "Linguistics and Reading." *The Elementary English Review* 19 (April and May 1942) : 125–130, 183–186.

Bloomfield, Leonard, and Barnhart, Clarence L. *Let's Read: A Linguistic Approach.* Detroit: Wayne State University Press, 1961.

Bond, Guy L., and Dykstra, Robert. "The Cooperative Research Program in First-Grade Reading Instruction." *Reading Research Quarterly* 2 (Summer 1967) : 5–142.

Bormuth, John R. "The Cloze Readability Procedure." *Elementary English* 45 (April 1968) : 429–436. Reprinted in John Bormuth, ed., *Readability in 1968.* Urbana, Ill.: National Council of Teachers of English, 1968, pp. 40–47.

Bormuth, John R., ed. *Readability in 1968.* Urbana, Ill.: National Council of Teachers of English, 1968.

Bormuth, John R. "Literacy in the Classroom." In *Help for the Reading Teacher: New Directions in Research,* edited by William D. Page. Urbana, Ill.: National Council of Teachers of English, 1975, pp. 60–89.

Bormuth, John R.; Manning, John; Carr, Julian; and Pearson, David. "Children's Comprehension of Between- and Within-Sentence Syntactic Structures." *Journal of Educational Psychology* 61 (October 1970) : 349–357.

Bortnick, Robert, and Lopardo, Genevieve S. "An Instructional Application of the Cloze Procedure." *Journal of Reading* 16 (January 1973) : 296–300.

Botel, Morton, and Granowsky, Alvin. "A Formula for Measuring Syntactic Complexity: A Directional Effort." *Elementary English* 49 (April 1972) : 513–516.

Bower, Thomas G.R. "Reading by Eye." In *Basic Studies on Reading,* edited by Harry Levin and Joanna P. Williams. New York: Basic Books, 1970, pp. 134–146.

Bradbury, Ray. *The Golden Apples of the Sun.* Garden City, N.Y.: Doubleday, 1953.

Bradbury, Ray. *Dandelion Wine.* Garden City, N.Y.: Doubleday, 1957.

Bransford, John D., and Franks, Jeffrey J. "The Abstraction of Linguistic Ideas." *Cognitive Psychology* 2 (October 1971) : 331–350.

Brause, Rita S. "Developmental Aspects of the Ability to Understand Semantic Ambiguity, with Implications for Teachers." *Research in the Teaching of English* 11 (Spring 1977) : 39–48.

Brown, Claude. *Manchild in the Promised Land.* New York: Macmillan, 1965.

Brown, Roger. "Psychology and Reading: Commentary on Chapters 5 to 10." In *Basic Studies on Reading,* edited by Harry Levin and Joanna P. Williams. New York: Basic Books, 1970, pp. 164–187.

Brown, Roger, and McNeill, David. "The 'Tip of the Tongue' Phenomenon." *Journal of Verbal Learning and Verbal Behavior* 5 (August 1966): 325–337.

Bruce, D.J. "The Effect of Listeners' Anticipations on the Intelligibility of Heard Speech." *Language and Speech* 1 (1958): 79–97.

Bruner, Jerome S., and O'Dowd, Donald. "A Note on the Informativeness of Parts of Words." *Language and Speech* 1 (1958): 98–101.

Burgess, Anthony. *A Clockwork Orange.* New York: Norton, 1963.

Burke, Carolyn. "Preparing Elementary Teachers to Teach Reading." In *Miscue Analysis: Applications to Reading Instruction,* edited by Kenneth S. Goodman (Urbana, Ill.: National Council of Teachers of English, 1973), pp. 15–29.

Burke, Carolyn. "Oral Reading Analysis: A View of the Reading Process." In *Help for the Reading Teacher: New Directions in Research,* edited by William D. Page. Urbana, Ill.: National Council of Teachers of English, 1975, pp. 23–33.

Burling, Robbins. *English in Black and White.* New York: Holt, Rinehart and Winston, 1973.

Burmeister, Lou E. "Usefulness of Phonic Generalizations." *The Reading Teacher* 21 (January 1968): 349–356, 360.

Buswell, Guy Thomas. *Non-Oral Reading: A Study of Its Use in the Chicago Public Schools.* Supplementary Educational Monographs, No. 60. Chicago: University of Chicago Press, 1945.

Cajon Valley Union School District. "Psycholinguistic Approach to Reading (PAR)." El Cajon, Calif., 1974. Available from the Educational Resources Information Center: ED 108 150.

Calvert, Kenneth H. "K-Ratio [Kernel Structure] Index." 1971. Available from the Educational Resources Information Center: ED 091 722.

Canney, George. "Reading Problems—Prevention Rather Than Cure." *Reading Horizons* 18 (Fall 1977): 7–12 .

Caplan, David. "Clause Boundaries and Recognition Latencies for Words in Sentences." *Perception and Psychophysics* 12 (1972): 73–76.

Carroll, John B. "The Nature of the Reading Process." In *Theoretical Models and Processes of Reading,* edited by Harry Singer and

Robert B. Ruddell. Newark, Del.: International Reading Association, 1970, pp. 292–303.

Carton, Aaron S. *Orientation to Reading*. Rowley, Mass.: Newbury House, 1976.

Chall, Jeanne. *Learning to Read: The Great Debate*. New York: McGraw-Hill, 1967.

Chenfeld, Mimi Brodsky. *Teaching Language Arts Creatively*. New York: Harcourt Brace Jovanovich, 1978.

Chomsky, Carol. *The Acquisition of Syntax in Children from 5 to 10*. Cambridge, Mass.: MIT Press, 1969.

Chomsky, Carol. "After Decoding: What?" *Language Arts* 53 (March 1976): 288–296, 314.

Chomsky, Noam. *Language and Mind*. New York: Harcourt Brace Jovanovich, 1968.

Clark, Herbert H., and Clark, Eve V. *Psychology and Language: An Introduction to Psycholinguistics*. New York: Harcourt Brace Jovanovich, 1977.

Clark, Mae Knight. *A Magic Box*. New York: Macmillan, 1965.

Clark, Mae Knight. *Opening Books*. New York: Macmillan, 1965.

Clay, Marie M. *What Did I Write?* London: Heinemann Educational Books, 1975.

Cleland, Donald L. "Vocalism in Silent Reading." In *Teaching Reading—Not by Decoding Alone*, edited by Joseph P. Kender. Danville, Ill.: Interstate Printers and Publishers, 1971, pp. 131–144.

Clymer, Theodore L. "The Utility of Phonic Generalizations in the Primary Grades." *The Reading Teacher* 16 (1963): 252–258.

Coleman, E.B. "Learning of Prose Written in Four Grammatical Transformations." *Journal of Applied Psychology* 49 (October 1965): 332–341.

Conrad, R. "Speech and Reading." In *Language by Ear and by Eye*, edited by James F. Kavanagh and Ignatius G. Mattingly. Cambridge, Mass.: MIT Press, 1972, pp. 205–240.

Cooper, Charles R. "An Outline for Writing Sentence-Combining Problems." *English Journal* 62 (January 1973): 96–102, 108.

Cooper, Charles R., and Petrosky, Anthony R. "A Psycholinguistic View of the Fluent Reading Process." *Journal of Reading* 20 (December 1976): 184–207.

Corcoran, D.W.J. "An Acoustic Factor in Letter Cancellation." *Nature* 210 (May 1966): 658.

Corcoran, D.W.J. "Acoustic Factor in Proof Reading." *Nature* 214 (May 1967) : 851–852.

Cox, Mary B. "The Effect of Conservation Ability on Reading Competency." *The Reading Teacher* 30 (December 1976) : 251–258.

Culhane, Joseph. "Close Procedures and Comprehension." *Reading Teacher* 23 (February 1970) : 410–413, 464.

Dahl, Patricia R., and Samuels, S. Jay. "Teaching Children to Read Using Hypothesis/Test Strategies." *The Reading Teacher* 30 (March 1977) : 603–606.

Dahl, Roald. *Someone Like You.* New York: Knopf, 1950.

Dawkins, John. *Syntax and Readability.* Newark, Del.: International Reading Association, 1975.

Dechant, Emerald V. *Improving the Teaching of Reading.* 2nd ed. Englewood Cliffs, N.J.: Prentice-Hall, 1970.

Diack, Hunter. *The Teaching of Reading in Spite of the Alphabet.* New York: Philosophical Library, 1965.

Diebold, A. Richard. "A Survey of Psycholinguistic Research, 1954–1964." In *Psycholinguistics: A Survey of Theory and Research Problems,* edited by Charles E. Osgood and Thomas A. Sebeok. Bloomington, Ind.: Indiana University Press, 1965, pp. 205–291.

Downing, John. "How Children Think about Reading." *The Reading Teacher* 23 (December 1969) : 217–230.

Durkin, Dolores. "Children Who Read before Grade One." *The Reading Teacher* 14, iii (January 1961) : 163–166.

Durkin, Dolores. *Children Who Read Early.* New York: Teachers College Press, Columbia University, 1966.

Durkin, Dolores. "A Six Year Study of Children Who Learned to Read in School at the Age of Four." *Reading Research Quarterly* 10, i (1974–1975) : 9–61.

Durkin, Dolores. *Teaching Young Children to Read.* 2nd ed. Boston: Allyn and Bacon, 1976.

Dykstra, Robert. "The Effectiveness of Code- and Meaning-Emphasis Beginning Reading Programs." *The Reading Teacher* 22 (October 1968) : 17–23.

Dykstra, Robert. "Summary of the Second-Grade Phase of the Cooperative Research Program in Primary Reading." *Reading Research Quarterly* 4 (Fall 1968) : 49–70.

Dykstra, Robert. "Phonics and Beginning Reading Instruction." In *Teaching Reading: A Phonic/Linguistic Approach to Developmental*

Reading, by Charles Child Walcutt, Joan Lamport, and Glenn McCracken. New York: Macmillan, 1974, pp. 373–397.

Edfeldt, Ake W. *Silent Speech and Silent Reading.* Chicago: University of Chicago Press, 1960.

Emans, Robert. "The Usefulness of Phonic Generalizations above the Primary Grades." *The Reading Teacher* 20 (1967): 419–425.

Endicott, A.L. "A Proposed Scale for Syntactic Complexity." *Research in the Teaching of English* 7 (1973): 5–12.

Epstein, William. "The Influence of Syntactical Structure on Learning." *American Journal of Psychology* 74 (1961): 80–85.

Erdmann, B., and Dodge, R. Psychologische Untersuchungen über das Lesen, auf Experimenteller Grundlage. Halle, 1898. As cited in Edmund Burke Huey, *The Psychology and Pedagogy of Reading* (1908; reprinted, Cambridge, Mass.: MIT Press, 1968).

Fagan, William T.; Cooper, Charles R.; and Jensen, Julie M. *Measures for Research and Evaluation in the English Language Arts.* Urbana, Ill.: National Council of Teachers of English, 1975.

Farnes, N.C. *Reading Purposes, Comprehension and the Use of Context.* Bletchley, Buckinghamshire, England: The Open University Press, 1973.

Fasold, Ralph W., and Wolfram, Walt. "Some Linguistic Features of Negro Dialect." In *Teaching Standard English in the Inner City*, edited by Ralph W. Fasold and Roger W. Shuy. Arlington, Va.: Center for Applied Linguistics, 1970, pp. 41–86.

Fisher, Kenneth David. "An Investigation to Determine If Selected Exercises in Sentence-Combining Can Improve Reading and Writing." Unpublished dissertation, Indiana University, 1973.

Flesch, Rudolf. *Why Johnny Can't Read.* New York: Harper & Row, 1955.

Fodor, J. A.; Bever, T. G.; and Garrett, M. F. *The Psychology of Language.* New York: McGraw-Hill, 1974.

Fodor, J., and Garrett, M. "Some Reflections on Competence and Performance." In *Psycholinguistic Papers*, edited by J. Lyons and R.J. Wales. Edinburgh: Edinburgh University Press, 1966, pp. 135–154.

Forester, Anne D. "What Teachers Can Learn from 'Natural Readers.'" *The Reading Teacher* 31 (November 1977): 160–166.

Forster, Kenneth I., and Ryder, Leonie A. "Perceiving the Structure and Meaning of Sentences." *Journal of Verbal Learning and Verbal Behavior* 10 (June 1971): 285–296.

Fries, Charles C. *Linguistics and Reading*. New York: Holt, Rinehart and Winston, 1963.

Gates, Arthur I. "Character and Purposes of the Yearbook." In *Reading in the Elementary School*, Part II of *The Forty-eighth Yearbook of the National Society for the Study of Education*. Chicago: University of Chicago Press, 1949, pp. 1–9.

Gates, Arthur I. *Teaching Reading: What Research Says to the Teacher*. 2nd ed. Washington, D.C.: National Education Association, 1962.

Gates, Arthur I., and Boeker, Eloise. "A Study of Initial Stages in Reading by Pre-School Children." *Teachers College Record* 24 (November 1923): 469–488.

Geissal, Mary Ann, and Knafle, June D. "A Linguistic View of Auditory Discrimination Tests and Exercises." *The Reading Teacher* 31 (November 1977): 134–140.

Gibson, Eleanor J. "Reading for Some Purpose." In *Language by Ear and by Eye*, edited by James F. Kavanagh and Ignatius G. Mattingly. Cambridge, Mass.: MIT Press, 1972, pp. 3–19.

Gibson, Eleanor J., and Levin, Harry. *The Psychology of Reading*. Cambridge, Mass.: MIT Press, 1975.

Gibson, Eleanor J.; Shurcliff, Arthur; and Yonas, Albert. "Utilization of Spelling Patterns by Deaf and Hearing Subjects." In *Basic Studies on Reading*, edited by Harry Levin and Joanna P. Williams. New York: Basic Books, 1970, pp. 57–73.

Glazer, Susan Mandel. "Is Sentence Length a Valid Measure of Difficulty in Readability Formulas?" *The Reading Teacher* 27 (February 1974): 464–467.

Goetz, Lee Garrett. *A Camel in the Sea*. New York: McGraw-Hill, 1966.

Goodman, Kenneth S. "A Linguistic Study of Cues and Miscues in Reading." *Elementary English* 42 (October 1965): 639–643.

Goodman, Kenneth S. "Reading: A Psycholinguistic Guessing Game." *Journal of the Reading Specialist* 6 (May 1967): 126–135.

Goodman, Kenneth S. "Behind the Eye: What Happens in Reading." In *Reading: Process and Program*, by Kenneth S. Goodman and Olive S. Niles. Urbana, Ill.: National Council of Teachers of English, 1970, pp. 3–38.

Goodman, Kenneth S. "Orthography in a Theory of Reading Instruction." *Elementary English* 49 (December 1972): 1254–1261.

Goodman, Kenneth S., ed. *Miscue Analysis: Applications to Reading Instruction*. Urbana, Ill.: National Council of Teachers of English, 1973.

Goodman, Kenneth S. "Testing in Reading: A General Critique." In *Accountability and Reading Instruction*, edited by Robert B. Ruddell. Urbana, Ill.: National Council of Teachers of English, 1973, pp. 21–33.

Goodman, Kenneth S. *Theoretically Based Studies of Patterns of Miscues in Oral Reading Performance.* Detroit: Wayne State University, 1973. Available from the Educational Resources Information Center: Ed 079 708.

Goodman, Kenneth S. "Effective Teachers of Reading Know Language and Kids." *Elementary English* 51 (September 1974): 823–828.

Goodman, Kenneth S. *Strategies for Increasing Comprehension in Reading.* Glenview, Ill.: Scott, Foresman, 1975.

Goodman, Kenneth S. "The Reading Process: A Psycholinguistic View." In E. Brooks Smith, Kenneth S. Goodman, and Robert Meredith, *Language and Thinking in School.* 2nd ed. New York: Holt, Rinehart and Winston, 1976, pp. 265–283.

Goodman, Kenneth S. "Teaching Reading: Developing Strategies for Comprehension." In E. Brooks Smith, Kenneth S. Goodman, and Robert Meredith, *Language and Thinking in School.* 2nd ed. New York: Holt, Rinehart and Winston, 1976, pp. 284–302.

Goodman, Kenneth S. "What We Know about Reading." In *Findings of Research in Miscue Analysis: Classroom Implications*, edited by P. David Allen and Dorothy J. Watson. Urbana, Ill.: ERIC Clearinghouse on Reading and Communication Skills and the National Council of Teachers of English, 1976, pp. 57–70.

Goodman, Kenneth, and Buck, Catherine. "Dialect Barriers to Reading Comprehension Revisited." *The Reading Teacher* 27 (October 1973): 6–12.

Goodman, Yetta. "Miscue Analysis for In-Service Reading Teachers." In *Miscue Analysis: Applications to Reading Instruction*, edited by Kenneth S. Goodman. Urbana, Ill.: National Council of Teachers of English, 1973, pp. 49–64.

Goodman, Yetta. "I Never Read Such a Long Story Before." *English Journal* 63 (November 1974): 65–71.

Goodman, Yetta M. "Reading Strategy Lessons: Expanding Reading Effectiveness." In *Help for the Reading Teacher: New Directions in Research*, edited by William D. Page. Urbana, Ill.: National Conference on Research in English, 1975, pp. 34–41.

Goodman, Yetta M. "Developing Reading Proficiency." In *Findings of Research in Miscue Analysis: Classroom Implications*, edited by

P. David Allen and Dorothy J. Watson. Urbana, Ill.: ERIC Clearinghouse on Reading and Communication Skills and the National
Council of Teachers of English, 1976, pp. 113–128.

Goodman, Yetta M. "Strategies for Comprehension." In *Findings of Research in Miscue Analysis: Classroom Implications*, edited by P.
David Allen and Dorothy J. Watson. Urbana, Ill.: ERIC Clearinghouse on Reading and Communication Skills and the National
Council of Teachers of English, 1976, pp. 94–102.

Goodman, Yetta M., and Burke, Carolyn L. *Reading Miscue Inventory
Complete Kit: Procedure for Diagnosis and Evaluation*. New
York: Macmillan, 1972.

Goodman, Yetta M., and Burke, Carolyn L. *Reading Miscue Inventory
Manual: Procedure for Diagnosis and Evaluation*. New York:
Macmillan, 1972.

Goodman, Yetta M., and Burke, Carolyn L. *Reading Miscue Inventory
Practice Analysis Manual*. New York: Macmillan, 1972.

Goodman, Yetta M.; Burke, Carolyn; and Sherman, Barry. *Strategies in
Reading Manual*. New York: Macmillan, 1974.

Goodman, Yetta, and Greene, Jennifer. "Grammar and Reading in the
Classroom." In *Linguistic Theory: What Can It Say about Read-
ing?* edited by Roger W. Shuy. Newark, Del.: International
Reading Association, 1977, pp. 18–30.

Gorman, Richard M. *Discovering Piaget: A Guide for Teachers*. Columbus,
Ohio: Charles E. Merrill, 1972.

Gough, Philip. "One Second of Reading." In *Language by Ear and by
Eye*, edited by James F. Kavanagh and Ignatius G. Mattingly.
Cambridge, Mass.: MIT Press, 1972, pp. 331–358.

Gray, William S. *On Their Own in Reading: How to Give Children Independence in Attacking New Words*. Glenview, Ill.: Scott, Foresman,
1948.

Gray, William S. *On Their Own in Reading: How to Give Children Independence in Analyzing New Words*. Rev. ed. Glenview, Ill.: Scott,
Foresman, 1960.

Greene, Graham. *The Power and the Glory*. New York: Viking Press, 1940.

Grimm Brothers. *Grimms' Fairy Tales*, translated by Mrs. E. V. Lucas,
Lucy Crane, and Marian Edwardes. New York: Grosset and Dun-
lap, 1945.

Guthrie, John T., ed. *Aspects of Reading Acquisition*. Baltimore: The
Johns Hopkins University Press, 1976.

Hall, MaryAnne. *Teaching Reading as a Language Experience*. 2nd ed.
Columbus, Ohio: Charles E. Merrill, 1976.

Hall, MaryAnne. *The Language Experience Approach for Teaching Reading: A Research Perspective.* 2nd ed. Newark, Del.: ERIC Clearinghouse on Reading and Communication Skills and the International Reading Association, 1978.

Hall, Robert A., Jr. *Sound and Spelling in English.* New York: Chilton, 1961.

Harper, Robert J., and Kilarr, Gary. "The Law and Reading Instruction." *Language Arts* 54 (November/December 1977): 913–919.

Harste, Jerome C. "Understanding the Hypothesis, It's the Teacher That Makes the Difference: Part I." *Reading Horizons* 18 (Fall 1977): 32–43.

Harste, Jerome. "Understanding the Hypothesis, It's the Teacher That Makes the Difference: Part II." *Reading Horizons* 18 (Winter 1978): 89–98.

Harste, Jerome C., and Burke, Carolyn L. "Toward a Socio-Psycholinguistic Model of Reading Comprehension." *Viewpoints in Teaching and Learning* 54 (July 1978): 9–34.

Heckleman, R. G. "A Neurological-Impress Method of Remedial-Reading Instruction." *Academic Therapy* 4 (Summer 1969): 277–282.

Heilman, Arthur W. *Principles and Practices of Teaching Reading.* Columbus, Ohio: Charles E. Merrill, 1972.

Hittleman, Daniel. "Seeking a Psycholinguistic Definition of Readability." *Elementary English* 26 (May 1973): 783–789.

Hittleman, Daniel R. *Developmental Reading: A Psycholinguistic Perspective.* Chicago: Rand McNally College Publishing, 1978.

Hochberg, Julian. "Components of Literacy: Speculations and Exploratory Research." In *Basic Studies on Reading,* edited by Harry Levin and Joanna P. Williams. New York: Basic Books, 1970, pp. 74–89.

Hollingsworth, Paul M. "An Experimental Approach to the Impress Method of Teaching Reading." *The Reading Teacher* 31 (March 1978): 624–626.

Hoskisson, Kenneth. "The Many Facets of Assisted Reading." *Elementary English* 52 (March 1975): 312–315.

Hoskisson, Kenneth, and Krohm, Bernadette. "Reading by Immersion: Assisted Reading." *Elementary English* 51 (September 1974): 832–836.

Huey, Edmund Burke. *The Psychology and Pedagogy of Reading.* 1908; reprinted, Cambridge, Mass.: MIT Press, 1968.

Hughes, Theone. "Sentence Combining: A Means of Increasing Reading Comprehension." Kalamazoo, Mich.: Western Michigan University, 1975. Educational Resources Information Center: ED 112 421.

Hunt, Barbara Carey. "Black Dialect and Third and Fourth Graders' Performance on the Gray Oral Reading Test." *Reading Research Quarterly* 10, i (1974–1975) : 103–123.

Hunt, Kellogg W. "Recent Measures in Syntactic Development." *Elementary English* 43 (November 1966) : 732–739.

Hunt, Kellogg W. *Syntactic Maturity in Schoolchildren and Adults.* Monographs of the Society for Research in Child Development, No. 134. Chicago: University of Chicago Press, 1970.

Hunt, Kellogg W., and O'Donnell, Roy C. "An Elementary School Curriculum to Develop Better Writing Skills." U. S. Office of Education Grant No. 4-9-08-903-0042-010. Tallahassee: Florida State University, 1970. Available from Educational Resources Information Center: ED 050 108.

Johns, Jerry, et al. *Assessing Reading Behavior: Informal Reading Inventories, An Annotated Bibliography.* Newark, Del.: International Reading Association, 1977.

Johnson, Ronald J.; Johnson, Karen Lamb; and Kerfoot, James F. "A Massive Oral Decoding Technique." *The Reading Teacher* 25 (February 1972) : 421–423.

Jongsma, Eugene. *The Cloze Procedure as a Teaching Technique.* Newark, Del.: International Reading Association, 1971.

Kennedy, Delores Kessler, and Weener, Paul. "Visual and Auditory Training with the Cloze Procedure to Improve Reading and Listening Comprehension." *Reading Research Quarterly* 8 (Summer 1973) : 524–541.

Kess, Joseph. *Psycholinguistics: Introductory Perspectives.* New York: Academic Press, 1976.

Klare, George R. "Assessing Readability." *Reading Research Quarterly* 10, i (1974–75) : 62–102.

Koch, Kenneth. *Wishes, Lies, and Dreams: Teaching Children to Write Poetry.* New York: Random House, Vintage Books/Chelsea House Publishers, 1970.

Kohler, Ivo. "Experiments with Goggles." *Scientific American* 206 (May 1962) : 62–72.

Kolers, Paul A. "Reading Is Only Incidentally Visual." In *Psycholinguistics and the Teaching of Reading,* edited by Kenneth S. Goodman and James T. Fleming. Newark, Del.: International Reading Association, 1969, pp. 8–16.

Kolers, Paul A. "Three Stages of Reading." In *Psycholinguistics and Reading*, edited by Frank Smith. New York: Holt, Rinehart and Winston, 1973, pp. 28–49.

Kreidler, Charles W. "Teaching English Spelling and Pronunciation." *TESOL Quarterly* 6 (March 1972): 3–12.

Labov, William. "The Reading of the *-ed* Suffix." In *Basic Studies on Reading*, edited by Harry Levin and Joanna P. Williams. New York: Basic Books, 1970, pp. 222–245.

Larrick, Nancy. "Wordless Picture Books and the Teaching of Reading." *The Reading Teacher* 29 (May 1976): 743–746.

Lefevre, Carl A. *Linguistics and the Teaching of Reading*. New York: McGraw-Hill, 1962.

Levin, Harry, and Kaplan, Eleanor L. "Grammatical Structure and Reading." In *Basic Studies on Reading*, edited by Harry Levin and Joanna P. Williams. New York: Basic Books, 1970, pp. 119–133.

Loban, Walter. *Language Development: Kindergarten through Grade Twelve*. Research report No. 18. Urbana, Ill.: National Council of Teachers of English, 1976.

Locke, John L., and Fehr, Fred S. "Subvocal Rehearsal as a Form of Speech." *Journal of Verbal Learning and Verbal Behavior* 9 (1970): 495–498.

McCracken, Robert A. "Initiating Sustained Silent Reading." *Journal of Reading* 14 (May 1971): 521–524, 582–583.

McCracken, Robert A., and McCracken, Marlene J. *Reading Is Only the Tiger's Tail*. San Raphael, Calif.: Leswing Press, 1972.

McCracken, Robert A., and McCracken, Marlene J. "Modeling Is the Key to Sustained Silent Reading." *The Reading Teacher* 31 (January 1978): 406–408.

McCracken, Glenn, and Walcutt, Charles C. *Lippincott's Basic Reading*, Teacher's Edition for Book E (grade 2¹), 2nd ed. Philadelphia: Lippincott, 1970.

McCullough, Constance M. "What Should the Reading Teacher Know about Language and Thinking?" In *Language and Learning to Read: What Teachers Should Know About Language*, edited by Richard E. Hodges and E. Hugh Rudorf. Boston: Houghton Mifflin, 1972, pp. 202–215.

McCullough, Constance M. "Pioneers of Research in Reading." In *Theoretical Models and Processes of Reading*, edited by Harry Singer and Robert B. Ruddell. 2nd ed. Newark, Del.: International Reading Association, 1976, pp. 2–7.

McDonell, Gloria M., and Osburn, E. Bess. "New Thoughts about Reading Readiness." *Language Arts* 55 (January 1978): 26–29.

McKee, Paul. *Primer for Parents.* 3rd ed. Boston: Houghton Mifflin, 1975.

McKenzie, Gary R., and Fowler, Elaine D. "A Recipe for Producing Student Discovery of Language Arts Generalizations." *Elementary English* 50 (April 1973): 593–598.

McLaughlin, G. Harry. "Reading at 'Impossible' Speeds." *Journal of Reading* 12 (March 1969): 449–454, 502–510.

McNeill, David. "Developmental Psycholinguistics." In *The Genesis of Language: A Psycholinguistic Approach,* edited by Frank Smith and George A. Miller. Cambridge, Mass.: MIT Press, 1966, pp. 15–84.

Mallitskaya, M. K. "K Metodike Ispol'zovania dl'a Razvitiya Ponimaniya Rechi u Detei v Kontse Pervogo i na Vtorom Godu Zhizni" (A Method for Using Pictures to Develop Speech Comprehension in Children at the End of the First and in the Second Year of Life). *Voprosy Psikhol* (1960): No. 3, 122–126.

Malmstrom, Jean, et al. *Course Book for English Language.* Kalamazoo, Mich.: Western Michigan University, 1965.

Marchbanks, Gabrielle, and Levin, Harry. "Cues by Which Children Recognize Words." *Journal of Educational Psychology* 56 (1965): 57–61.

Marcus, A. "The Development of a Diagnostic Test of Syntactic Meaning Clues in Reading." In *Diagnostic Viewpoints in Reading,* edited by R. E. Leibert. Newark, Del.: International Reading Association, 1970.

Marks, Lawrence E., and Miller, George A. "The Role of Semantic and Syntactic Constraints in the Memorization of English Sentences." *Journal of Verbal Learning and Verbal Behavior* 3 (February 1964): 1–5.

Martin, Bill Jr., with Brogan, Peggy. *Sounds of a Powwow.* Holt, Rinehart and Winston, 1974.

Martin, Bill Jr., with Brogan, Peggy. *Sounds of Language Readers.* New York: Holt, Rinehart and Winston, 1972 ff.

Mathews, Mitford M. *Learning to Read: Historically Considered.* Chicago: University of Chicago Press, 1966.

Max, Louis William. "Experimental Study of the Motor Theory of Consciousness: IV. Action-Current Responses in the Deaf during Awakening, Kinaesthetic Imagery and Abstract Thinking." *Journal of Comparative Psychology* 24 (October 1937): 301–344.

May, Frank B. *To Help Children Read: Mastery Performance Modules for Teachers in Training.* Columbus, Ohio: Charles E. Merrill, 1973.

May, Frank B., and Eliot, Susan B. *To Help Children Read: Mastery Performance Modules for Teachers in Training.* 2nd ed. Columbus, Ohio: Charles E. Merrill, 1978.

Mehler, Jacques. "Some Effects of Grammatical Transformation on the Recall of English Sentences." *Journal of Verbal Learning and Verbal Behavior* 2 (November 1963): 346–351.

Menyuk, Paula. *Sentences Children Use.* Cambridge, Mass.: MIT Press, 1969.

Miller, George A. "The Magical Number Seven, Plus or Minus Two: Some Limits on Our Capacity for Processing Information." *Psychological Review* 63 (1956): 81–97.

Miller, George A. "Some Psychological Studies of Grammar." *American Psychologist* 17 (1962): 748–762.

Miller, George A. "The Psycholinguists." *Encounter* 23 (July 1964): 29–37.

Miller, George A.; Bruner, Jerome S.; and Postman, Leo. "Familiarity of Letter Sequences and Tachistoscopic Identification." *Journal of General Psychology* 50 (1954): 129–139.

Miller, George A., and Chomsky, Noam. "Finitary Models of Language Users." In *Handbook of Mathematical Psychology,* vol. 2, edited by Robert D. Luce, Robert R. Bush, and Eugene Galanter. New York: John Wiley, 1963, pp. 420–491.

Miller, George A., and Isard, Stephen. "Free Recall of Self-Embedded English Sentences." *Information and Control* 7 (1964): 292–303.

Moses, Joseph. *The Great Rain Robbery.* Boston: Houghton Mifflin, 1975.

National Council of Teachers of English, Commission on the English Curriculum. *The English Language Arts.* New York: Appleton-Century-Crofts, Inc., 1952.

Nelson, Ruth. "The First Literate Computers?" *Psychology Today* 11 (March 1978): 73–74, 78, 80.

"News from the Professional Studies and Standards Committee: Department of Education Definition of Reading." *The Michigan Reading Journal* 11, ii (Spring 1977): 35–36.

Ney, James W. "Notes toward a Psycholinguistic Model of the Writing Process." *Research in the Teaching of English* 8 (Summer 1974): 157–169.

O'Donnell, Roy C.; Griffin, William J.; and Norris, Raymond C. *Syntax of Kindergarten and Elementary School Children: A Transforma-*

tional Analysis. Research report no. 8. Urbana, Ill.: National Council of Teachers of English, 1967.

O'Donnell, Roy C., and King, F.J. "An Exploration of Deep Structure Recovery and Reading Comprehension Skills." *Research in the Teaching of English* 8 (Winter 1974) : 327–338.

O'Hare, Frank. *Sentence Combining: Improving Student Writing without Formal Grammar Instruction.* Research report no. 15. Urbana, Ill.: National Council of Teachers of English, 1973.

O'Hare, Frank. *Sentencecraft.* Lexington, Mass.: Ginn, 1974.

Olsen, Hans C., Jr. "Linguistics and Materials for Beginning Reading Instruction." In *The Psycholinguistic Nature of the Reading Process,* edited by Kenneth S. Goodman. Detroit: Wayne State University Press, 1968, pp. 273–287.

Page, William D., ed. *Help for the Reading Teacher: New Directions in Research.* Urbana, Ill.: National Conference on Research in English and the National Council of Teachers of English, 1975.

Palermo, David S. *Psychology of Language.* Glenview, Ill.: Scott, Foresman, 1978.

Palermo, David S., and Molfese, Dennis L. "Language Acquisition from Age Five Onward." *Psychological Bulletin* 78 (December 1972) : 409–428.

Pearson, P. David. "The Effects of Grammatical Complexity on Children's Comprehension, Recall, and Conception of Certain Semantic Relations." *Reading Research Quarterly* 10, 2 (1974–1975) : 155–192.

Pearson, P. David, and Johnson, Dale D. *Teaching Reading Comprehension.* New York: Holt, Rinehart and Winston, 1978.

Peltz, Fillmore Kenneth. "The Effect upon Comprehension of Repatterning Based on Students' Writing Patterns." *Reading Research Quarterly* 9, iv (1973–1974) : 603–621.

Perkins, Al. *Hand, Hand, Fingers, Thumb.* Bright and Early Book series. New York: Random House, 1969.

Pikulski, John. "A Critical Review: Informal Reading Inventories." *Reading Teacher* 28 (November 1974) : 141–151.

Pikulski, John. "Readiness for Reading: A Practical Approach." *Language Arts* 55 (February 1978) : 192–197.

Porter, William S. *The Complete Works of O. Henry.* Garden City, N.Y. Doubleday, Doran, 1936.

Poulton, E.G. "Peripheral Vision, Refractoriness and Eye Movements in Fast Oral Reading." *British Journal of Psychology* 53 (1962) : 409–419.

Read, Charles. "Pre-school Children's Knowledge of English Phonology." *Harvard Educational Review* 41 (1971) : 1–34.

Read, Charles. *Children's Categorization of Speech Sounds in English.* Research report No. 17. Urbana, Ill.: National Council of Teachers of English, 1975.

Reid, Jessie F. "An Investigation of Thirteen Beginners in Reading." *Acta Psychologica* 14, 4 (1958) : 295–313.

Reid, Jessie F. "Learning to Think about Reading." *Educational Research* 9 (1966) : 56–62.

Reynolds, Quentin. "A Secret for Two." *Colliers* 97 (May 16, 1936) : 44.

Rhodes, Lynn K. "Predictable Books: An Instructional Resource for Meaningful Reading and Writing." In *The Affective Dimension of Reading,* edited by Darryl J. Strickler. Bloomington: Indiana University, 1977, pp. 195–213.

Rigg, Pat. "Dialect and/in/for Reading." *Language Arts* 55 (March 1978) : 285–290.

Roberts, Kathleen Piegdon. "Piaget's Theory of Conservation and Reading Readiness." *The Reading Teacher* 30 (December 1976) : 246–250.

Robinson, Francis P. *Effective Reading.* New York: Harper and Brothers, 1962.

Robinson, Richard D. *Introduction to the Cloze Procedure.* Newark, Del.: International Reading Association, 1972.

Rode, Sara S. "Development of Phrase and Clause Boundary Reading in Children." *Reading Research Quarterly* 10, i (1974–1975) : 124–142.

Ruddell, Robert B. "The Effect of Oral and Written Patterns of Language Structure on Reading Comprehension." *Reading Teacher* 18 (1965) : 270–275.

Ruddell, Robert B. "Psycholinguistic Implications for a Systems of Communication Model." In *Psycholinguistics and the Teaching of Reading,* edited by Kenneth S. Goodman and James T. Fleming. Newark, Del.: International Reading Association, 1969, pp. 61–78.

Ruddell, Robert B. "Language Acquisition and the Reading Process." In *Theoretical Models and Processes of Reading,* edited by Harry Singer and Robert B. Ruddell. Newark, Del.: International Reading Association, 1970, pp. 1–19.

Rupley, William H., and Robeck, Carol. "ERIC/RCS: Black Dialect and Reading Achievement." *The Reading Teacher* 31 (February 1978) : 598–601.

Samuels, S. Jay. "Modes of Word Recognition." In *Theoretical Models and Processes of Reading,* edited by Harry Singer and Robert B.

Ruddell. Newark, Del.: International Reading Association, 1970, pp. 23–37.

Saporta, Sol, ed. *Psycholinguistics: A Book of Readings.* New York: Holt, Rinehart and Winston, 1962.

Savin, Harris B. "What the Child Knows about Speech When He Starts to Learn to Read." In *Language by Ear and by Eye*, edited by James F. Kavanagh and Ignatius G. Mattingly. Cambridge, Mass.: MIT Press, 1972, pp. 319–326.

Savin, Harris B., and Perchonock, Ellen. "Grammatical Structure and the Immediate Recall of English Sentences." *Journal of Verbal Learning and Verbal Behavior* 4 (October 1965): 348–353.

Schneyer, J. Wesley. "Use of the Cloze Procedure for Improving Reading Comprehension." *The Reading Teacher* 19 (December 1965): 174–179.

Sendak, Maurice. *Chicken Soup with Rice.* New York: Harper & Row, 1962. Available from Scholastic Book Services.

Seton, Anya. *Devil Water.* Boston: Houghton Mifflin, 1962.

Simon, Herbert A. *The Sciences of the Artificial.* Cambridge, Mass.: MIT Press, 1969.

Singer, Harry, and Ruddell, Robert B., eds. *Theoretical Models and Processes of Reading.* 2nd ed. Newark, Del.: International Reading Association, 1976.

Singer, Harry; Samuels, Jay; and Spiroff, Jean. "The Effect of Pictures and Contextual Conditions on Learning Responses to Printed Words." *Reading Research Quarterly* 9, iv (1973–1974): 555–567.

Smith, E. Brooks; Goodman, Kenneth S.; and Meredith, Robert. *Language and Thinking in the Elementary School.* New York: Holt, Rinehart and Winston, 1970.

Smith, E. Brooks; Goodman, Kenneth S.; and Meredith, Robert. *Language and Thinking in School.* 2nd ed. New York: Holt, Rinehart and Winston, 1976.

Smith, Frank. *Understanding Reading.* New York: Holt, Rinehart and Winston, 1971, 1978.

Smith, Frank, ed. *Psycholinguistics and Reading.* New York: Holt, Rinehart and Winston, 1973.

Smith, Frank. *Comprehension and Learning: A Conceptual Framework for Teachers.* New York: Holt, Rinehart and Winston, 1975.

Smith, Frank. "The Role of Prediction in Reading." *Elementary English* 52 (March 1975): 305–311.

Smith, Frank, with Holmes, Deborah Lott. "The Independence of Letter, Word, and Meaning Identification in Reading." In *Psycholinguistics and Reading*, edited by Frank Smith. New York: Holt, Rinehart and Winston, 1973, pp. 50–69.

Smith, Laura A., and Lindberg, Margaret. "Building Instructional Materials." In *Miscue Analysis: Applications to Reading Instruction*, edited by Kenneth S. Goodman. Urbana, Ill.: National Council of Teachers of English, 1973, pp. 77–90.

Smith, Nila Banton. *American Reading Instruction: Its Development and Its Significance in Gaining a Perspective on Current Practices in Reading*. Newark, Del.: International Reading Association, 1965.

Smith, Richard J., and Barrett, Thomas C. *Teaching Reading in the Middle Grades*. Reading, Mass.: Addison-Wesley, 1974.

Smith, William L. "The Effect of Transformed Syntactic Structures on Reading." In *Language, Reading, and the Communication Process*, edited by Carl Braun. Newark, Del.: International Reading Association, 1971, pp. 52–62.

Soffietti, James P. "Why Children Fail to Read: A Linguistic Analysis." *Harvard Education Review* 25 (1955): 63–84.

Standal, Timothy C. "Readability Formulas: What's Out, What's In?" *The Reading Teacher* 31 (March 1978): 642–646.

Stauffer, Russell G. "Productive Reading-Thinking at the First Grade Level." *The Reading Teacher* 13 (February 1960): 183–187.

Stauffer, Russell G., and Cramer, Ronald. *Teaching Critical Reading at the Primary Level*. Newark, Del.: International Reading Association, 1968.

Steiner, R.; Weiner, M.; and Cromer, W. "Comprehension Training and Identification of Good and Poor Readers." *Journal of Educational Psychology* 62 (1971): 506–513.

Stewig, John Warren. "Alphabet Books: A Neglected Genre." *Language Arts* 55 (January 1978): 6–11.

Stotsky, Sandra L. "Sentence-Combining as a Curricular Activity: Its Effect on Written Language Development and Reading Comprehension." *Research in the Teaching of English* 9 (Spring 1975): 30–71.

Strickland, Ruth G. *The Contribution of Structural Linguistics to the Teaching of Reading, Writing, and Grammar in the Elementary School*. Bloomington, Ind.: Indiana University, *Bulletin of the School of Education* 40, i (January 1964).

Strong, William. *Sentence Combining.* New York: Random House, 1973.

Tallon, Robert. *Zoophabets.* Indianapolis: Bobbs Merrill, 1971.

Tatham, Susan Masland. "Reading Comprehension of Materials Written with Select Oral Language Patterns: A Study at Grades Two and Four." *Reading Research Quarterly* 5 (Spring 1970) : 402–426.

Taylor, Insup. *Introduction to Psycholinguistics.* New York: Holt, Rinehart and Winston, 1976.

Taylor, Stanford E.; Frackenpohl, Helen; and Pettee, James L. *Grade Level Norms for the Components of the Fundamental Reading Skill.* Huntington, N.Y.: Educational Developmental Laboratories, Bulletin No. 3, 1960.

Terman, Sibyl, and Walcutt, Charles C. *Reading: Chaos and Cure.* New York: McGraw-Hill, 1958.

Thurber, James. *The Wonderful O.* New York: Simon and Schuster, 1957.

Tull, Maxine Boatner, and Gates, John Edward. *A Dictionary of American Idioms,* updated by Adam Makkai. Rev. ed. Woodbury, N.Y.: Barron's Educational Series, 1975.

Tulving, Endel, and Gold, Cecille. "Stimulus Information and Contextual Information as Determinants of Tachistoscopic Recognition of Words." *Journal of Experimental Psychology* 66 (October 1963) : 319–327.

Venezky, Richard L. "English Orthography: Its Graphical Structure and Its Relation to Sound." *Reading Research Quarterly* 2 (1967) : 75–106.

Venezky, Richard L. "Regularity in Reading and Spelling." In *Basic Studies on Reading,* edited by Harry Levin and Joanna P. Williams. New York: Basic Books, 1970, pp. 30–42.

Venezky, Richard L. *The Structure of English Orthography.* The Hague: Mouton, 1970.

Venezky, Richard L., and Calfee, Robert C. "The Reading Competency Model." In *Theoretical Models and Processes of Reading,* edited by Harry Singer and Robert B. Ruddell. Newark, Del.: International Reading Association, 1970, pp. 273–291.

Walcutt, Charles Child. *Tomorrow's Illiterates: The State of Reading Instruction Today.* Boston: Little, Brown, 1961.

Walcutt, Charles Child; Lamport, Joan; and McCracken, Glenn. *Teaching Reading: A Phonic/Linguistic Approach to Developmental Reading.* New York: Macmillan, 1974.

Waller, T. Gary. *Think First, Read Later! Piagetian Prerequisites for Reading.* Newark, Del.: International Reading Association, 1977.

Wardhaugh, Ronald. *Reading: A Linguistic Perspective*. New York: Harcourt Brace Jovanovich, 1969.

Wardhaugh, Ronald. "The Teaching of Phonics and Comprehension: A Linguistic Evalution." In *Psycholinguistics and the Teaching of Reading*, edited by Kenneth S. Goodman and James T. Fleming. Newark, Del.: International Reading Association, 1969, pp. 79–90.

Watson, Dorothy J. "Helping the Reader: From Miscue Analysis to Strategy Lessons." In *Miscue Analysis: Applications to Reading Instruction*, edited by Kenneth S. Goodman. Urbana, Ill.: National Council of Teachers of English, 1973, pp. 103–115.

Weaver, Constance. "Using Context: Before or After?" *Language Arts* 54 (November/December 1977): 880–886.

Weaver, Constance. *Grammar for Teachers: Perspectives and Definitions*. Urbana, Ill.: National Council of Teachers of English, 1979.

Weaver, Constance, and Smith, Laura. "A Psycholinguistic Look at the Informal Reading Inventory, Part II: Inappropriate Inferences from an Informal Reading Inventory." *Reading Horizons* 19 (Winter 1979), pp. 103–111.

Weber, Rose-Marie. "First-Graders' Use of Grammatical Context in Reading." In *Basic Studies on Reading*, edited by Harry Levin and Joanna P. Williams. New York: Basic Books, 1970, pp. 147–163.

Weber, Rose-Marie. "Linguistics and Reading." In *Psychological Factors in the Teaching of Reading*, compiled by Eldon Ekwall. Columbus, Ohio: Charles E. Merrill, 1973, pp. 268–291.

Weinstein, Rhona, and Rabinovitch, M. Sam. "Sentence Structure and Retention in Good and Poor Readers." *Journal of Educational Psychology* 62 (February 1971): 25–30.

Wharton, Edith. *Ethan Frome*. New York: C. Scribner's, 1911. Available in large type from Watts, Franklin, a subsidiary of Grolier.

Williams, Joanna P. "Reactions to Modes of Word Recognition." In *Theoretical Models and Processes of Reading*, edited by Harry Singer and Robert B. Ruddell. Newark, Del.: International Reading Association, 1970, pp. 38–46.

Williamson, Joanne. *The Glorious Conspiracy*. New York, Knopf, 1961.

Wiseman, Bernard. *Morris Has a Cold*. New York: Dodd, Mead, 1978.

Wolfram, Walter A., and Fasold, Ralph W. "Toward Reading Materials for Speakers of Black English: Three Linguistically Appropriate Passages." In *Teaching Black Children to Read*, edited by Joan C. Baratz and Roger W. Shuy. Arlington, Va.: Center for Applied Linguistics, 1969, pp. 138–155.

Woodworth, Robert S. *Experimental Psychology.* New York: Holt, Rinehart and Winston, 1938.

Yngve, Victor H. "Computer Programs for Translation." *Scientific American* 206 (June 1962) : 68–76.

SUGGESTED READINGS

At the end of each chapter in this book, there is a list of readings for further exploration. In most cases these suggested readings have been articles, or chapters from a book. And in most cases, these articles or chapters have been suitable for the newcomer to psycholinguistics and reading. In the original draft of this book, I attempted to include a fairly thorough list of such articles and chapters in the final bibliography. But with the rapid proliferation of articles on psycholinguistics and reading, that original aim has become unrealistic.

For those primarily interested in the instructional relevance of psycholinguistics, I would simply recommend browsing through the appropriate professional journals from about 1976 onward. In particular, I would recommend the following:

Published by the National Council of Teachers of English (*NCTE*)

Language Arts	for elementary teachers
English Journal	for secondary teachers

Published by the International Reading Association (*IRA*)

The Reading Teacher	for elementary teachers
Journal of Reading	for secondary teachers

Those with a scholarly bent will also be interested in the IRA's *Reading Research Quarterly* and the NCTE's *Research in the Teaching of English.*

The following books are primarily for those who want a more thorough understanding of psycholinguistics in general, the nature of the reading process, the implications and applications of miscue research, and the history of the teaching of reading. In each section, I have placed an asterisk before two books that are especially recommended as starting points for further exploration.

Psycholinguistics in General

*Aitchison, Jean. *The Articulate Mammal: An Introduction to Psycholinguistics.* New York: McGraw-Hill, 1977.

Clark, Herbert H., and Clark, Eve V. *Psychology and Language: An Introduction to Psycholinguistics.* New York: Harcourt Brace Jovanovich, 1977.

Kess, Joseph. *Psycholinguistics: Introductory Perspectives.* New York: Academic Press, 1976.

Palermo, David S. *Psychology of Language.* Glenview, Ill.: Scott, Foresman, 1978.

Taylor, Insup. *Introduction to Psycholinguistics.* New York: Holt, Rinehart and Winston, 1976.

*Weaver, Constance. *Grammar for Teachers: Perspectives and Definitions.* Urbana, Ill.: National Council of Teachers of English, 1979.

The Nature of the Reading Process

Allen, P. David, and Watson, Dorothy J., eds. *Findings of Research in Miscue Analysis: Classroom Implications.* Urbana, Ill.: ERIC Clearinghouse on Reading and Communication Skills and the National Council of Teachers of English, 1976.

Anderson, Irving H., and Dearborn, Walter F. *The Psychology of Teaching Reading.* New York: Ronald Press, 1952.

*Carton, Aaron S. *Orientation to Reading.* Rowley, Mass.: Newbury House, 1976.

Ekwall, Eldon E., comp. *Psychological Factors in the Teaching of Reading.* Columbus, Ohio: Charles E. Merrill, 1973.

Farnes, N.C. *Reading Purposes, Comprehension and the Use of Context.* Bletchley, Buckinghamshire, England: The Open University Press, 1973.

Gibson, Eleanor J., and Levin, Harry. *The Psychology of Reading.* Cambridge, Mass.: MIT Press, 1975.

Goodman, Kenneth S., ed. *The Psycholinguistic Nature of the Reading Process.* Detroit: Wayne State University Press, 1968.

Goodman, Kenneth S. *Theoretically Based Studies of Patterns of Miscues in Oral Reading Performance.* Detroit: Wayne State University, 1973. Available from the Educational Resources Information Center: ED 079 708.

Goodman, Kenneth S., and Fleming, James T., eds. *Psycholinguistics and the Teaching of Reading.* Newark, Del.: International Reading Association, 1969.

Goodman, Kenneth S., and Niles, Olive S. *Reading: Process and Program.* Urbana, Ill.: National Council of Teachers of English, 1970.

Gunderson, Doris V., ed. *Language and Reading: An Interdisciplinary Approach.* Arlington, Va.: Center for Applied Linguistics, 1970.

Guthrie, John T., ed. *Aspects of Reading Acquisition.* Baltimore: The Johns Hopkins University Press, 1976.

Hodges, Richard D., and Rudorf, E. Hugh, eds. *Language and Learning to Read: What Teachers Should Know about Language.* Boston: Houghton Mifflin, 1972.

Huey, Edmund Burke. *The Psychology and Pedagogy of Reading.* 1908; reprinted, Cambridge, Mass.: MIT Press, 1968.

Kavanagh, James F., and Mattingly, Ignatius G., eds. *Language by Ear and by Eye: The Relationship Between Speech and Reading.* Cambridge, Mass.: MIT Press, 1972.

Kender, Joseph P., ed. *Teaching Reading—Not by Decoding Alone.* Danville, Ill.: Interstate, 1971.

Levin, Harry, and Williams, Joanna P., eds. *Basic Studies on Reading.* New York: Basic Books, 1970.

Page, William D., ed. *Help for the Reading Teacher: New Directions in Research.* Urbana, Ill.: National Conference on Research in English and the National Council of Teachers of English, 1975.

Singer, Harry, and Ruddell, Robert B., eds. *Theoretical Models and Processes of Reading.* Newark, Del.: International Reading Association, 1970, 1976. Three-fourths of the articles in the 1976 edition are new to that edition.

Smith, Frank, ed. *Psycholinguistics and Reading.* New York: Holt, Rinehart and Winston, 1973.

Smith, Frank. *Comprehension and Learning: A Conceptual Framework for Teachers.* New York: Holt, Rinehart and Winston, 1975.

Smith, Frank. *Understanding Reading.* 2nd ed. New York: Holt, Rinehart and Winston, 1978.

*Smith, Frank. *Reading Without Nonsense.* New York: Teachers College Press, 1978.

Wardhaugh, Ronald. *Reading: A Linguistic Perspective.* New York: Harcourt Brace Jovanovich, 1969.

Miscue Research and Its Implications and Applications

*Allen, P. David, and Watson, Dorothy J., eds. *Findings of Research in Miscue Analysis: Classroom Implications.* Urbana, Ill.: ERIC Clearinghouse on Reading and Communication Skills and the National Council of Teachers of English, 1976.

Goodman, Kenneth S., ed. *Miscue Analysis: Applications to Reading Instruction.* Urbana, Ill.: National Council of Teachers of English, 1973.

Goodman, Kenneth S. *Theoretically Based Studies of Patterns of Miscues in Oral Reading Performance.* Detroit: Wayne State University, 1973. Available from the Educational Resources Information Center: ED 079 708.

Goodman, Yetta M., and Burke, Carolyn L. *Reading Miscue Inventory Complete Kit: Procedure for Diagnosis and Evaluation.* New York: Macmillan, 1972.

*Goodman, Yetta M., and Burke, Carolyn L. *Reading Miscue Inventory Manual: Procedure for Diagnosis and Evaluation.* New York: Macmillan, 1972.

Page, William D., ed. *Help for the Reading Teacher: New Directions in Research.* Urbana, Ill.: National Conference on Research in English and the National Council of Teachers of English, 1975.

The Teaching of Reading: History and Controversies

Chall, Jeanne. *Learning to Read: The Great Debate.* New York: McGraw-Hill, 1967.

Diack, Hunter. *The Teaching of Reading in Spite of the Alphabet.* New York: Philosophical Library, 1965.

Downing, John. *Evaluating the Initial Teaching Alphabet.* London: Cassell, 1967.

Flesch, Rudolf. *Why Johnny Can't Read.* New York: Harper & Row, 1955.

Gray, William S. *On Their Own in Reading: How to Give Children Independence in Attacking New Words.* Glenview, Ill.: Scott, Foresman, 1948.

Gray, William S. *On Their Own in Reading: How to Give Children Independence in Analyzing New Words.* Glenview, Ill.: Scott, Foresman, 1960.

Harrison, Maurice. *The Story of the Initial Teaching Alphabet.* New York: Pitman, 1964.

*Mathews, Mitford M. *Teaching to Read, Historically Considered.* Chicago: University of Chicago Press, 1966.

*Smith, Nila Banton. *American Reading Instruction: Its Development and Its Significance in Gaining a Perspective on Current Practices in Reading.* Newark, Del.: International Reading Association, 1965.

Staiger, Ralph C., ed. *The Teaching of Reading.* Paris: UNESCO, and Lexington, Mass.: Ginn, 1973.

Walcutt, Charles Child; Lamport, Joan; and McCracken, Glenn. *Teaching Reading: A Phonic/Linguistic Approach to Developmental Reading.* New York: Macmillan, 1974.

index